D1544888

The Transgender Issue

The Transgender Issue

An Argument for Justice

SHON FAYE

ALLEN LANE
an imprint of
PENGUIN BOOKS

ALLEN LANE

UK | USA | Canada | Ireland | Australia
India | New Zealand | South Africa

Allen Lane is part of the Penguin Random House group of companies
whose addresses can be found at global.penguinrandomhouse.com

Penguin
Random House
UK

First published 2021

007

Copyright © Shon Faye, 2021

Set in 12/14.75 pt Dante MT Std
Typeset by Jouve (UK), Milton Keynes
Printed and bound in Great Britain by Clays Ltd, Elcograf S.p.A.

The authorized representative in the EEA is Penguin Random House Ireland,
Morrison Chambers, 32 Nassau Street, Dublin D02 YH68

A CIP catalogue record for this book is available from the British Library

ISBN: 978–0–241–42314–1

www.greenpenguin.co.uk

This book is dedicated to my mother, in a frankly insufficient attempt to reciprocate her dedication to me.

When I say trans, I also mean escape. I mean choice. I mean autonomy. I mean wanting something greater than what you told me. Wanting more possibilities than the one you forced on me.

Travis Alabanza

Contents

Prologue

The liberation of trans people would improve the lives of everyone in our society. I say 'liberation' because I believe that the humbler goals of 'trans rights' or 'trans equality' are insufficient. Trans people should not aspire to be equals in a world that remains both capitalist and patriarchal and which exploits and degrades those who live in it. Rather, we ought to seek justice – for ourselves and others alike.

Trans people have endured over a century of injustice. We have been discriminated against, pathologized and victimized. Our full emancipation will only be achieved if we can imagine a society that is completely transformed from the one in which we live. This book is primarily concerned with explaining how society, as it is currently arranged, often makes trans people's lives unnecessarily difficult. Yet, in posing solutions to these problems, it does not limit itself to thinking solely about trans people, but also encompasses anyone who is routinely disempowered and dispossessed.

Full autonomy over our bodies, free and universal healthcare, affordable housing for all, power in the hands of those who work rather than those privileged few who extract profit from our vastly inequitable system, sexual freedom (including freedom from sexual violence) and the end to the mass incarceration of human beings are all crucial ingredients in the construction of a society in which trans people are no longer abused, mistreated or subjected to violence. Such systemic changes would also particularly benefit everyone else forced to the margins of society, both in the UK and across the world.

The demand for true trans liberation echoes and overlaps with the demands of workers, socialists, feminists, anti-racists and queer people. They are *radical* demands, in that they go to the root of what our society is and what it could be. For this reason, the existence of trans people is a source of constant anxiety for many who are either invested in the status quo or fearful about what would replace it.

In order to neutralize the potential threat to social norms posed by trans people's existence, the establishment has always sought to confine and curtail their freedom. In twenty-first-century Britain, this has been achieved in large part by belittling our political needs and turning them into a culture war 'issue'. Typically, trans people are lumped together as 'the transgender issue', dismissing and erasing the complexity of trans lives, reducing them to a set of stereotypes on which various social anxieties can be brought to bear. By and large, the transgender issue is seen as a 'toxic debate', a 'difficult topic' chewed over (usually by people who are not trans themselves) on television shows, in newspaper opinion pieces and in university philosophy departments. Actual trans people are rarely to be seen. This book intentionally and deliberately reappropriates the phrase 'transgender issue', in order to outline the reality of the issues facing trans people today, rather than as they are imagined by people who do not face them.

In doing so, this book takes a wide-ranging look at different aspects of trans experience. The introduction looks at the ways in which the media has warped and distorted the conversation around trans people in Britain. The first chapter is a broad survey of everyday trans life, in family relationships, education and housing, from childhood to old age. The second chapter moves to one of the most specific areas of trans oppression, examining healthcare and the denial of bodily autonomy.

While trans people's rights are often considered a liberal

human rights issue, and liberals tend to argue for trans equality as a matter of individual freedom, trans people endure incessant discrimination both in trying to get work and, if they can get it, in the workplace. The third chapter, accordingly, situates them in this broader class struggle, examining trans experiences in the employment market. Worldwide, sex work remains one of the most common ways for trans people to earn a living; accordingly, Chapter 4 focuses on the political struggle of trans sex workers.

Discrimination and violence against trans people aren't always interpersonal. State violence – the state's monopoly on legal force through policing, prisons and migrant detention centres, and its consequent power to restrict trans people from moving freely in public spaces with privacy and dignity – is examined in the fifth chapter.

In this struggle for freedom from oppression and violence, trans people often fight alongside other marginalized people. However, the relationship between trans people and lesbians, gay men and bisexual people and the feminist movement are the subject of much controversy, both historically and in our present times. Greater acknowledgement of gender variance in the twenty-first century has led to wider recognition of the fact that the spectrum of human sexuality is much more complex and less rigid than previously thought, which can and does unsettle some people. This disquiet is exploited by conservatives and religious groups whose aim is to undermine LGBTQ+ power by promoting in-fighting. Similarly, the common fight against the oppression of women can all too frequently beome mired in anxiety over who should even be included in the category of 'woman'. In this book, however, I argue in the final chapters that the central demands of trans liberation are not merely aligned with, and no threat to, gay rights and feminism, but are synonymous with the goals of those movements.

When writing about trans people, it is still customary to

explain what 'trans' itself means. This in itself is telling. Despite all the headlines and media coverage, most people who don't know a trans person would struggle to define the term. In general, there are a few aspects of trans terminology that often confuse people new to the topic. One is that trans politics uses umbrella terms for convenience – that is, using one word to describe a vast range of very different experiences or identities. Another is that the language evolves so rapidly that specialist terms commonly used even five years previously soon become redundant through changes in linguistic fashion and in society or simply through the development of new perspectives that change the way language is used. Much of the contemporary jargon associated with trans campaigning, politics and identity originated on the internet; thus it can surge and fade in popularity very quickly. In what follows, I've tried to make my own language as clear as possible, while accepting the risk that my terminology may seem dated in a few years' time.

'Trans', as I use it in this book, is an umbrella term that describes people whose gender identity (their personal sense of their own gender) varies from, does not sit comfortably with, or is different from, the biological sex recorded on their birth certificate based on the appearance of their external genitalia.

The standard view of how sex and gender manifest in the world is as follows. Babies born with observable penises are recorded as male, referred to and raised as boys, and as adults are men; babies born with observable vulvas are recorded as female, referred to and raised as girls, and as adults are women. To be trans is, on some level, to feel that this standardized relationship between one's genitalia at birth and the assignment of one of two fixed gender identities that are supposed to accurately reflect your feelings about your own body has been interrupted. How the person who experiences this interruption reacts to it can vary hugely – which is why 'trans' is a catch-all word for a diverse range of identities and experiences. It's also worth pointing out that 'trans' is a twentieth-century word used to describe a Western way of thinking about gender variance, which assumes that there is a neat binary. Other cultures and societies have had different ways of understanding the relationship between genitalia, reproductive capacity and social role, and do not have the same Western tradition of rigidly forcing people into the two categories of man and woman. The phrase 'two-spirit', for example, has become the most common term in the English language to describe a diverse range of gender-variant ceremonial and social roles among indigenous North American communities. Similarly, examples of third-gender cultures exist across the world, such as the waria of Indonesia, the Samoan Fa'afafine, the hijra in India and the muxe of the Zapotec cultures in southern Mexico.

When we talk about trans people, we're usually referring to individuals who were either recorded as male at birth but who understand themselves to be women (trans women) or, vice versa, were recorded as female at birth but who understand themselves to be men (trans men). Not all trans people, however, find simply moving between the pre-existing categories of man and woman satisfactory, accurate or desirable. Such trans people, who are less well understood, generally unsettle mainstream society more than trans men and women, because they challenge not only the prevailing idea that birth genitals and gender are inseparable, but also the idea that there are just two gender categories. Often, these people are accused of making up their experience out of a need for attention or a desire to feel special – though in reality the political, economic and social costs for such 'non-binary' trans people (who don't straightforwardly see themselves as men or women) can be immense. Throughout this book, when I refer to 'trans people' I am talking about all trans men, trans women and non-binary people, unless otherwise specified. I also refer, throughout, to the LGBTQ+ community.

'LGBTQ+' is another umbrella term: a now widely accepted acronym to refer to the political coalition between lesbians, gay men, bi people, trans people and those who otherwise identify as queer. In some cases, such as in Chapter 6, I mention the 'LGBT' community, either because my sources do or because the research I am citing or the organizations I am discussing limit themselves to the first four letters only.

Finally, the term most commonly used now to describe people who are not trans is 'cis', short for 'cisgender'. 'Cisgender' is the Latin antonym for 'transgender'. If you were born with a penis, registered as male, your parents then called you a boy and raised you as such and you would still describe yourself as a man today, this book, when it mentions 'cis men' or 'cisgender men', is referring to someone like you.

The term 'cis' is relatively new, and its use can prove controversial. Some people clearly do not like the way it redefines as a majority experience a state that was previously thought of simply as 'normal'. Others hear in it an accusation or slur. Some feminists reject the term 'cis' because they believe it implies that all cisgender women are comfortable with femininity, or that it minimizes the way millennia of patriarchy has imposed constraints on women in a sexist world. This is not my interpretation of the term. As I see it, a cisgender woman can be a gender nonconforming woman who defies sexist norms but still wishes to be legally, socially and politically categorized as a woman.

When I use 'cis' in this book, I do so simply to denote non-trans people. We need a word for the 99 per cent of people in our society who do not have the experience of being trans, who fill almost all positions of power and authority, who control access to healthcare and education, and who make our laws. Simply by being a majority, cisgender people create the world that trans people live in.

Prologue

Not all cis people behave in oppressive ways towards trans people, and not all cis people experience perfect comfort with their bodies or their gender; but, in general, it is fair to say that there are some automatic benefits that come from being a cis person. Gender is one of the first things we look for, ask about or intuit in a person. Cis men and women have the immeasurable benefit of never being thought to be mistaken, deluded or deceptive about this very fundamental fact about their personhood. This means that, in many contexts, they tend to be automatically credited with more authority, insight or expertise on both their own identity and on trans people's identities than trans people themselves are. In considering the reality of trans lives, it is my hope that this book will overturn that implicit, and often unjust, authority.

Introduction: Seen but Not Heard

> Mr Upton has recently made a significant change in his life and
> will be transitioning to live as a woman. After the Christmas
> break, she will return to work as Miss Meadows.

This brief announcement in the parents' newsletter of St Mary
Magdalen's School in Accrington, Lancashire, was easy to miss.
It was buried, casually, amid a number of other staff changes
being announced at the start of the 2012 Christmas break: a Year
1 teacher was increasing her hours to full time; another was
reducing them; one teacher was leaving the school for a new
position in Spain; one was becoming a woman. The headteacher,
Karen Hardman, later admitted that she thought Miss Meadows'
transition was 'bound to arouse interest' in the school community; perhaps the announcement was placed among a list of more
routine staff changes in the hope of minimizing any undue reaction, or to avoid sensationalizing the transition of a member of
staff. If this was this case, it was a vain hope.

Within a few days of the school newsletter's publication, the
name Lucy Meadows – the name by which she wished to be
called following her transition – was splashed across the national
press, alongside her previous, male, name. Soon afterwards, journalists were encamped around her home. Within three months,
Lucy Meadows, aged 32, was found dead under the stairs at her
home; she had taken her own life.

The school and its headteacher had tried their best to support
Lucy Meadows publicly, and the letter unleashed a wave of hys-
teria that they could not have anticipated. The first response

came in a local newspaper, the *Accrington Observer*, which reported how the announcement had 'provoked concerns from some parents, who claim it has confused pupils who have got to know him [*sic*] as a man', adding that Lucy Meadows had given a statement in which she 'thanked school governors and colleagues for their support, and asked for his [*sic*] privacy to be respected'.

The next day, the story went national, in rather less measured tones. 'He's Not Only in the Wrong Body . . . He's in the Wrong Job', shouted the headline of the *Daily Mail* columnist Richard Littlejohn's weekly column, which was dedicated to an attack on Meadows. Referring to Meadows by her male name and with male pronouns throughout, the columnist's tone was contemptuous. 'He started turning up for class wearing pink nail varnish and sparkly headbands,' Littlejohn wrote of Meadows. 'The school might be extremely proud of its "commitment to equality and diversity",' he sneered, 'but has anyone stopped for a moment to think of the devastating effect all this is having on those who really matter? Children as young as seven aren't equipped to compute this kind of information.' Despite insisting that he supported the right of trans people to 'seek sex-changes', Littlejohn placed the blame for the children's possible confusion not on society but on Meadows herself: 'By insisting on returning to St Mary Magdalen's, he is putting his own selfish needs ahead of the well-being of the children he has taught for the past few years . . . if he cares so little for the sensibilities of the children he is paid to teach, he's not only trapped in the wrong body, he's in the wrong job.'

The *Daily Mail* kickstarted a media storm. Reporters lay in wait outside Meadows' house; parents dropping off children at the school were harassed for negative comments; and – so Meadows said to friends – those trying to give supportive remarks to journalists were ignored. 'I know the press offered parents money if they could get a picture of me,' she wrote in an email to a friend on New Year's Day 2013. In the end, unable to get their hands on such an image, media outlets lifted an old picture from the Facebook pages of Meadows' brother and sister without permission. A Year 5 pupil's drawing of Meadows after her transition, which had been removed from her school's website to protect her, was accessed through caching (Littlejohn's piece described this drawing). Meadows' ex-partner, Ruth, with whom Meadows had had a son before she came out as trans, later said that Meadows had been very low, especially because of the death of a close friend and the strain of her own transition and the ensuing media coverage. In fact, Meadows had grown suicidal well before her death: on 7 February 2013, she had tried unsuccessfully to end her life. A month later, she tried again. This time, she didn't survive the attempt.

It would be reductive to suggest that the gross and gratuitous invasion of her privacy was the sole reason for Lucy Meadows' suicide. Suicide attempts occur at a higher rate among trans people than the general population. Indeed, the statistics are truly alarming: research by the UK charity Stonewall published in 2017 found that 45 per cent of trans young people had attempted suicide at least once. Yet, behind the statistics are individuals, suffering in private and leading complex human lives: there is rarely one simple explanation for such a tragedy. But we can surely say this: in the final months of her life, when she must have been experiencing a degree of mental anguish, Lucy Meadows was bullied, harassed, ridiculed and demonized by the British media. Her death remains one of the darkest chapters in the British trans community's history, and one of the most shameful episodes in the long and shameful history of the British tabloid press. Even if she was struggling in other ways, Meadows had not been a public figure or a celebrity, nor had she ever sought to be. She had wrestled privately with gender for many years, and her decision to transition was, by all accounts, not taken lightly. All she had done was to be trans and to be honest about who she was, continuing with a job she had been good at in a school that supported her. Her story was not remotely in the public interest. At the inquest into her death, the coroner, Michael Singleton, stated that the media should be ashamed of their treatment of Meadows. Summing up his verdict, Singleton turned to the assembled press in the court gallery and told them, 'Shame on all of you.'

One of the grimmest aspects of the Lucy Meadows story was that so much of it was foreseeable. In December 2011, a year before the Christmas newsletter announcing Meadows' transition, the Leveson Inquiry – the judicial public inquiry into the British press following the News International phone-hacking scandal – had received written submissions by Trans Media Watch, a charity founded in 2009 to encourage improvement in media coverage of transgender issues. The submissions detailed how the British press systematically misrepresents and maligns trans individuals, or makes them figures of fun. They would be chillingly prophetic in the case of Lucy Meadows. 'Members of the press would not deny that they can be a force to shape society for good,' the submissions state, 'yet, in the case of transgender people, they have largely acted as self-appointed moral police. The defence the press uses in situations such as these is that they are simply reflecting public unease – downplaying its role in creating and shaping that unease to begin with.' The press, Trans Media Watch told the inquiry, achieved this in two ways: first, by creating and sustaining a climate of ridicule and humiliation through mocking headlines and juvenile language, which invites abuse from the public, especially online; and, second, 'singling out individual transgender people and their families for sustained personal intrusion'. Trans Media Watch asked the Inquiry to recommend better protections for trans people, including anonymity in cases where the subject was not a public figure, better regulation and improved access to justice. To this day, their recommendations have not been implemented.

Following Lucy Meadows' death, there was briefly some hope that the British media's long pattern of cruelty towards trans people would change for the better. Since the *Sunday People* outed the trans model April Ashley back in 1961 with the headline ' "Her" Secret is Out' – thereby instantly ending her modelling career – the media have tended to be less interested in informing the public about trans people and more interested in creating profitable cycles of mockery and suspicion. But while, since Lucy Meadows' death, there have been some small improvements in press conduct towards trans *individuals*, such gains have been more than offset by the dramatic rise of another phenomenon: a huge ramping up of press hostility towards trans people *as a minority group*.

By the end of the 2010s, trans people weren't the occasional freak show in the pages of a red-top tabloid. Rather, we were in the headlines of almost every major newspaper every single day. We were no longer portrayed as the ridiculous but unthreatening provincial mechanic who was having a 'sex swap'; now, we were depicted as the proponents of a powerful new 'ideology' that was capturing institutions and dominating public life. No longer something to be jeered at, we were instead something to be feared. Soon after the Lucy Meadows inquest, that fleeting opportunity to shed light on the bullying of trans people evaporated. In the intervening years, the press flipped the narrative: it was trans people who were the bullies. Five years after Meadows' death, the tone of even one of the country's most respected broadsheets, *The Times*, dripped with contempt: 'A worthy movement to help a minority group has become a form of McCarthyism in bad wigs and fishnets, thanks to a bunch of bullies, trolls and humourless misogynists,' one 2018 article on trans people read. 'Feel too daunted to venture an opinion on anything "transgender"? Great! That's exactly how the bullies like it.'[1]

Britain is in the midst of a heated national conversation about the 'issue' of transgender people. Perhaps no topic – other than Brexit and, latterly, the coronavirus pandemic – has received such a consistently high and recurring level of popular media coverage in the past few years. In 2020 alone *The Times* and its sister paper *The Sunday Times* between them ran over 300 articles – almost one a day – on trans people. The free *Metro* newspaper accepted a full-page ad in 2018 from a campaign group urging the public to resist reform to the Gender Recognition Act, a piece of legislation designed to make the process of changing your legal gender less costly and invasive, in line with other European countries. The previous year, the tabloid *Daily Star* ran an entirely false series of stories claiming that the notorious child murderer Ian Huntley was transgender, before – two years later – finally admitting the story wasn't true.

At the same time, televised debates on the topic became a staple fixture of daytime TV shows like *Good Morning Britain*, *This Morning*, *Victoria Derbyshire* and *Loose Women*, whose hosts solemnly weighed up the rights of trans people to participate fully in public life. In May 2018 Channel 4 hosted *Genderquake*, a televised live debate on the 'transgender issue' that became so hostile that the trans participants were heckled with graphic abuse live on primetime television, resulting in over 200 complaints to Ofcom.

Naturally, celebrities got involved. In 2017, on *Good Morning Britain*, the TV presenter Piers Morgan asked two trans guests if trans identities were just 'gobbledigook' and wondered – live on air – whether he could identify as a 'black woman' or an 'elephant', generating a row which unsurprisingly spilled over on to Twitter. Meanwhile, in June 2020, the most successful British author of all time, J. K. Rowling, immersed herself in international controversy when she published an essay, 'TERF Wars', on her website. Rowling's position on trans people's identities was already controversial from December 2019, when she had publicly supported Maya Forstater, a tax expert who lost her job at a thinktank following an investigation into tweets her employer judged to be transphobic. 'I'm deeply concerned about the consequences of the current trans activism,' Rowling wrote. 'I'm concerned about the huge explosion in young women wishing to transition . . . and also about the increasing numbers who seem to be detransitioning (returning to their original sex), because they regret taking steps that have, in some cases, altered their bodies irrevocably.' Her criticisms of trans womanhood were even more blunt: ' "woman" is not a costume. "Woman" is not an idea in a man's head. "Woman" is not a pink brain, a liking for Jimmy Choos or any of the other sexist ideas now somehow touted as progressive.'

Another British celebrity who can be relied on to weigh in with an opinion on trans people is the comedian Ricky Gervais: 'We need to protect the rights of women. Not erode them because some men have found a new cunning way to dominate and demonize an entire sex.' This was not Gervais's first commentary on the existence of trans people, having previously tweeted jokes riffing on the idea of transgender people's bodies as inherently absurd. 'It should be every woman's right to show her cock to whomever she likes,' gives an idea of Gervais's brand of humour on the subject. Unsurprisingly, this often facile public interrogation of trans people's identities by the likes of Morgan, Rowling and Gervais – who have a combined reach of 36 million Twitter followers – further entrenched in the public imagination a sense that trans people were fair game.

A similar shift could be seen in politics. During the 2019 UK general election campaign, the Liberal Democrat leader Jo Swinson was constantly challenged in the media about her progressive stance on trans issues. This questioning set a precedent for the subsequent Labour Party leadership contest in 2020, in which every candidate was asked about trans people's rights. Trans people were suddenly the issue everyone needed an opinion on: what did it mean to be a man or a woman, or to assert your existence as something else entirely? If anyone could determine their own gender, was the same true of race – could a white person 'identify' as black? Were trans children being fast tracked to irreversible decisions about their bodies, or were increased waiting times leaving them without the care they need? Were those who crossed the lines of gender to be embraced or feared?

So, yes, Britain is immersed in a deafening conversation about trans people. But there is also no doubt that we've been having – and are having – the wrong conversation. I am a trans woman who has worked within the media during this time, so I know a bit about it. I have worked both within LGBTQ+ organizations lobbying for trans rights, and as a writer at several newspapers and magazines, and have been regularly asked to argue – on radio and television as well as in print – on behalf of the rights and freedoms of trans people. I almost always turn down such invitations. Here's why. The media agenda with respect to 'the transgender issue' is often cynical and unhelpful to the cause of trans justice and liberation. Media coverage of the trans community rarely seems to be driven by a desire to inform and educate the public about the actual issues and challenges facing a group who – as all evidence indicates – are likely to experience severe discrimination throughout their lives. Today, the typical news item on trans people features a debate between a trans advocate on one side and a person with 'concerns' on the other – as if both parties were equally affected by the discussion. As trans people face a broken healthcare system – which in turn leaves them with a desperate lack of support both with their gender and the mental health impacts of the all-too-commonly associated problems of family rejection, bullying, homelessness and unemployment – trans people with any kind of platform or access have tried to focus media reporting on these issues, to no avail. Instead, we are invited on television to debate whether trans people should be allowed to use public toilets. Trans people have been dehumanized, reduced to a talking point or conceptual problem: an 'issue' to be discussed and debated endlessly. It turns out that when the media want to talk about trans issues, it means they want to talk about *their* issues with *us*, not the challenges *facing us*.

Time and again, when trying to raise the systemic issues affecting trans people's lives, I have found myself frustrated, even silenced. It's not so surprising. At the time of writing, despite the media myth of a powerful trans lobby, in the UK there are no openly trans newspaper editors and no trans staff writers at any major newspapers, no trans television commissioners, no trans High Court judges, no trans MPs, no trans members of the devolved legislatures of Wales, Scotland or Northern Ireland, and no trans chief executives at major charities. (Jay Stewart, chief executive of the youth charity Gendered Intelligence, is the only trans person to head any of the British charities specifically campaigning on trans issues.) This, then, is a question of power: the terms of the conversation that is happening *about* trans people are rarely set *by* trans people. In part, this is because the trans population in Britain is small; indeed, we don't even have a solid figure for the number. The largest and most inclusive estimate of anyone who falls within the definition of 'trans' used by official bodies is between 200,000 and 500,000 trans people in the UK. By any measurement, then, we are less than 1 per cent of the population.

Many people who pick up this book will not, to their knowledge, be in regular contact with a trans person. Human beings rely on familiarity to understand and empathize with others, and we find it easier to extend compassion to those we can relate to. Given that, like any minority, trans people are unfamiliar to the average person, we rely more heavily on media representation, on political solidarity from people who aren't trans and vocal, and ongoing support from public institutions to create the right conditions for understanding and compassion from the rest of society. By the same token, we're especially vulnerable to the spread of misinformation, harmful stereotypes and repeated prejudicial tropes. And the latter, unfortunately, are widespread in public culture, just as they have been throughout history. Trans people are discriminated against, harassed and subjected to violence around the world because of deep prejudices that have been embedded into the fabric of our culture, poisoning our capacity to empathize, and even to accept trans people as fully human.

In the 2010s, many campaigners and activists in the trans community hoped that this desperately needed understanding would come from 'visibility politics' and better representation: the idea being that if a handful of selected trans people in culture and the arts were to attain greater visibility in the media then their presence might make trans people as a whole more familiar, and consequently less stigmatized and misunderstood. In the US, a key milestone of trans visibility politics came with the cover of the May 2014 issue of *Time* magazine. This featured Laverne Cox, a working-class black trans actress then playing a trans character on the hit Netflix television series *Orange is the New Black*. Alongside the image of Cox ran a caption, 'The transgender tipping point: America's next civil rights frontier'. The image and headline were both bold and instantly iconic. Cox became a ferocious advocate for trans people, many of whom (myself included) have felt more welcome to come out or be open in public because of the climate around her cover and similar cultural representations in the mid 2010s. But they were also reductive and naïve in their optimism about what might follow on from Cox's personal rise to celebrity. Two years later, America elected Donald Trump, whose government introduced a series of anti-trans legislative measures designed to roll back any advancement American trans people had made in civil rights or healthcare access. In some trans communities – particularly those deemed 'criminal' by the state, because of their race, social class or participation in criminalized economies like drugs or sex work – the line between visibility and increased surveillance was so fine that to be more widely seen by society was potentially more harmful than liberating. Visibility politics may not have completely failed to help the US trans community, but its success in improving the lives of the majority of trans people (who would never be on magazine covers) has been vastly overstated.

The same was true in Britain during the mid to late 2010s. To some extent, trans people started to become more visible in the wider culture: beloved national soap operas like *EastEnders* and *Emmerdale* hired trans actors to play trans roles; trans people began to appear on the covers of magazines, as panellists on news shows, and so on. Like many others, I volunteered with new organizations like All About Trans, which worked to host non-confrontational meetings between television producers and newspaper editors and 'ordinary' trans people. While these had some positive benefits, their success depended very much on the benevolence of particular individuals inside media organizations and also on the 'right kind' of trans people making the 'right impression': having the right look (whatever that might be), or speaking and behaving in the right way.

Alongside this organized, deliberate work on better representation in traditional media came the explosion of social media networks, which allowed some trans people more scope to talk to each other, to create their own content, and to organize themselves politically online. Until then, geography and the need for discretion about their trans identity had barred many trans people from engaging in community work. The rapid expansion of a varied and highly engaged online trans subculture came as a surprise to most commentators in the traditional media. Suddenly, platforms like Twitter allowed trans people access and an un-fettered right of reply – far removed from the days where any-one who took issue with media coverage would have to write in privately. Now, those with media platforms were no longer able to publish misinformation with impunity: they could be chal-lenged and publicly held to account. Some of the British com-mentariat adapted to this new accountability more easily than others: for most of us under the age of 35 working in the media, it is all we have ever known. Others, though, responded with hos-tility to such public challenges: trans people active on social media platforms were condemned as angry activists, as a mob that were trying to silence debate, or simply, as *The Times* had it, as 'bullies'.

The increasingly polarized discussion of trans people and their rights on social media platforms was a boon to a media outrage cycle that was by the end of the 2010s financially driven by engage-ment, clickbait, shares and soundbites. Where many trans people had begun the decade hopeful about social media's potential for democratizing representation and visibility, many ended it exhausted and demoralized by an increasingly toxic online environment, in which prominent trans social media users were expected to with-stand daily abuse and harassment. As with mainstream media, online visibility politics had been, at best, a limited success.

Although visibility helps redress a representational inequality, it does nothing on its own to achieve redistributive justice. This is a larger, more complex and ultimately more important fight, one whose aim is to reallocate resources to the most vulnerable trans communities in their struggle to resist state violence (like police harassment, imprisonment or deportation), poverty and dispossession, and achieve better labour conditions. The most noteworthy ally that British trans people once appeared to have in this fight was the Women and Equalities Select Committee Inquiry on Transgender Equality, a cross-party parliamentary investigation into the political realities of being British and trans, which published its findings in January 2016. The inquiry found that 'there is a complex and extensive hierarchy of issues that need to be addressed' to achieve trans equality in the UK. And, it stated emphatically, trans people were being failed:

> A litmus test for any society that upholds the principles of fairness and equality is the extent to which it supports and protects the rights and interests of every citizen, even the most marginalized groups . . . our society is still failing this test in respect of trans people, despite welcome progress in recent years.[2]

The report made several wide-ranging recommendations for legislative and policy changes to improve trans people's lives, in a number of areas: from healthcare and schools to hate crime and the care of trans prisoners. To date, however, none of these recommendations have been implemented, and none of them seem to have any prospect of being realized in the foreseeable future. What's more, since the report was published, the situation for trans people has in many respects deteriorated. At the time, Theresa May's Tory government agreed to adopt one single recommendation: reform of the Gender Recognition Act 2004, which governs the process by which some trans people are able to change their legal gender and obtain a replacement birth certificate. In order to make the process more accessible and less pathologizing, the Trans Inquiry recommended removing the need for extensive medical evidence from clinicians. May hoped this simple legislative change, which would cost less to implement than more systemic reforms recommended in the NHS or schools, would give her ailing government a much-needed PR boost and bring her kudos as a progressive Conservative, much as introducing same-sex marriage had done for her predecessor, David Cameron.

Yet when the proposed reform was trailed, the media backlash was overwhelming. Several grassroots campaign groups claiming to protect women and children began a determined campaign to halt it, insisting that a more humane process for gender recognition would allow sexual predators greater access to vulnerable people like cisgender women or children. The issue blew up so spectacularly that the government's consultation with members of the public on how best to reform the Gender Recognition Act in 2018 received over 100,000 responses. While most were pro-reform, many thousands were boilerplate responses from campaign groups opposed to it. When Theresa May resigned after failing to secure support for her Brexit deal in 2019, the proposed reforms were shelved entirely.

Today, representational equality and true redistributive politics elude trans people, even as more and more trans people are coming out than ever before. Trans people have now become one of a number of targets in right-wing media, alongside, for instance, Muslims, immigrants generally, Gypsy, Roma and Traveller communities, Black Lives Matter, the fat acceptance movement, and feminists challenging state violence against women. All these groups and more have been reduced to issues in a toxic and polarized public rivalry between value systems. The past few years have seen discussions around trans people become not only poisonous but, crucially, banal. The 'topic' of trans has now been limited to a handful of repetitive talking points: whether non-binary people exist and whether gender neutral pronouns are reasonable; whether trans children living with dysphoria should be allowed to start their transition; whether trans women will dominate women's events in the Olympics; and the endless debate over toilets and changing rooms.

This book will not regurgitate these talking points yet again. I believe that forcing trans people to involve themselves in these closed-loop debates *ad infinitum* is itself a tactic of those who wish to oppress us. Such debates are time-consuming, exhausting distractions from what we should really be focusing on: the material ways in which we are oppressed. The author Toni Morrison once spoke about how precisely this tactic is employed by white people against people of colour: 'The function, the very serious function of racism, is distraction,' she told students at Portland State University in 1975. 'It keeps you from doing your work. It keeps you explaining, over and over again, your reason for being . . . None of this is necessary. There will always be one more thing.' In much the same way, the public discourse over trans people's experience is distorted and derailed.

With this book, I want to change the trajectory, to move beyond this discussion of trans people as framed by those who want to stoke a so-called culture war, and to start a new, healthier, conversation about trans people in the UK and beyond. Something that this book is not: a memoir. Ever since the travel writer Jan Morris published a memoir of her own transition, *Conundrum*, back in 1974, trans writers in Britain and around the world have tended to restrict themselves to publishing confessional texts in which the writer's own body is the starting point for any commentary on the society in which it exists. While the trans memoir has been important in destigmatizing and demystifying trans people's understanding of themselves, confession and candour ought not to be the only basis for trans people's right to public and political speech. In this we have much in common with cisgender women writers, who are also pushed into memoir over analysis. You don't have to know the intimate details of my private life to support me. Don't worry about the 'why'; act on the 'what'. What does being a trans person in a transphobic society produce? At the moment, too often, it is still violence, prejudice and discrimination.

In any event, my personal story would not be much use to you, since, as I am a middle-class, white trans woman with a university degree and a strong support network of friends and family, it is wholly unrepresentative of the vast majority of trans people's lives. The media platform which gave me the opportunity to write this book is derived from very real advantages afforded to me because of my social class, ethnicity and education. This has always been the case. As the feminist academic Viviane Namaste wrote twenty years ago: 'Professional and middle-class norms determine not only what transsexuals can say and in what spaces. They also confer the right to speak to those transsexuals who will abide by the codes of a middle-class discourse.'[3] In writing this book, I have tried to use these privileges as an instrument to amplify the voices of trans people who are not as routinely heard or discussed. My hope is that this book will contribute to an ongoing conversation in trans texts, while recognizing that the discussion of trans liberation will always remain limited without achieving greater diversity in trans publishing and dismantling the hierarchies found in a well-resourced trans activism that is carried out by middle-class professionals, many of whom are not trans themselves, in a few well-funded LGBTQ+ charities.

Throughout this book, cis readers will recognize inequalities often endured by trans people that they personally, or other minority groups they are familiar with, are also experiencing. This is a good thing: the framing of trans people as 'the transgender issue' has the effect of cutting us off from solidarity and making us the 'other'. A new conversation, then, must necessarily start to undo this estrangement and consider what we share and where we overlap with other minorities or marginalized groups. It is only through solidarity, compassion and radical reimagining that we can build a more just and joyful world for all of us.

I.

Trans Life Now

'My preconceptions about trans people came from the media, and I certainly hadn't heard of trans children. I thought it was all about stereotypes. So it just flummoxed me having an assigned male child who didn't have especially "feminine" interests and yet was saying consistently, "I'm a girl." '

Kate is telling me about her eldest daughter, Alex.* It's a warm July evening, and we're sitting in the kitchen of their family home, in a comfortable suburb peopled by middle-class couples with young families. Alex, still at primary school, is trans. A few years ago, her mum assumed she was a boy who was clumsily trying to ask for typically feminine things:

> I remember I used to have conversations with her at a very young age in the car because she'd get really upset. I'd say, 'But I don't understand what would be different if you were a girl? What can't you do that you could do if you were a girl?' I'd ask, 'Do you want a doll?' She'd just reply 'I don't like dolls!'

When Kate and her husband Joe agreed to speak to me to help me with research for this book, I suggested visiting them at their home, partly because I felt that meeting anywhere else would be a logistical challenge for a couple with young kids. I also thought

* Names of all trans young people, and of their parents, have been changed for their privacy.

it would put both parents at ease: people in their position are often extremely reluctant to publicize their stories, because of the media hostility towards trans children and their parents. They'd invited me to dinner, and earlier that evening I'd sat with the entire family as we ate pizza and garlic bread. Sitting next to me, Alex seemed like a typical kid of her age who accepted me casually as a stranger at the table. As Alex's parents later pointed out, there wasn't anything especially feminine about her dress sense; she wasn't what people call a 'girly girl'.

'She was very into books from a really young age and still is,' Joe tells me. 'We have to tell her to stop reading to sleep.' He and Kate describe their daughter proudly as 'someone with a strong sense of herself and a sense of justice – what's right and wrong. She thinks very deeply about things.' But, Kate chips in, 'she can also be really immature at times, too; I mean, she's not perfect.'

Alex was around three years old when she began to correct her mother if she called her a boy. 'I'd try and encourage her good behaviour, as any parent does, by saying things like "good boy",' Kate explains. 'She began to reply, "No. Good *girl*."'

Joe and Kate soon felt a little out of their depth. 'Like a lot of parents with young kids, I thought there was something I was meant to teach her that I had missed,' says Kate. 'I just didn't get it.'

Joe tells me how Alex soon started to tell other children and the staff at nursery that she was a girl – but would regularly be corrected. Soon she started to become frequently upset, particularly before bed. The source of her distress, says Joe, was always clear: 'It was "Why can't you call me a girl?" "Why won't you call me a girl?" "I'm a girl" "I'm a girl" "I'm a girl" "Why can't I be a girl?".' Joe is careful to stress how fixated his daughter had become on being regarded as female by those around her. It wasn't long before Alex had convinced half her nursery class to refer to her with female pronouns; the staff, meanwhile, were as unsure as her parents about how to respond to this unusual situation.

Children are known for being more accepting of difference than adults, after all. One thing, though, was clear to everyone around her: Alex was really unhappy.

Now, for those unacquainted with trans people, it might seem that in the past decade there has been a huge rise in children expressing issues with their birth-assigned gender. This is a perilous misunderstanding of the reality; in fact, there aren't greater numbers of children asserting a trans identity than there were in times past. There are simply more children who feel able to talk about it openly and seek support and advocacy from their parents. In March 2017 a ninety-year-old Second World War veteran called Patricia Davies came out as a transgender woman and began taking hormones, shortly after discussing her lifelong gender dysphoria with her doctor. Speaking to the *Daily Mirror*, Patricia said she first realized she was a girl back in 1930, when she was just three years old – the same age as Alex, when she began to assert her gender identity to her parents.

'I've known I was transgender since I was three years old. I knew a girl called Patricia and I decided I wanted to be known by that name, but it didn't stick.'[1] Patricia recalled that, even though her mother was initially tolerant of her interest in femininity, she soon sensed wider society would not be so understanding and learned to repress her own instincts about her gender: 'They thought they could make you better. They didn't realize it was something that you could not cure. Because of the general hostility of people I kept quiet.'

Patricia and Alex may be three generations apart, but their experiences attest to the importance of family, education and wider societal attitudes in determining the course of the rest of a trans person's life. Patricia's parents came from a time where they had no reference or model for how to help her, and she struggled to repress her gender for most of her adult life. Alex will not have that same struggle, because of her parents' acceptance.

Alex and Patricia have something else in common. They are both part of two growing trans populations – children and older people – who are more likely to be dependent on the benevolence of institutions, such as schools (in the case of children), or health and social care professionals (in the case of elderly people). This chapter, then, will act as a broad survey of the challenges many trans people experience in their daily lives. It will consider how trans people, of all ages, navigate life in their own homes, families and communities. What are the challenges facing trans children when they go through the school gates in the morning? What are the effects on those trans young people who are rejected by those closest to them? How can being trans make a person vulnerable to domestic abuse from their partner? How do we as a society make space for an ageing trans population alongside their cisgender counterparts? These are vital questions and, in many instances, they are questions of broader social justice that affect other disadvantaged groups. It is as much a matter of systemic failure as it is of personal bigotry. The effect of transphobic prejudice in many contexts is to magnify other hardships such as class, racism, sexism or ableism. For example, many of the practical actions needed to help homeless trans people are much the same as those needed to help homeless people generally. However, there are specific ways in which transphobia creates particular vulnerabilities in the homeless trans population which policy usually fails to take into consideration.

For many trans people, experiences of shame, suppression and discrimination start early in life, often in their family home. If the existence of adult trans people has in recent decades become increasingly accepted, even normalized, the same isn't true for trans children, whose existence is more often disputed and who risk censure, even punishment, from adults for expressing their trans identity. In Britain, the national conversation about trans children, driven by the media, focuses on the question of why children are trans (or, in some cases, whether trans children exist at all). And, as far as trans children and young people are concerned, the views expressed are often particularly intolerant and demeaning, with reactions varying from concern for their welfare to outright derision. Back in 2017, the BBC made a TV documentary entitled 'Transgender Kids: Who Knows Best?' It featured Kenneth Zucker, a Canadian clinician whose approach with gender-variant children remains highly controversial: it's alleged that he was in effect practising reparative or conversion therapy. (Zucker completely denies such allegations.) Conversion therapy is typically understood as a damaging pseudoscientific practice which attempts to change a person's sexual orientation or gender identity. When asked about young children expressing their trans identity, Zucker replied: 'A four-year-old might say that he's a dog – do you go out and buy dog food?' Though extreme, the sentiment expressed – portraying trans children's claims about their own identities as absurd and deluded – is typical of much media coverage of trans young people's lives.

Such attitudes are encouraged and bolstered by ongoing misinformation about children and transition surgery. The reality – and it needs to be clearly and emphatically stated – is that children under 18 *never* have genital surgeries in the UK. That many people I have personally encountered believe otherwise is largely due to a hostile press and sensationalist headlines: one such, published in *The Sunday Times* in June 2019, referred to Mermaids, the UK's leading charity supporting families of trans children, as a 'child sex change charity'.[2] Apart from anything else, this is entirely erroneous. Young trans children, prior to puberty, only ever transition socially – that is to say, changing names, pronouns and, in some cases, clothes or hairstyles.

Media discussion of trans children frequently oscillates between seeing them as innocents to be rescued from the grip of a malign ideology, or as dangers to be feared. An example of the latter came in an exchange between the broadcaster Nick Robinson, the BBC's former political editor, and the trans writer Paris Lees on BBC Radio 4's *Political Thinking* podcast in February 2018. Lees was on the podcast to discuss trans representation in the media. Robinson, instead, took the opportunity to challenge her about the rights of trans people to access spaces such as toilets and changing rooms: what about 'blokes having a sex change going into girls' changing rooms in schools'?[3] When Lees challenged him on his choice of language and asked why he thought an adult would be in a girls' changing room, Robinson replied, 'No, not an adult. Could be someone at a younger age.'[4] Though Robinson eventually retracted his original language, his – at best careless – conflation of young trans girls with (predatory) adult 'blokes' is precisely the kind of rhetorical sleight of hand that impacts on healthy discussion of trans children's experiences.

I can empathize with Lees. In June 2018, I was invited on to the BBC's *Newsnight* programme to discuss the Girl Guides' trans inclusion policy (which allowed trans girls to join the Guides like any other girl). Before the show, I was told that the discussion would centre on 'concerns' about a policy that allows transgender girls to participate in camping trips and overnight stays without the parents of the other girls being told. I told the producers I found this framing dangerous, insinuating as it did that trans children as a group carry an elevated sexual risk to other children. All else aside, I was struck by the producers' sloppy understanding of the basics: disclosure of a trans child's medical and personal history to their peers' parents was self-evidently unlawful and a breach of fundamental human rights, particularly the right to privacy. It quickly dawned on me that the discussion wasn't intended to inform the public about the rights of trans children and the responsibilities of adults to safeguard their wellbeing, but rather to entertain viewers by means of confected controversy and debate. I turned the invitation down.

While the media seems all too happy to focus on trans

children's right to participate in activities alongside their peers (or, indeed, on trans children's very existence), there is little coverage of one of the most pressing problems: the fact that they are significantly more likely to experience discrimination, harassment and violence at home or at school. Sometimes, horrific stories hit local news headlines, such as the trans teenage boy whose face was slashed by a gang of teenagers in Witham, Essex, or the eleven-year-old trans girl in Manchester who, after months of bullying, was shot with a BB gun at school. To date, though, the national media has more or less completely failed to explore the ways in which such egregious incidents form part of a wider pattern of abuse of trans children. According to 2017 research by the LGBTQ+ charity Stonewall, 64 per cent of British trans schoolchildren report being bullied for being trans or for their perceived sexual orientation (sometimes trans young people are instead perceived as gay); 13 per cent of trans pupils experience physical violence as part of this culture of bullying.[5] Any connections between the prevalence of bullying and mental health issues among trans children (a shocking 84 per cent of British trans young people have self-harmed[6]) remain woefully underexamined in the media or in education policy.

For all this – with little thanks to the media – progress is being made in one of the relationships that matters most. Parents like Joe and Kate, who have supported their trans daughter Alex in her gender identity since she was three years old, are becoming increasingly common. Joe and Kate's willingness and ability to support Alex, they tell me, is due to greater availability of information about trans children and gender dysphoria.

'This is where we were in a really fortunate situation,' Kate explains,

in that, when we looked at the internet, there was masses of information. Whereas parents in our exact shoes, even five years earlier, would have done a search and not really found anything. We found a lot of stuff and we found particularly blogs and articles written by American parents – they were five years ahead of the UK.

As their certainty that they merely had a confused son started to crumble, Kate and Joe realized they had much research to do. Alex was determined to assert a female identity, and her parents dropping the use of male pronouns in the family home could hardly alleviate her daily distress in a world that still treated her as a boy. 'Being gender neutral when everyone else was being gendered wasn't an acceptable solution,' Kate tells me. 'That was when I started properly reading and thinking, OK, we need to actually have a plan.'

As the couple read up on the subject, they came across hundreds of accounts of families with a young child identifying as a gender different from the one they were assigned at birth. They were surprised to find how close these accounts were to their own experience. 'It can be spookily similar, even with quite diverse stories, among the kids who feel really, really strongly and are able to vocalize it at that young age.'

Kate points out that these similarities between the various accounts of parents with trans children attract criticism from those commentators who argue that trans children do not exist or should not be affirmed in their gender. 'That's why some of the haters don't believe it,' she says,

> because they think families are following 'the script', whereas we know we experienced it long before we'd read it in anyone else's account. And now I've read it and I've talked to tons of people and the story is similar! This gender identity that just seems to *be there* with a three-year-old as the thing that matters to her more than anything else.

One theme in Kate and Joe's story, which recurs in many accounts of trans children attempting to express a variant identity, is the initial reluctance of most parents to fully affirm that their child is another gender. This reluctance is in stark contrast to a widespread misconception that parents of young trans children might have helped them affirm too quickly in what might have otherwise been 'a phase'. In reality, many supportive parents acknowledge that, if anything, they tried to resist their child's happiness for too long because of their own ignorance or fear. Kate and Joe's story is a case in point: their acceptance of Alex's identity was a gradual process. After some initial research, they spoke to their GP and contacted England's Gender Identity Development Service (GIDS), the specialist service for gender identity issues in children, which told them that Alex would need to be formally referred for any advice to be given. The waiting list was ten months. Kate and Joe also contacted the charity Mermaids. By now, Alex was, with her parents' support, presenting in an increasingly feminine way, which was drawing attention from extended family and other parents at nursery. Mermaids put them in touch with other parents of trans children; they in turn were able to comfort Alex by telling her she was not the only child who felt 'different'. Sharing these experiences also allowed Kate and Joe to fully comprehend Alex's situation. After one shopping trip to buy clothes – entirely from the girls' section – Alex still got upset in the car home, at which point, Joe says, he finally asked his child what would make her happy.

'When I've been good', Alex replied, 'I want you to say, "You've been a good girl today."'

Joe replied, 'Well, today you've been a good girl.'

In that moment, Joe and Kate acknowledged that they would be spending much of their lives fighting for acceptance, not on behalf of their confused and distressed son, but on behalf of their trans daughter.

★

Parental acceptance is the most crucial factor in the future well-being of any trans child. A 2017 study published in the *Journal of the American Academy of Child and Adolescent Psychiatry* found that parents allowing trans children to transition socially virtually eliminates the higher rates of depression and low self-worth trans children experience compared to their cisgender siblings and control groups. Another study looked at trans young people who had chosen a new name to better reflect their gender identity. It found that, compared with peers who were not able to use their chosen name in any context, trans young people who were allowed and encouraged by parents and other adults to use their name at home, at school and with friends experienced a 71 per cent decrease in symptoms of severe depression, a 34 per cent decrease in reported thoughts of suicide and a 65 per cent decrease in suicide attempts.[7] Naturally, using chosen names is not the only factor in improving the mental health of trans children – but they function as a pretty strong indicator of how much the person in question is accepted by those around them. In his 2016 book *Straight Jacket: How to be Gay and Happy*, the writer Matthew Todd describes how parents' non-acceptance of their LGBTQ+ kids' 'difference' (which, he suggests, usually involves breaking gender norms) can begin a chain reaction of negative shame which continues into adulthood, producing unhappiness and maladaptive behaviour linked to problems like depression, anxiety and addiction. In this, Todd draws upon the work of the self-help author John Bradshaw, who makes a distinction between healthy shame – which we use to deter children from dangerous or harmful behaviour – and a more toxic kind of shame that is directed at children for being who they fundamentally are. Todd insists there's a crucial difference between shaming bad behaviour while continuing to affirm that the child is loved, and shaming a child's innate characteristics – such as flamboyance in little boys – for making them a bad kind of person:

it's not a choice or thing we've done, it's a natural part of us, so we can't correct the thing perceived as the problem . . . It's as if receiving the love of our parents is conditional on changing the colour of our eyes. As children we are not equipped to understand that it is just the actions and beliefs of other human beings – our parents – that are wrong. We internalise the negative feelings and believe it is *we* that are wrong.[8]

The idea of parents supporting their gay, lesbian and bi kids has gradually and thankfully become less controversial, whereas it remains so for trans children. Parents who decide to support a child in their wish to transition and live socially in a different gender are still usually regarded as controversial by much of the population. This can range from school-gate whispers and pointed questions at best, to outright accusations of child abuse or Munchausen's by proxy at worst. Even worse, some parents fear losing their children because of misguided intervention by authorities. Joe recalls how the primary reason he wanted Alex to be referred to GIDS was his fear that he and Kate might get into trouble with social services for allowing Alex to present publicly as a girl.

'We were quite worried at that point. We'd heard about families like ours who got into trouble, who had been reported to social services, and we felt quite vulnerable. And,' Joe adds, he and Kate were 'worried that a lot of people would think that we were making it up.'

Joe's fears weren't unfounded. In May 2019 a case was referred to the High Court in which social workers for Lancashire County Council had sought orders against the parents of two trans children to take the children into care. Social services were alerted when H, the couple's three-year-old foster child, born male, had gone into school presenting as a girl. H's apparent transition alarmed social workers, in particular because the couple's biological child – R, aged seven and also born male – had also transitioned to live as a girl. Perhaps suspicious of two trans children being raised in the same family, social workers wanted to remove the children from their parents on the basis that 'H and R have suffered and are at risk of suffering significant emotional harm because their complete social transition into females occurred at a very young age and was actively encouraged.' The High Court hearing, which took into account expert evidence from specialists, dismissed the claim, ruling that the parents had instead 'appropriately supported' the child. The judge, Mr Justice Williams, added that there was no evidence of harm in the parents' supporting H in her social transition and that it was 'overwhelmingly obvious' that the couple were good parents who were 'attuned and careful'; the question of any risk to their children was 'comprehensively dispelled'. Despite the outcome, this case must still have had a hugely negative impact on the family involved – and families in a similar position who, following the case closely, feared being involved in such proceedings themselves.

Cases like this show a need for better training for the relevant professionals. A 2018 review by the National Institute of Economic and Social Research found that training for child and family social workers on transgender issues is 'largely deficient' and that social workers' knowledge was 'very mixed'.[9] All of which, I'd argue, speaks of the enduring societal prejudice against trans people, and staff-training modules alone won't fix the problem. In this cisgender worldview, being trans is always considered an undesirable – if sometimes tolerable – result for a human being. Certain unfortunate individuals may wish to transition as adults, such a belief goes, but innocent children risk being too easily encouraged into this potential disaster and will grow up with bitter regret at what has happened to them. The irony of this prejudice is self-evident: it utterly disregards the harm involved in *not* supporting a trans child who is certain of their identity and who vocalizes it. Many trans adults have memories of trying to articulate their identity to parents who did not or could not support them and instead sought to suppress their identity through denial, punishment and shame. As Matthew Todd explains, these tactics have a profound impact on the child, who learns from adults that a fundamental aspect of themselves and their psychological makeup is wrong, but still cannot be changed. If we want to do right by trans children, we must first understand that attempts to suppress trans children who persistently express their identity can be the greatest source of lifelong harm. By contrast, parents who support their child's exploration of gender – in whatever form it may take – should be praised for fulfilling their responsibility to create a secure and loving home for their child.

As well as parental and family acceptance, one of the biggest, most unavoidable influences on trans young people's everyday lives is school. When Kate and Joe decided to support Alex in socially transitioning to live as a girl and be referred to as 'she' and 'her', she was still at nursery. Concerned that this would confuse parents of Alex's peers, Joe and Kate wrote them a letter explaining that Alex had wrestled for a long time with her identity, had felt distressed to be identified as a boy, and so would now be living as a girl.

'I think the response to that letter was quite positive,' says Joe cautiously. 'People saying, "Totally fine," or "You must be going through a difficult time," and "It's lovely that she's happy." Quite a lot of responses like that.' He pauses. 'But then people just started dropping out of our life.'

The initial positive responses to their letter gave way to hostility, as they found themselves confronted by parents who said they were doing the wrong thing. 'The responses that hurt were where people thought that their child could be confused and/or that our child was contagious. So people stopped their kid hanging out with ours, or quit some of the groups that she was part of.' Kate recalls how people pulled their children out of the swimming lessons and gym club that Alex attended: 'We had people ask to be put in a different class, saying, "My child can't be around a trans child or a confused child."'

Things did get better. At the time of writing, Alex is at primary school. Here, most pupils have only ever known her as a girl – though she has also chosen to be open with her classmates about her past and being trans. Alex's distress and angst about gender dissipated 'literally overnight', Kate says, as soon as she began using female pronouns and was referred to as a girl at home and in school. While the family still came across teachers and parents with negative attitudes, they were able to carve out space for Alex to be herself.

'It's quite simple at the moment,' Kate says. 'At this age, the kids are just running around and there's not really any bullying I've seen. She's popular and she has really good friends.'

It is the adult world, though, that instils and nurtures prejudice, and, Kate explains, adult acceptance can be tentative:

> I don't think a lot of the parents are properly accepting. And that worries me. The kids are fine because they're not really understanding or thinking about it. I don't know how that's going to work as they all get older, because I don't think they're going to get educated properly about these issues.

When 64 per cent of trans pupils say they are bullied for being LGBTQ+ at school, almost half of those bullied never tell anyone about the bullying, and 46 per cent say they hear transphobic language 'frequently' at school,[10] it's fair to say there is a crisis in our education system around tackling bullying, violence, harassment and social exclusion. The origins of this crisis go back decades. After a series of right-wing-media-induced panics in the 1980s about a 'gay agenda' being promoted in schools, the Thatcher government responded by promising to clamp down on the problem. In a speech to the Conservative Party conference in October 1987, Margaret Thatcher bemoaned a society in which

Too often, our children don't get the education they need – the education they deserve . . . that opportunity is all too often snatched from them by hard-left education authorities and extremist teachers . . . Children who need to be taught to respect traditional moral values are being taught that they have an inalienable right to be gay.

Acting to stem this tide, in 1988 her government passed Section 28, a legislative measure banning schools from promoting 'the teaching in any maintained school of the acceptability of homosexuality as a pretended family relationship'. The effect of the legislation was to gag teachers both from explicitly teaching about gay and lesbian issues and from offering support to individual LGBTQ+ pupils. Given that much behaviour in children that becomes the focus of bullying is actually about breaking gender norms, this legislation, while primarily directed against 'homosexuals', undoubtedly stunted and warped British society's awareness of trans people too. While Section 28 was eventually repealed in 2000 in Scotland, and in 2003 in England and Wales, its poisonous legacy endured in a generation of teachers who had been trained not to tackle LGBTQ+ issues and the bullying that arose from them.

Section 28 came into force two months after I was born, and remained in place until I was in sixth form. Like many trans teenagers still presenting as their birth sex, I was often perceived as gay. From around the age of eleven, I became a target of homophobic taunting: this persisted daily through my early teen-age years. The basis for this was a cluster of various traits and mannerisms which my peers coded as feminine: from my in-tonation, to the way I walked, to my interests. When I relay these experiences now, I find that non-LGBTQ+ people assume this bullying took the form of name-calling (homophobic slurs like 'queer', 'batty boy' or 'faggot') and, sometimes, being physically intimidated or even assaulted. What people tend not to realize as instinctively was how sexualized some of this harassment was. If I was gay, the assumption was that I must be sex-mad: I was pub-licly taunted and humiliated by being graphically told how much I wanted anal sex, or to 'suck my cock' by boys a few years older than me. On one school trip where we shared dormitories, I woke up to find a porn magazine left open on my face. When I was thirteen, a boy in another year grabbed my crotch through my trousers, to 'check' if I was a girl or not. I was never really beaten up, though, and things improved at school as I got older. It's a sad indictment of the widespread homophobia and transphobia in schools at the time that I actually consider myself lucky: some of my friends and many of the trans people I've met in my work spent their school years in total misery, being terror-ized daily.

My own experience made me acutely aware of the complex web of shame that homophobic and transphobic bullying can instil. It was confusing to be taunted and harassed by people who had formed conclusions about my sexuality, when even I wasn't sure what my orientation was. Furthermore, I didn't feel like I could discuss the situation with anyone, either at school or at home, because doing so would have only drawn more attention to my queerness and provoked questions from adults that I didn't feel prepared or safe to answer. Though a couple of progressive-minded teachers did bring up the subject of gay people favourably in the course of PSHE lessons, they were few and far between – and there was no mention whatsoever of trans people throughout my entire education. Most teachers, whatever their personal beliefs, were silent on these matters; worse, a minority were as prejudiced as my bullying peers. On more than one occasion I was advised to 'tone it down': a victim-blaming euphemism for repressing the femininity that was attracting negative attention. When, on a school trip to London, we walked through Soho, the deputy headmaster, no less, quipped, 'Keep your backs against the wall here, boys.' The shadow of Section 28 fell heavily: the effect of suppressing education about LGBTQ+ issues was not only to prevent LGBTQ+ children existing openly at school but, just as perniciously, to create a culture of silence that allowed prejudice among kids and staff alike to flourish unchallenged. Queer young people, for their part, were forced to internalize a constant drip-feed of humiliation, often (like me) not wanting to speak out for fear of making a horrible situation even worse. Having to absorb such humiliation in childhood is, unsurprisingly, something associated with a range of negative mental health outcomes later in life. Section 28 must be remembered and condemned for what it was: a staggering dereliction of duty on behalf of Britain's policymakers towards the country's young people.

In the decades since Section 28's repeal, there are signs that things have slowly – very, very slowly – improved for lesbian, gay and bisexual pupils. Research carried out by Stonewall has found that, since 2007, the number of lesbian, gay and bi pupils bullied because of their sexual orientation has fallen by almost a third. The number of schools who overtly condemn such bullying has nearly trebled, and homophobic remarks are far less likely to be heard in classrooms, corridors and playgrounds.[11] There is increasing public recognition that formal education about same-sex relationships and sexual orientation in schools is necessary. (Although not universally: in March 2019, twenty-one MPs voted against LGBTQ+-inclusive guidance for relationships and sex education in English schools, while in the same month protesters held rallies against the introduction of LGBTQ+-inclusive relationship and sex education outside Parkfield Community School, a Birmingham primary school.)

This growing acceptance of the need to create an inclusive school environment has not been extended so readily to trans pupils. Just as, back in the 1980s, the British media feared a 'gay agenda' in schools, so in the late 2010s a similar panic was created about the idea of 'gender ideology' infiltrating the education system. While opposition to LGB-inclusive education is now the preserve of religious conservatives and the ultra-right wing of the Tory party, resistance to teaching children about the existence of trans people occurs across the political spectrum, while media attacks on organizations providing support to families and training to schools and public bodies, particularly the charity Mermaids, are all too frequent. Worse still, specific organizations have been founded to actively campaign against trans inclusion in schools, both in the media and by mounting legal challenges to local councils that implement trans-inclusion guidelines. One such organization, Transgender Trend, is a regular source of quotes for topical articles in newspapers such as *The Sunday Times* and *Daily Mail*. In its own words, Transgender Trend was founded in 2015 by a 'group of concerned parents' for 'everyone who is concerned about the social and medical "transition" of children, the introduction of "gender identity" teaching into schools and new policies and legislation based on subjective ideas of "gender" rather than the biological reality of sex'. In 2018, it published a resource pack for schools – markedly similar in appearance to the resources provided by major LGBTQ+ and trans organizations – purportedly to assist teachers in supporting children struggling with their gender identity. On closer examination, the guidance provided does precisely the opposite, by encouraging the suspicion and suppression of trans children's needs. 'Advice given by transgender organizations is focused upon the transgender individual and may not look at the holistic duties that the school has to the whole community,' it ominously insists. The same resource pack also states, on no evidence whatsoever, that trans children and young people are 'a very new phenomenon. Schools need to be aware that there is no long-term evidence base to support the "transition" of children, including social transition.'[12]

Anti-trans groups like Transgender Trend are strangers to research – precisely because, exposed to research, their assertions evaporate. Rather, they rely on unevidenced myths, speculation and insinuation: that trans people are a new phenomenon, for example, or that there is a social prestige attached to being trans which must be discouraged. 'The school should aim to avoid any transgender child becoming a "cause célèbre" through the actions of the school,' the same schools pack warns, while also referring to 'the risk of "social contagion" from celebrity trans internet vloggers who glamorize medical transition'.[13] According to Transgender Trend, coming out as trans 'also may be used by the child as an excuse for bad behaviour or failing in class, or a pass to gaining special rights and exemptions not afforded to other children'.[14] In other words, not only does being trans make a child more glamorous and popular but being trans can confer special privileges or operate as a 'get out of jail free' card.

All these assertions, it must be emphasized, are total nonsense. In fact, research reveals that the reality for trans pupils in British schools is starkly different from the one imagined by anti-trans campaign groups. Seventy-seven per cent of LGBTQ+ pupils say they have never received any school-based education about gender identity and what being 'trans' means; 33 per cent of trans pupils are not able to be known by their preferred name at school; 58 per cent are not allowed to use the toilets in which they feel comfortable.[15] This environment, created by the failings of adults, only increases hostility and bullying among pupils. Horrifyingly, almost one in ten trans young people have received a death threat while at school. Rather than being indulged or given special treatment, the stark truth is that many trans children are receiving little institutional support and, in some cases, are explicitly discouraged from being fully themselves at school.

Yet, just when greater inclusion, full commitment to anti-bullying practices and more robust safeguarding is needed, there emerges a false political narrative of trans children being disruptive to their peers, being extended privileged treatment, and carrying a risk of social contagion, converting other children to their 'gender ideology'. Taking all of the above into account, it is clear that Britain is in the grip of a moral panic about trans children and young people.

In their classic analysis of moral panics, sociologists Erich Goode and Nachman Ben-Yehuda outline five key characteristics: 'concern', or the belief that the behaviour of the group in question are likely to have a negative effect on society; 'hostility' – fairly self-explanatory – to the point where the group in question are seen as 'folk devils', that is, a group of people who are portrayed in media as outsiders and deviant, and who are blamed for crimes or other sorts of social problems; 'consensus', or widespread acceptance that the group in question poses a very real threat to society; 'disproportionality' – the resulting societal action taken against the group is entirely disproportionate to the actual threat posed by it; and, finally, 'volatility' – moral panics typically appear and subside very quickly, often vanishing abruptly because media, and therefore public, interest wanes or a new panic supplants the previous one.[16]

The narratives perpetuated about trans children, particularly in schools, by headlines like 'Children Sacrificed to Appease Trans Lobby' or 'Cult of Gender Identity is Harming Children',[17] are intended to alarm the public – it's impossible to draw any other conclusion from the language used – and they certainly fit Goode and Ben-Yehuda's description of a moral panic. The framing of trans people as 'folk devils' relies on three key factors.[18] First, reducing trans children into crass stereotypes, such as Nick Robinson's conflation of young trans girls with the more familiar and well-worn caricature of adult 'blokes who've had sex changes'. Second, exaggeration, such as overhyping the increase in children coming out as trans by use of language like 'surge' and carefully selected statistics for headlines such as 'Minister to Order Inquiry into 4000 per cent Rise in Children Wanting to Change Sex'.[19] Between 2015 and 2020, 10,478 children (defined as under eighteen) were referred to England's Gender Identity Development Service. The total child population of England is approximately 12 million. So, even with the increased numbers of children who are presenting to the NHS with gender issues, and even if all of them are persistently identifying as trans, these referrals would constitute at most approximately 0.09 per cent of the total child population of England. The influence of LGBTQ+ organizations over schools – almost invariably portrayed as nefarious – is also exaggerated (the UK's largest LGBTQ+ charity, Stonewall, works with around 1,500 of the UK's 32,770 schools); so too is the ease with which families can access medical treatments and the age at which these treatments are made available. Finally, the creation of folk devils relies on predictions about the group's behaviour. Hostile media headlines regularly use the word 'grooming'[20] to describe the supposed influence of 'the trans lobby' over children: a term that intentionally hints at sexual predation. In transphobic blogs, anti-trans online forums and social media, wild claims are made of a homophobic conspiracy to turn gay children straight, and of the existence of an online trans cult that attempts to recruit autistic young people. This last claim is based on the fact that there is some evidence of a link between being trans and autism: that autistic people may be more likely to have gender dysphoria and thereby identify themselves as trans – though as yet there is little evidence as to why this should be so. More important than explaining any potential link is the evidence that trans young people who are also autistic or otherwise neuro-diverse are at an even higher risk of bullying and social exclusion at school than trans young people who are not.[21] It's also notable that anti-trans theories can trade in negative stereotypes about autism as much as transphobic stereotypes.

Sociologists broadly agree that moral panics can result in retrograde policy changes and punitive measures that impact significantly on civil rights; just as significantly, they can also make institutions – like schools – more hesitant in acting to defend the group being targeted. It is more important than ever that those responsible for the wellbeing and education of children are properly trained and informed of the facts so that they can protect trans children.

The moral panic surrounding trans children and their families not only obscures the bullying and exclusion trans kids already face, but actively encourages it.

'I feel like it's quite shaky acceptance, or tolerance,' Kate says of the attitudes she and her daughter Alex experience in their daily lives. 'If there's some negative article about how trans kids don't exist, and parents are abusive, it really worries me how that affects the way parents perceive Alex and therefore how they feed that on to their own kids.'

Kate is especially concerned about how media coverage has already affected Alex's experience of school. 'The one proper problem we had at school was in the week after the BBC documentary [*Transgender Kids: Who Knows Best?*]. It's not a coincidence, the timing, and so, I don't know which parents watched that and what they then said to their kids, and then their kids say something hostile to Alex. It definitely has an impact.'

Joe tells me that many parents in their situation share similar stories of the connection between bullying and media misrepresentation: 'If there's a documentary out, or a newspaper article, then kids are being bullied in school. They're getting abused on Snapchat, they get beaten up, they get a brick through the window. You know this is happening, and we see it, anecdotally, in the groups we're part of.'

As trans children like Alex grow up and move to secondary school, they, like all teenagers, enter an environment in which they cannot be as sheltered from prejudice or as easily protected by their parents as they were before. Like other teenage girls, Alex will look to assert her own identity in the world as an individual above and beyond her gender. But her parents worry that, unlike other girls, she'll face unique challenges, given that teenagers may be more inclined than younger children to pick on anyone different.

'The secondary school thing?' Kate says; 'I just don't imagine it's going to be very easy, particularly as we don't exactly live in one of the more progressive areas for LGBTQ+ kids, like Brighton.'

Still, though the current state of the UK media and its discussion of trans children alarms Kate and Joe, they acknowledge that there is an upside: the greater visibility of trans people in public life gives them hope for their daughter's future. Societal attitudes, they believe, are changing and will continue to change for the better. Joe says,

> I used to be very worried about her future relationships and life prospects, her life expectancy and her health and everything else. And now? Honestly, I think she's going to be absolutely fine. Everyone's got something going on with them. Everyone's got their own battles to fight. Of course, I worry for her; everyone worries for their kids. We've already got examples of people in the public

eye who are trans who are just getting on with it and excelling and I think you'll see more and more and she's just going to fly.

I left the family convinced that, despite almost inevitable difficulties ahead, Alex would ultimately thrive because of the love and support of two parents who were prepared to defend her to the hilt. Meeting Alex had also given me hope for the future; she and I were trans female people born only one generation apart, yet the world she is growing up in seems to have far more space in it for trans people than the one I knew.

Yet it also raises another question about growing up trans in Britain today. Alex's family home was a place of love and security, but this is by no means the case for all trans children The UK government's National LGBT Survey, conducted in 2018, the largest survey of LGBT people ever carried out anywhere, found that 44 per cent of trans people avoided being open about their gender identity at home for fear of a negative reaction. The survey also provides some insight into the kinds of negative reaction trans young people fear: 27 per cent said they had experienced verbal harassment from someone they lived with in the past year; 5 per cent said they had experienced physical violence at the hands of someone they lived with. Shockingly, the most frequent perpetrators in both cases were parents.[22]

Family rejection and estrangement have devastating long-term health implications. They also have a material impact. For some kids, the only option is leaving home. Others have no option at all: their parents kick them out. As a result, trans teenagers and young adults in Britain are much more likely to experience homelessness than their cisgender peers. According to research by akt (formerly the Albert Kennedy Trust), a charity that has been providing safe homes and supporting LGBTQ+ youth since 1989, 24 per cent of homeless young people identify as LGBTQ+, and in 77 per cent of these cases homelessness was due to family abuse or rejection, usually related to their sexuality or gender identity.[23] A minority within a minority, trans young people are disproportionately over-represented in the homeless population: one in four trans people have experienced homelessness.

'The numbers have increased significantly', akt's CEO Tim Sigsworth tells me at the charity's head office in London. 'When I started at akt twelve years ago, less than 5 per cent of our service users identified as trans. Now, we are looking at around 35 per cent.' Later, I speak to Dawn, a regional services manager for akt in Newcastle, who says that in the north-east of England about half of the young people accessing akt's services are trans. The reason for this dramatic increase in a little over a decade, Tim and Dawn both suggest, is that more people are coming out younger, but family and community attitudes aren't evolving fast enough – meaning that trans teens and young adults are facing a wave of hostility. Dawn says that this negative reaction is the key difference in the situations facing trans young people and the lesbian, gay and bi young people she also works with: 'Things are getting easier on sexuality in terms of understanding, but gender identity remains hard for people to grasp, and parents don't know what is happening for the young person. They can react badly.'

On a chilly November evening, at a weekly meet-up for trans young people in Cardiff, I am introduced to twenty-five-year-old Rudy Harries, a trans man. Today, Rudy is studying for a master's degree at Cardiff University; he has good friends and is engaged to be married. Life is good. Yet just one year ago, Rudy tells me, he was homeless. Before I leave, he hands me a copy of a speech he gave a few days previously to a meeting organized by Cymorth Cymru (the umbrella body for providers of housing support in Wales), saying that it provided the fullest description of his own experience. I read the speech on the train home.

'I graduated from university in the summer of 2016,' the speech starts. 'I was forced to return home to South Wales because I wasn't mentally well enough to start a graduate job. My family are part of an incredibly conservative religious sect.' Rudy had been openly queer since he was seventeen. First coming out as bisexual, at university he had begun to transition medically to male, taking testosterone, which gave him a more masculine presentation and voice. His immediate family struggled with the idea and, when he moved back into the family home, one close relative in particular made his life hell.

'The abuse there escalated from verbal to physical,' Rudy went on, 'and after talking to my partner, who lives away, I was convinced to go to a local domestic violence centre and ask for help.' Professionals at the domestic violence centre were genuinely concerned Rudy's life was in danger: 'they did an assessment and decided that I was at imminent threat of homicide. "If you stay there," they told me, "you will be dead in six months or less."'

Despite the gravity of his situation, Rudy found that existing provision for victims of domestic abuse wasn't designed with someone like him – a transitioning trans man – in mind. Indeed, the domestic violence provision was heavily gendered. 'I was given three options,' he continued: 'a woman's shelter, a man's shelter, or presenting myself to the council as homeless. It should tell you all you need to know about the fear that British trans people live in right now, in 2019, when I tell you I chose homelessness.'

Rudy believed that the option of highly gendered domestic violence shelters could make him a target as someone in the process of transitioning to male: 'My figure and voice [were] becoming more masculine by the day as the result of hormone treatment. I feared that if I tried to access a gendered refuge, someone would report me to the tabloids.'

Rudy had come up against a common problem for trans people seeking crisis services: not simply a lack of specialist provision, but a lack of understanding of how trans people's fear of highly gendered services can lead them to self-exclude – as Rudy felt he had to – because of the risk of further harassment and prejudice within those services. Presenting as homeless to his local authority hardly brought an end to Rudy's problems. Homelessness has increased year on year across the UK in the past decade. The huge numbers of homeless people waiting to be accommodated in Wales alone meant that, even though he was fleeing domestic violence, Rudy was placed in 'Band C' priority – the third of four bandings for the most urgent cases. He was placed in a bed and breakfast, as is customary for those waiting to be housed. There, things took a turn for the worse.

'A couple of weeks into my stay, a new man joined our breakfast table. He'd just got out of prison for beating up a gay man. He seemed proud of it. I knew that if I didn't get out of there I would be at serious risk of further abuse.'

Here, Rudy encountered another key problem for trans people experiencing housing issues or homelessness: the risk of harassment that accompanies living in shared accommodation with homophobic or transphobic people. The default position in the UK for benefit claims is that all single people under the age of thirty-five who claim universal credit (formerly housing benefit) to help pay rent should live in shared accommodation with housemates to keep costs to the state down (there are some exceptions, such as those leaving the care system and people with certain disabilities). For those driven to the brink of homelessness, emergency accommodation – like the bed and breakfast Rudy was placed in – lacks even the most basic privacy.

'We see cases where trans young people are just put in hostels with shared bathroom facilities,' Dawn at akt tells me. 'I had a case where a young trans woman who was transitioning was having to share a bathroom. It isn't acceptable.' This lack of privacy can become particularly pressing for trans young people who either cannot – or do not want to – 'pass' as a non-trans person, which often means they are subject to harassment in private spaces like bathrooms. 'Another example would be a trans man who is wearing chest binders all day and sharing facilities with people,' Dawn explains. 'If he doesn't want other residents to know he's hiding it all the time and binding longer than he safely should until late at night when other people are asleep, that's a huge problem.'

As the akt CEO Tim Sigsworth says emphatically, 'Shared accommodation does not work if you are going through a very private and personal transition process.'

When Rudy was forced to share accommodation with someone convicted of a violent homophobic hate crime, he wrote to his member of the Senedd (Welsh Parliament) and was transferred, though he remained in emergency accommodation for three months as the council struggled to place him in proper temporary housing. According to his November 2019 speech at Cymorth Cymru, this difficulty in finding him somewhere to live stemmed directly from his trans identity: the available hostels, shared housing and temporary accommodation were either gender segregated or had specific age requirements.

'I was too old for some places, not woman enough for some, not man enough for others. I was in a state of limbo. My existence as a transgender man who was a victim of domestic violence was not part of anybody's protocol'. Some of this will be about appearance: a trans man currently transitioning may feel anxious about going to a women's shelter while presenting as male, but also fear being subject to hostility if they are identified as trans in a men's shelter.

This, Tim Sigsworth tells me, is a fundamental problem for vulnerable people with multifaceted identities: 'Services will compartmentalize us, because they can only deal with one problem at a time. So they will not see the whole person. It's a massive issue. So a lot is lost.'

Rudy finally got back on his feet thanks to the help of a support worker working for the Welsh homeless charity Llamau, which ran the emergency accommodation he was placed in. 'They got me into longer-term supported accommodation where I could put down roots, and work to get my life back together again.' Rudy concurs with Tim: 'People are more complex than tick-boxes. One size does not fit all.'

The ways in which different forms of marginalization, prejudice and oppression can combine in certain contexts – known as 'intersectionality' – have in recent years become more widely acknowledged in activist circles. Yet, for those working in front-line community services, there's often neither the time nor the resources to consider the intersecting vulnerabilities facing those trans young people who have been rejected by their families and are consequently struggling to find somewhere to live. For instance, trans young people from certain ethnic, cultural and religious backgrounds are more likely to need help. Tim tells me that, in London, 80 per cent of akt's service users are BAME and that, even outside London, the overall proportion of BAME service users is 58 per cent. Trans young people of colour, then, are disproportionately in need of support with housing – and, in addition to the institutional barriers they may face for being trans, it is also fair to assume they experience similar hurdles because of race. In part, as Tim explains, this is because in the charity and housing sector the people providing support don't reflect the communities they're serving: 'I think for people of colour, it's mainly secular, white-led services that are responding to their needs. So often in services the young people we work with won't be seen by another trans person or they won't see another person of colour, and they often will not see somebody who is a person of faith.'

Akt, on the other hand, tries to ensure that both its staff and its own volunteer base is representative of the young people it works with. One of these volunteers – who was previously supported by akt – is Robyn, a twenty-seven-year-old non-binary trans person, whose identity is trans feminine (meaning that she was assigned male at birth, but her gender identity now sits closer to feminine/female on the gender spectrum and she consequently uses feminine pronouns).

'I was born and raised in Birmingham and grew up in a pretty small neighbourhood of almost 100 per cent Muslims, mainly Pakistani Muslims,' Robyn tells me. She attended Parkfield Community School – the school which in 2019 made headlines when its LGBTQ+-inclusive relationships education attracted protests outside the school gates. 'I'm not surprised that that school is where the protest began,' Robyn acknowledges. Though her own family is Muslim, they were not 'super religious'; rather, their faith was expressed 'culturally'. Long before her sexuality or gender became an issue, Robyn felt like the 'black sheep' of her family.

'I wasn't interested in the same things as them. At times, they could be very bigoted. I just didn't agree with their views on a lot of things. We had wildly different personalities and politics and it made me stick out.' Her childhood was unhappy: 'It was a pretty abusive home, even without gender coming into play.'

Was it violent, I ask.

'Really violent, just incessantly violent, almost exclusively from my dad, but my older brother joined in a lot of it once he got a little older, because the age difference between me and him is six years.'

Early in adolescence, Robyn became aware that she was attracted to people of all genders and felt confused about whether she was gay or bi. 'I didn't really know trans people existed. It took till probably my late teens to realize that was even a thing people felt that they could put a word on. I was definitely thinking I was just very feminine, gay, or bi man, and thinking I just wanted to really present as feminine. I thought, "Am I a drag queen? I don't understand." '

University gave Robyn space to come out as bi; soon, she had come to the realization that she was also trans. But, at twenty-two years old, she had to drop out of her course because of mental health issues. She had no job – and now, no accommodation: her family, she believes, suspected she might be gay, and had grown overtly homophobic as a form of discouragement. Rather than return home, she turned to akt, who helped her find accommodation. Eventually, she decided to come out to her friends on Facebook, a step that inevitably meant having to tell her family. 'I was so torn up about telling them and stressed about it. And in my head, it was like, well, they're abusive. So I expected them to react badly. Just from the stress of not wanting to tell them, I got really ill.'

Robyn's mental health deteriorated to the point where she attempted suicide. She was placed on a men's psychiatric ward; there, she decided to text her entire family to tell them she was trans and to ask if that was OK with them. She received no response. 'Then I got a call from my sister, who said, "Well, you need to stay in hospital, obviously, because you're saying all this crazy stuff about being a girl. And don't worry, they can fix that for you, you know." '

Robyn says she thinks her family would have accepted her back as a son and brother if she had conceded that she was mentally ill and apologized. As it is, only one family member, a younger brother, still speaks to her.

Robyn is at pains to point out that, even when she has accessed support from LGBTQ+ organizations, she has been nervous about being 'pigeonholed' by white people because of her ethnic and religious background. 'I often didn't feel comfortable talking about my family's religion. I worried people would just say, "Oh, so you're trans, your family is Muslim? Obviously, those two things can't go together." So that's it. That's the entire story. Well, no, it's not always that easy.'

Speaking about how race has shaped her experience of being trans, Robyn says a key problem is that she feels she fights bigotry on both fronts, having to deal with transphobia in her family's community and racist assumptions within the trans community from which she seeks support. 'I have tried really hard to socialize with trans groups, and it's super white; to the point almost where it feels intentional. It's really difficult to feel like I finally found my people, they understand what I'm going through. And then you see that they're all white and they understand such a small part of what I experienced as a trans woman of colour.'

She says one racialized assumption is that she must be or have been a sex worker, something she's been asked directly. 'That's a hugely messed up thing to say, first of all, and you've just assumed that there's just one narrative. You wouldn't say that to a white person. You wouldn't feel comfortable saying that. But you think you know my entire story? Because obviously, we must all have the exact same one.'

Robyn's description of a trans movement conceived as being for and run by white people, when in fact it is predominantly trans people of colour who are experiencing homelessness at disproportionate rates, raises the question of priorities in the political movement for trans liberation. In the media, much of the focus on 'trans rights' in recent years has been on legislative rights (such as streamlining the process for legal gender recognition or having a gender-neutral passport), and on social conduct, such as checking a person's pronouns. This emphasis stems in part from a media agenda set by cisgender people, often – as we've seen – for the purposes of creating controversy and fuelling a culture war. As a result, like many movements formed around an aspect of personal identity, class politics and a broader critique of capitalism have become sidelined in the trans movement. Besides the time and energy trans people have to spend defending civil rights and social courtesies, there's a pretty straightforward reason for this. In any minority group, those who have the time, resources and political access to lead the charge for recognition and better treatment tend to be the middle-class members, who don't appreciate the urgent issues of poverty and homelessness that for many can impede participation in activist movements. This representational imbalance leads to 'single issue' priorities, which emphasize the personal freedoms of the individual over the economic liberation of the entire minority group.

Trans politics is no different. Poverty and homelessness are rarely framed as 'trans issues' in the media – or even by large LGBTQ+ lobby groups. Yet the introduction of Universal Credit by the Conservative-led coalition government in 2013, as part of its wider programme of austerity measures, had perhaps the most damaging impact on vulnerable trans people of any policy in recent memory. Universal Credit, which involves a six-week delay before a claimant can receive any benefit, is one of the key ways a trans young person can slide into hardship. As Tim Sigsworth notes, 'That's long enough for a landlord to throw somebody out. That's long enough for a young person's finances to unravel very quickly.'

What's more, in the intervening years, the ravages of austerity have left a housing crisis in which vulnerable tenants are subject to the prejudices of private landlords. These include refusing to rent to a trans person because they are trans, and refusing to rent to people on benefits in general: a prejudice against poverty itself. As Tim says, 'Landlords are now more interested in somebody who has a stable job, who is earning at a certain level, who they see as a sure bet to pay the rent.'

Many homeless trans people stay off the streets by 'sofa surfing': either staying with friends or, in some cases, exchanging sex for a place to stay. Inevitably, some end up sleeping rough. For trans people on the streets, life can be brutal. 'Being homeless, you get attacked. Being trans and homeless, you get attacked more,' Anna, a homeless twenty-four-year-old trans woman told her local newspaper, the *Bristol Cable*.[24] Anna had 'always known' she was trans, 'but by the time I was old enough to put words to what I was feeling, I was about thirteen. I hid it for a year – I'd sneak away, dress up, trying to build confidence in myself. Then I told my mum, and that was that – she battered me and threw me out on the streets. Kicked out of home aged fourteen, Anna was homeless for the subsequent decade. Being a trans woman on the streets made her especially vulnerable: 'You'd be amazed the amount of people that treat transgender people as if they're sex objects. It's disgusting – makes me feel shit about myself.'

On the street, the propositioning and threats of sexual violence were relentless: '"Do you want to come and suck my dick?" . . . "I'll give you a place to stay for the night, if you give me some" . . . "I'll pay you sixty quid if you give me a blow job." That's the value people hold on us. It's worse because I'm homeless and vulnerable. People have tried to rape me.'

Anna's case is all too common. In July 2017, the *Bristol Post* reported that another homeless trans woman based in Bristol, known as Jo, returned from church to find that the bus shelter she had been living in had been deliberately set on fire. She sat on a nearby wall and watched, helpless, as the flames turned all her possessions to ash. Residents familiar with Jo told the newspaper that she 'suffered abuse because she was transgender and because she lived outside'.[25]

The stories of both Anna and Jo highlight the violence to which homeless trans people are subjected. Despite this, many feel forced to remain on the streets because of transphobia in mainstream homeless shelters. 'They need to set up an LGBT hostel. They won't put me into a male hostel because I'll be attacked, and other things could happen. But they won't put me into a woman's hostel because I'm still "equipped",' Anna told the *Bristol Cable*, describing once again how the gendering of services allows many trans people to slip between the cracks.[26]

Change will only be brought about by bringing class politics back on to the political agenda. This would mean, for example, incorporating a broader criticism of Universal Credit, the lack of social housing and the unchecked power of private landlords into the heart of LGBTQ+ and trans politics. Action on trans (and wider LGBTQ+) homelessness is desperately needed, and one group of activists in London is rising to the challenge. The Outside Project, launched in winter 2017, is the UK's first dedicated LGBTQ+ homeless shelter. Originally consisting of a twelve-bed tour bus bought through crowdfunding, the project now has local authority grant funding and a fixed home in a former fire station in Clerkenwell, which doubles as a daytime community centre for LGBTQ+ groups.

On the eve of Pride in London 2019, a hot July evening, I was given a tour of the shelter by the project's campaigns manager, Harry Gay. The Outside Project, he explains, was set up by a group of people who worked in the homeless sector in mainstream services. 'They were seeing lots of people from across the LGBT spectrum coming in, and then struggling in mainstream shelters,' Harry tells me. 'There are housing charities, but there was nothing really there for people that were in crisis.'

Music is blaring, and the atmosphere is buzzing as we walk through the yard outside: guests and volunteers are spray-painting signs and banners for the march the following day. Inside, it's equally lively. The slogans on the project's placards are unabashedly radical: solidarity with LGBTQ+ migrants and abolition of borders; demands for housing and an end to capitalism.

Earlier that day, I had watched Harry on national television arguing that Pride had become too commercialized: the Pride in London organizers, he said, seemed more preoccupied with the Outside Project's radical image than the important work it does.

I ask Harry if he's a socialist: 'Yes, absolutely,' he says. What about the project? 'Well, everything that we do is, yes. I think otherwise, if activism is just liberal, it's just all marketing ploys and it's all about increasing capital and nothing is actually to benefit the community.' In particular, activists at the Outside Project see themselves as offering a critique of mainstream LGBTQ+ campaigning, which does focus on corporations and the middle-class experience. 'We can work from the grassroots up and look at the needs of the guests,' Harry tells me. 'I think the movement at the moment is all about workplace inclusion policies, and the celebration of workplace inclusion, and that's great, but it's completely overlooking people that have been left behind in the movement – like trans people and those who are homeless. Our line is that we don't need a workplace inclusion policy, we need housing. That's what we say when anyone says, "Don't you think it's great that this organization has gender neutral toilets?" Yeah, sure, but that should be a blanket rule anyway.'

Harry says his political stance arises from looking at the root causes of the guests' homelessness: 'An employer having an inclusion policy is fine, but what about zero-hour contracts and minimum wage? They're the reasons that people do end up in contact with our organization. It's a working-class issue. Those are the people that are going to end up in our shelter.'

The shelter itself has thirteen spaces. Sometimes people stay just one night, sometimes they come and go sporadically, some stay for long stretches. The aim is usually to get guests into longer-term housing, and in this the project works with Stonewall Housing, a more traditional LGBTQ+ housing charity (completely separate from the Stonewall I have previously mentioned, both taking their name from the Stonewall Inn in New York City). Harry says the Outside Project is fulfilling a critical need: 'I guess the best thing about the shelter is that, in a mainstream service, guests will be fixated on their identity and whether they need to conceal it, because of homophobia and transphobia, from staff members and other guests. But here we just focus on housing. It's a space where everything else can just be normal.'

As with the larger charities, Harry tells me that trans people, mainly trans women, are over-represented among their guests. 'There's a couple of things that are extra traumatic for a trans person on the streets. There was one guest staying with us that had to go back to presenting as male on the streets because of safety; she was a trans woman. When she would come and stay, it would just be a few days she could take to settle back into herself and present how she felt most comfortable.'

Addiction and sex work are reasonably common among trans guests. The Outside Project seeks to take a less judgemental or prescriptive approach than other services: 'If people do turn up and they're high or they're drunk, that's fine as long as they don't bring it in with them. Because a lot of shelters will just say "No", but then they're out on the streets. We know some trans guests rely on going out and doing sex work to survive, and they don't have to hide that. We will always accept people.'

The Outside Project is a genuinely inspiring example of grassroots activism benefiting the trans people who are most vulnerable, and I found myself agreeing with Harry that the wider movement – particularly those parts that have the ear of government and the media – seems to have forgotten them. Sadly, it is the only service of its kind in the UK: most trans people living on the streets are still struggling with services that weren't designed for them. Projects like this take an impressive level of commitment to manage, run and fund – and that isn't easy to find, particularly in an era of under-funding by successive right-wing governments, in which demand for specialist crisis services vastly outstrips supply. Ending homelessness is an important political goal for society as a whole; it is especially important for trans people.

Another sector that has seen swingeing cuts in funding is domestic and sexual violence services, as Rudy's story of trying to escape domestic violence shows. Refuges are in crisis. Since 2010, most councils in England, Wales and Scotland have slashed funding for refuges, with cuts of nearly £7 million over the past eight years. Nearly two thirds of referrals to all refuges are currently refused because there is insufficient funding or no space for the victim. Conversations around domestic abuse and the dwindling provision for survivors usually focus on the most common scenario: heterosexual couples with a (cisgender) male perpetrator and a (cisgender) female survivor. Yet trans people face extraordinarily high rates of domestic abuse at the hands of their partners: according to research by Stonewall, one in five trans people (19 per cent) had experienced domestic abuse from a partner in the previous year.[27] This included 21 per cent of trans men and 16 per cent of trans women, which is significantly higher than the recorded rate of domestic abuse among the wider population – 7.9 per cent of women and 4.2 per cent of men, according to the Office for National Statistics (the ONS believe their own figures may underestimate the true extent of domestic abuse, though this is also probably true of the figures for trans people: research by the Scottish Transgender Alliance and the LGBT Domestic Abuse Project found that one in four survivors told no one about the domestic abuse that they had experienced).

The invisibility of domestic abuse among trans people is in large part due to the invisibility of trans people's romantic and sexual lives in the wider culture as a whole. The most commonly referenced figures in the media, whether Caitlyn Jenner in the US or the former boxing manager Kellie Maloney in the UK, are late-transitioning trans women who, prior to transition, had heterosexual marriages with women. Yet trans people's romantic lives are much more diverse than this, especially as the visible community has grown and people are coming out younger. Trans people may have relationships with cisgender people or other trans people, and date men, women or non-binary people. This reality is not often represented in mainstream media, with the result that lots of trans people are led to believe that transitioning may mean the end of their love life. At one point, I was one of the many trans people who believed, incorrectly, that I would be fundamentally unlovable to anyone who knew I was assigned a different gender at birth. While I soon learned that this wasn't the case, I also realized – as a trans woman who only dated men – that there were men out there who could simultaneously be attracted to me and also be abusive. This was particularly apparent on dating apps, where I was always open about being trans. If men initiated messaging and I declined their advances, it was not uncommon to receive a torrent of misogynist and transphobic abuse.

Online, you can simply block a stranger who exhibits such malicious behaviour. Real-life domestic abuse, however, is often insidious and incremental, with the abuser creating a sense of dependence in the abused while eroding their self-esteem. The negative messages trans people receive from society about their bodies, their desirability as partners, and their worth as individuals can make them especially susceptible to emotional, sexual and physical abuse by partners. According to GALOP, the LGBT+ anti-violence charity, while trans and cis people may face similar patterns of abuse, many trans survivors also face specific forms of abuse related to their trans identity. Perpetrators might withhold medication or prevent treatment related to the victim's transition, refuse to use correct pronouns and prevent the victim from telling other people about their trans history or identity, or convince their partner that nobody would believe them about the abuse because they are trans. Trans people's higher rates of unemployment and lack of contact with their birth family also minimize potential escape routes from such situations. Globally, cis male intimate partners or ex-partners are the most common perpetrators of murders of trans people (particularly trans women). These include, in the UK, thirty-six-year-old Naomi Hersi, who was murdered in 2018 by Jesse McDonald, a man she met on a dating website, and thirty-three-year-old Vanessa Santillan, who in 2015 was beaten and strangled by her husband Joaquin Gomez Hernandez.

Despite this, there are currently no LGBTQ+-specific refuge services in England, and there are only two refuges, both in London, that provide specialist support to LGBTQ+ survivors. As with homelessness services, trans people often fear being greeted with ignorance or even hostility in mainstream services, which are highly gendered. Barriers to accessing support can vary according to the specific trans person's experience. Trans men and non-binary people who were assigned female at birth may be nervous about accessing support services that are targeted at women, despite the fact that their abuse pre-dates their transition or their abuser still perceives and treats them as a woman, so making their experience different from that of other male survivors. Faced with disavowing their identity as men in women's services or fearing transphobia in men's services, many trans men are left without access to specialist support.

For trans women and other trans people who were assigned male at birth, there can be anxiety about accessing appropriate women's services because of trans women's perception that they are not welcome, and media narratives framing them as a risk to cisgender women. While most of the key women's organizations in the UK state publicly that they can and do support trans women survivors, hostile attitudes to trans women are still found within the sector. 'Many of the women and children we work with are terrified of males. And yes, this includes males who identify as transgender,' one chief executive of a women's charity providing support services said at an anti-trans campaign meeting in January 2019.[28] In another speech, given at the Scottish Parliament, the same chief executive went so far as to suggest that trans women's identities were themselves a form of abuse for cisgender female survivors: 'You are not offering a trauma-informed environment if you, in your position of power, gaslight traumatized women and pretend that someone that you both really know is a man is actually a woman.'[29]

A February 2021 investigative report by *gal-dem* magazine into transphobia in the gender-based violence support sector spoke to several frontline workers, many of whom had concerns about prejudice against trans women (also known as transmisogyny – a term to which I'll return later) in organizations supporting women escaping violence. 'Workers say,' the report stated, 'that hierarchical power structures mean transmisogyny is often sanctioned from the top. Close ties between powerful names in the sector mean it is hard to challenge for fear of being blacklisted from multiple organizations.'[30] One of the cited examples of such transphobia occurred when workers were trying to set up a new helpline for clients at a women's service. Unclear on the organization's inclusion policy, some junior staff asked for clarity on who the helpline was for, to ensure it would support trans women: 'The reply from [the director of operations at the organization] and another senior staff member was, "If they sound like a woman on the phone, talk to them . . . If they don't sound like a woman, it doesn't matter if they say they are, hang up. We're not supporting them."'

The same investigation also found that workers had overheard colleagues making prejudiced comments about trans women. These included referring to trans women as 'men-women'; asserting that only 'biological women' should have access to refuges; and senior staff telling junior employees that they themselves were behaving like 'perpetrators' by supporting trans-inclusivity, as it put them on the side of 'men'. Even when openly discussing trans women who may need access to services, the language used was dehumanizing: 'There is a real focus on the penis,' one worker told the magazine. Some women working in the sector revealed they had been instructed to stop tweeting in support of trans women from their personal social media accounts.

That people in leadership positions within the support sector will openly call trans women 'men', and conflate trans women's existence with the gaslighting of cisgender male perpetrators, may go some way to explaining the institutional barriers many trans women have come up against while attempting to access support in gendered services. The British media conversation about trans women and 'women only' domestic violence services has been instrumental in blocking legal gender recognition reforms and has prevented genuine engagement with the reality of trans women's experiences of domestic abuse – which are, as a result, simply erased.

Here, it's crucial to point out that the struggles faced by trans women in this regard are very similar to the struggles faced by BAME, lesbian and disabled women.[31] There is a wider structural reality at work: the hostility and bad-faith discussion of trans inclusion in domestic violence services is in the interests of a right-wing government that does not wish to fund these services *at all*. This manufactured controversy over trans inclusion is a deliberate distraction: the bitter debate over trans women makes political solidarity and organizing among LGBTQ+ people and cisgender straight women more difficult. But such solidarity is desperately needed in order to fight cuts and the changes to welfare provision that make it harder for people to leave their abusers. Instead of solidarity, transphobic commentary rejects any responsibility towards trans survivors, often insisting that trans people should create their own services and refuges if they need them so badly. While specialist provision for trans survivors is to be encouraged, there is a difference between advocating for tailored services designed to help people with specific experiences and championing enforced segregation.[32] There is also a lack of practicality in the idea of these hypothetical 'third' spaces, often touted as a specious solution to the 'problem' of trans women accessing women's services: the trans population is so small and geographically disparate it would be difficult to provide a specialist service in every location where a trans person is in need of help. The choice can't be between tailored services or no provision at all: accommodation in mainstream services will always need to be an option. Many services for women already do precisely this; as one refuge manager put it:

> If somebody comes to a service, if they say they're a trans woman then we would say do you want to be referred to a specialist LGBT service or do you want to stay within our service. Whether it was sexuality or gender or ethnicity or race or disability, if we know of another organization that's got specialist support we would offer them that, as well as saying that they can come into the general organization if they choose to.[33]

Many people, whether trans or cis, will be fortunate enough never to require the services of a homeless shelter or domestic violence refuge. As we age, however, many of us will become reliant on care homes and hospitals, which are in many ways analogous to the public housing and hostels discussed above, and which carry many of the same problems regarding gender segregation. With a growing older population – over the next fifty years there are projected to be an additional 8.6 million people in the UK aged 65 years and over, a population roughly equivalent to the size of London – there is growing pressure on the system and ever more trans people reaching old age, so addressing their needs will become more and more urgent.

One such need is protecting the dignity of older trans people in care homes, where they may experience greater discrimination than they did living independently. Older trans people today will have lived through a period where being trans, or behaviour associated with it (including offences related to homosexuality), was criminalized or pathologized. Older LGBTQ+ people, including trans people, are more likely to experience isolation, too – partly because they are less likely to have children. Nearly half of transgender people who do have children have no contact with them.[34] The prospect of entering care homes, however, is daunting, as trans people worry about a loss of personal agency and hostility from care workers and other residents. Speaking in a video about older trans people for the My Genderation campaign 'Growing Older As Me', Cat Burton, a sixty-six-year-old retired pilot, described some of the simple ways in which trans people may lose control over their appearance and self-expression:

> Transgender people might have needs that are not necessarily obvious to care workers. A trans woman that suddenly isn't capable of looking after her facial hair in a way that she has grown accustomed to, or a trans woman that has to wear a wig, and then has to be seen by care workers without it, who may not perhaps take the greatest care of presenting them [with the gender expression they feel most comfortable with] to the other people living in the home.[35]

For older trans people who come out late in life, particularly those who wish to surgically transition, there can be anxiety about requiring intimate and personal care when their genitals or other sex characteristics are 'incongruous' with their gender. Jenny-Anne Bishop, a trans campaigner who, as part of Swansea University's Trans Ageing and Care Project, spoke to multiple trans people about their experiences and fears of growing older, raised precisely this concern about intimate care:

[A trans person's] body may not match their gender presentation. If somebody needs help with dressing, undressing, and washing, there's always the danger a carer is going to be surprised or just laugh at them or be derogatory.[36]

Bishop also gave examples of trans people who had been ostracized in their care home by other residents. Of one trans woman who had been excluded, she says:

They wouldn't sit with her for meals, they wouldn't let her join in the games, they deliberately made sure she couldn't watch her programmes on the television. The caregiver then started giving her less care, and nobody checked to see if she had eaten her food. She's fine now because our group in Liverpool found out about it and got her moved to her a care home where they are very accepting.[37]

Trans people with dementia are particularly vulnerable, given that they may regress and forget they have transitioned and find their own anatomy or dress alien and frightening. 'This can result in them becoming very disoriented and anxious,' Sean Page, a consultant nurse for dementia at Betsi Cadwaladr University Health Board, told BBC News. 'They may not understand why they are being referred to as being a certain gender as they cannot recall publicly voicing this preference.'[38] Such challenges will only become greater as the openly trans population continues to grow in both size and age.

The reality of trans life today is often hidden from public view.

Thinking back to my visit to Kate, Joe and Alex, I am struck by how nervous their family was to speak publicly about their situation because of the hostile media climate invested in moral panic and false narratives. Yet, talking to trans people about their own priorities demonstrated to me that an urgent redirection of focus and political energy is needed. School bullying, family rejection, homelessness, domestic abuse and discrimination in care services are major issues that continue to affect huge numbers of trans people, even as societal attitudes appear to be growing more tolerant. These difficulties affect trans people in their most intimate lives and shape their happiness day to day. All raise deep questions about how a lack of family and community acceptance, a sustained political attack on the social safety net by successive neoliberal governments, and a society that imposes a strict gender binary by punishing or excluding anyone who cannot fit neatly into that binary, are at the core of what it means to be trans in Britain today. The liberation and prosperity of trans people as a group will require a transformation of how the family and the community embrace difference and of the allocation of proper resources – specifically money – to those whose immediate social and familial circles have cast them out.

In all this, it cannot be emphasized enough that the political demands of trans people align with those of disabled people, migrants, people with mental illnesses, LGB people and ethnic minorities (and, needless to say, trans people can be found within all of these groups). This overlap between the needs of different marginalized people must be stressed because the illusion that trans people's concerns are niche and highly complex is often a way to disempower them. The emphasis on the 'minority' status of minorities keeps them focused on explaining their difference in public discourse, so that they can be continuously batted away as an aberration or minor concern. In the specific case of trans people, this disempowerment begins at the most fundamental level: with our bodies and our right to exercise autonomy over them without interference by society. If we are to liberate all trans people socially, we must begin with the liberation of the physical trans body.

2

Right and Wrong Bodies

When someone learns that a person is trans, their first instinct is usually to ask details about that person's surgical status. When my mother told a next-door neighbour, who'd known me since I was a child, that I had transitioned to live as a woman, his first instinct was to ask when I was due to undergo surgical genital reconstruction. I don't believe he realized how invasive his question was – particularly in asking my mother, of all people, about the genital configuration of her daughter. While, anecdotally, it does seem that increasing awareness and visibility of trans people correlates with a greater courtesy towards us, this curiosity about medical details persists. It's just dressed up in more euphemistic language. At a party, I was once asked if I had gone through or was going through 'the full process'. Many people with whom I've discussed this book asked if I was going to extensively describe my own medical transition. (If that's what you're here for, prepare to be disappointed.)

The long tradition of sensationalist, degrading exhibition of trans people as medical freaks has persisted in twenty-first-century culture. 'Transsexual Former Builder Left "half man, half woman" After being "refused NHS boob job"' was typical of headlines attached to stories about trans healthcare in the mainstream UK media until well into the 2010s.[1] Such stories – inviting ridicule of people who sought medical gender reassignment, as well as disdain for the reality of gender dysphoria and the NHS itself for providing care to trans people – were the dominant register of most discussions until relatively recently. Such narratives, of demanding and entitled trans patients expecting a surgical shopping list to be paid for by the public purse, have shaped a culture in which it's still considered acceptable to discuss trans people's bodies in this way. Failure to move beyond lurid accounts of the specific hormonal and surgical treatments some trans people seek is part of the problem.

Talking about 'trans healthcare' must also mean talking about the general physical health, sexual health and mental health of trans people. Failing to consider trans health in a holistic way will simply allow the dire state of trans people's experiences of the health service in the UK to remain hidden.

In 2016, the UK parliamentary Women and Equalities Select Committee Inquiry into Transgender Equality, chaired by the then Women and Equalities Minister, Maria Miller MP, published a report which found that 'the NHS is letting down trans people, with too much evidence of an approach that can be said to be discriminatory and in breach of the Equality Act.'[2] In what follows, I want to explore how healthcare is often an oppressive experience for trans people in Britain today and to consider the ways these experiences resonate with the struggles of other groups whose lives can be shaped and defined by the prejudices of clinicians.

First, one of the most important – and, for many, confusing – questions: why do some trans people need medical intervention at all? Dysphoria, the antonym of 'euphoria', is the clinical term now used to describe the intense feeling of anxiety, distress or unhappiness some trans people feel in relation to their primary sex characteristics (genitals), their secondary sex characteristics (breasts, facial hair, menstruation, face shape, voice) or how these physical traits cause society to interact with them, by perceiving them as a male or female. Previously called 'gender identity disorder' and, before that, 'transsexualism', gender dysphoria is the name given to an experience many trans people struggle with, which can be helped by medical intervention. Although the term is widely used within the community, different trans people can experience dysphoria in very different ways, and so might have different clinical needs.

Gender dysphoria is a rare experience in society as a whole, affecting about 0.4 per cent of the population, which can make it hard to explain to the vast majority of people, who have not experienced it. To get around this, we often rely on metaphors. The clumsy phrase 'born in the wrong body' has become the favoured soundbite in popular media. Clumsy because – and this must be stressed – many trans people do not think this describes dysphoria at all well. To my mind, the trans writer Andrea Long Chu expresses it more accurately: 'Dysphoria,' she says, 'can feel like heartbreak.'[3] Heartbreak, its incapacitating grief and the sense of absence and loss which activate the same parts of the brain as physical pain, can be so all-consuming it interferes with your everyday life. So, too, dysphoria. For me, at least, this is a much richer way of describing how many trans people experience distress with their bodies – indeed, how I felt until I medically transitioned.

Dysphoria, it should be said, is not a precondition of being trans. According to some research, as many as 10 per cent of those who positively identify as trans men, trans women, non-binary people and various other terms do so without any feelings of dysphoria. It is sometimes incorrectly assumed that trans men and women experience dysphoria and non-binary people do not, when in fact some non-binary people feel themselves to be in great need of medical assistance, and some trans men and women seek none at all. Nevertheless, most trans people experience dysphoria to some degree – which is why, here, I focus on them.

In response to the shoddy, sensationalist tradition of media coverage, the mainstream trans visibility movement in recent years has mostly tried to avoid discussion of trans people's bodies and healthcare. *Time* magazine's 2014 cover featuring the US actress and high-profile trans advocate Laverne Cox was intended to proclaim a new era in the transgender civil rights struggle. One notable characteristic of Cox's advocacy was a categorical refusal to discuss her own medical transition, insisting that this was the wrong focus. In an exchange that went viral online, she told the television host Katie Couric:

> The preoccupation with transition and surgery objectifies trans people. And then we don't get to really deal with the real lived experiences. The reality of trans people's lives is that so often we are targets of violence. We experience discrimination disproportionately to the rest of the community. Our unemployment rate is twice the national average; if you are a trans person of colour, that rate is four times the national average. The homicide rate is highest among trans women. If we focus on transition, we don't actually get to talk about those things.[4]

Cox's deft rebuff of Couric's prurient line of questioning expressed the frustration of many trans people who are constantly told that, to be given any platform to speak about their lives, they must be willing to be candid about their bodies. At the time, Cox's refusal of this tawdry exchange was new and exhilarating. Her refusal to be coerced into speaking personally about medical transition in the media was a catalyst for a wider refusal among trans people, particularly the younger generation, to engage in the surgical show-and-tell demanded by cisgender people.

But while this refusal has been a vital aspect of trans people taking back control of their own stories, it has not given way to a new and much-needed discussion of the general and systemic healthcare challenges that trans people face in every aspect of medical care, including routine health matters, mental health issues, sexual health access, fertility and even palliative care. With this lack of debate, this silence, comes a new risk: that in rightly avoiding the pressure to disclose personal details about transition, we have lost any residual public interest in our health and wellbeing.

Yet trans people in Britain have tried to bring about change in healthcare. In February 2013, the General Medical Council (GMC) was presented with ninety-eight cases of alleged misconduct by British doctors and other medics towards their trans patients. After a grassroots campaign on social media had allowed hundreds of ordinary trans people to speak out about medical mistreatment, their cases were compiled by the campaigner and Liberal Democrat parliamentary candidate Helen Belcher. The individual allegations were made confidentially but, Belcher said, they involved 'allegations of sexual abuse, physical abuse, verbal abuse, inappropriate and sometimes damaging treatment, treatment withheld, threats of withholding treatment, poor administration, acting against the patient's best interests'. It was, she concluded, 'pretty horrific reading'.[5] While the GMC displayed an initial interest in taking formal action, technicalities and the anonymity of the complainants meant that only thirty-nine out of the ninety-eight cases were taken forward. Of these, in the end only three of the complaints were fully investigated. Ultimately, none were upheld.

Despite failing to gain formal restitution, the attempt was a watershed moment, involving trans people coming together and sharing their experiences of medical mistreatment with each other, which in turn galvanized them to fight for genuine institutional change. As with so much political activity for trans liberation in the 2010s, the GMC investigation was only made possible by social media. The details of widespread abuse of British trans people by those who were supposed to be helping them wasn't a story broken by a newspaper or uncovered by an inquiry. It began with a hashtag. #TransDocFail was created by a trans woman in 2013 as a space for British trans Twitter users to discuss failures in healthcare publicly and with each other. Within twenty-four hours of its creation the hashtag was used over a thousand times. Thanks to the permanence of the internet, many anonymized versions of these accounts are still available to read online. Collectively, they paint a vivid picture of the power dynamic between trans people and their doctors, and the prevalence of ignorance and outright prejudice in the medical profession. They also reveal the powerlessness felt by trans patients in the face of sustained mistreatment.

Such protests and demands for better treatment are synonymous with the trans movement. Back in 1972, a group of transsexuals and transvestites, meeting regularly in Notting Hill, in London, as a branch of the new Gay Liberation Front, wrote a piece for the activist pamphlet *Lesbian Come Together*. As many as 60,000 people in Britain were taking cross-sex hormones, they stated; more wanted to do so but were refused by doctors. They described the stigma to which trans people were subjected by the medical profession when accessing hormone and surgical treatment, and their struggle for autonomy: 'the psychiatrists who electro-shock us think we're pathetic or tragic . . . one sister said that after six months of psychiatric treatment she discovered that no one knew her like herself.'[6]

Trans patients in Britain are no longer electro-shocked (this particular barbarism died out in the early 1970s), but, even today, they still face persecution and injustice in their encounters with the medical establishment. This is not simply a matter of a few 'bad apples' practising psychiatry, or well-meaning ignorance on the part of GPs' receptionists that can be quickly remedied by an afternoon training session. The medical establishment in Britain is systemically and institutionally discriminatory towards trans people.

This may come as a surprise to those who argue that transgender

identity is a fad being pushed by 'Big Pharma', private plastic surgeons and a nefarious global medical industry: a conspiracy
theory rehearsed among groups as apparently disparate as the
US Christian right and some anti-trans feminist writers. In 2018,
the American conservative magazine *The Federalist* argued that
'exceedingly rich, white men (and women) who invest in bio-
medical companies are funding myriad transgender organizations
whose agenda will make them gobs of money.'[7] Trans people,
these conspiracy theorists believe, are part of a body-modification
pyramid scheme: having been preyed on and been sold lies about
'our sex' by rich people in white coats, we aim to recruit new
members in order to affirm our poor choices. The insinuation
that trans people and their doctors are co-conspirators in a dangerous medical fad has worked its way obliquely into the pages
of liberal newspapers and news programmes. It becomes especially pernicious when the discussion turns to the small number
of trans children whose gender dysphoria interferes with their
mental health enough to warrant intervention to delay their
puberty. But the idea that trans people and their doctors are in
cahoots is laughable: the reality is starkly different.

The entire trans healthcare infrastructure emerged in the course
of the twentieth century under the mantle of the highly patriarchal
field of psychiatry. Institutionally, doctors came to understand hormone treatment and surgery as a means to police the parameters
of what they deemed was or wasn't an 'acceptable' trans person –
and, by logical extension, the boundaries of gender itself. When
medical transitioning was first devised as a technology, its primary purpose was not to help the trans patient, but to control
and manage gender variance in society while leaving the gender
binary intact. Movement between the two sexes could be made
possible by hormones and surgery, but the semblance of two
mutually exclusive categories, male and female, would remain. In

order to sustain this fixed binary, cis people created paternalist, prejudiced requirements that trans patients had to meet in order to merit healthcare. Some of these requirements still exist to this day, in slightly less draconian forms.

Historically, then, transgender health has been less about empowering trans people and more about tying up the loose ends of binary gender in a society where some people's lives seemed to threaten such a notion.[8] In this sense, the development of trans healthcare is more analogous to that of women's* reproductive health – particularly access to free, safe and legal abortion – than it is to the cosmetic-surgery Ponzi scheme dreamed up in the fevered minds of conspiracy theorists.

Here, it's worth reminding ourselves of the progress of attitudes to abortion – which, in the UK, is still not a legal right (in Northern Ireland, the decriminalization of abortion only occurred as recently as 2019). The default legal position on abortion is that termination of pregnancy is a serious criminal offence. It only ceases to be an offence when the procedure is procured under the strict conditions of the Abortion Act 1967, which requires the permission of two doctors and an approved justification for the termination to proceed. The Abortion Act was not passed out of a feminist desire to grant women full bodily autonomy, but to manage the crisis of women's deaths resulting from unsafe 'back

---

* Reproductive healthcare like abortion, contraception and fertility treatment directly affects everyone with a uterus, which also includes some trans men and non-binary people who are capable of becoming pregnant. For this reason, it is most accurate to say that reproductive health is not *entirely* a women's issue and it also forms a constituent part of trans health for the trans people who can bear children. However, given that this area has historically and predominantly affected women at a global level and is understood politically by conservative and regressive political forces to be bound up with the role of women in society, I here use the term 'women's reproductive health' for expediency.

street' abortions, which had become the leading cause of maternal deaths in the decade up to 1967, killing between fifty and sixty British women a year.[9] At the time, limited access to abortion had also become more agreeable to the (largely male) medical profession as a result of the Thalidomide scandal of 1962, in which a drug prescribed to pregnant women for morning sickness led to thousands of children born with severe disabilities, and many women had been compelled by law to deliver children with severe, life-limiting abnormalities or health problems. In short, while social and professional attitudes to abortion have changed since the 1960s, the legal and political foundations of abortion access do not emphasize the agency of the patient. Such access therefore remains precarious and vulnerable to attack from conservative forces.

Since its inception, access to trans healthcare has similarly been an ideological battleground. For those who need them, medical transition and contraception or abortion are – or should be – about the bodily autonomy of the individual, their right to mental well-being and the freedom to carve out their own destiny in defiance of prevailing gender roles. (These roles, should we need reminding, frame women as vessels for reproduction and trans people as threats to the strict separation of male and female sex roles on which patriarchy depends.) Access to abortion and access to trans healthcare are often attacked in similar ways: principally by overstating the incidence and likelihood of regretting either process, and an intense, disproportionate focus in the media on the stories of individuals who do regret their personal choices, as a way to undermine the principle of choice generally. Only about 5 per cent of women experience any degree of regret over their abortion. Multiple studies show the regret rate for gender reassignment surgery is even lower: about 0–2 per cent.[10] Despite this, the fear of regret has become a powerful tool used to justify the delay or withholding of treatment.

Little wonder, then, that it is conservative politicians who attack trans healthcare and women's reproductive rights in the same breath. Recently, the most egregious examples of this attitude are to be found, unsurprisingly enough, in the actions of the 2016–2020 Trump administration. In 2017, Trump reinstated the Reagan-era 'Mexico City policy', banning US federal funding for overseas organizations that conduct abortions or advocate for abortion rights (also known as the 'global gag rule'), and used his Supreme Court nominations to establish a judicial bench hostile to pregnancy termination. At the same time, it banned US trans people from the military (in part because trans service people had their healthcare funded by the federal government); reversed federal protections for trans children in schools instituted by President Barack Obama; and, in May 2019, signalled its desire to attack the federal statute protecting trans people from discrimination in healthcare and insurance – in other words, to give providers the right to refuse trans people health treatment for any reason. The two policy positions are linked: restriction of access to abortion and restriction of access to trans healthcare both emerge from conservative ideological positions about gender roles and the degree to which an individual is entitled to autonomy over their body.

In the UK, while the culture war over bodily autonomy is less pronounced, there are similar overlaps between the anti-abortion and anti-trans movements. Between 2015 and 2020 the Conservative MP for Monmouth, David T. C. Davies, sponsored events at Parliament for anti-trans lobby groups, and personally led a Westminster Hall debate on the legitimacy of trans rights. Davies also voted against same-sex marriage and – ignoring international medical consensus – for reducing the abortion limit from twenty-four weeks to twelve.

The analogy with abortion is useful primarily because people are generally less aware of the struggle for good trans healthcare than they are of the political warfare over reproductive rights, which affects so many more people. But it is also a helpful comparison given the general confusion among the public about whether they ought to consider being trans as a mental illness and, if not, why the NHS provides treatment for it. I think the distress associated with unwanted pregnancy (which is not an illness but may require medical intervention) serves as a better analogy for explaining why trans healthcare is available on the NHS: to preserve wellbeing and prevent personal distress.

What we choose to define (and stigmatize) as 'mental illness' is itself a matter of politics. For instance, our perception of homosexuality as an identity instead of a disorder is a relatively recent development, made possible by decades of campaigning to depathologize it. Similar efforts to depathologize transgender people have met with some success. In May 2019, the World Health Organization removed 'gender identity disorder' from its diagnostic chapter on mental disorders in the eleventh edition of the International Classification of Diseases, which comes into effect in 2022. Instead, 'gender incongruence' will be listed under the section on sexual health issues. And, back in October 2017, the then British prime minister, Theresa May, announced her government's plans to streamline and de-medicalize the legal process for legal gender recognition in England and Wales, 'because being trans is not an illness and shouldn't be treated as such'.[11]

Yet there is a tension between this move to redress the historical association between trans people's identities and mental imbalance, and the importance of access to free healthcare for many trans people's wellbeing. In the context of successive Conservative governments' squeeze on NHS and social care funding, Theresa May's apparently positive words on 'not treating' trans people as if they're ill should be viewed with suspicion. Both trans and cis patients alike have good reason to fear the increasing NHS reliance on the private sector, which drives up costs and introduces a profit motive to healthcare, including gender identity services and surgeries. There is an irony here: it is generally conservatives who make specious claims about money-making schemes preying on trans people, but, in fact, it is conservatives' own policies of cuts and privatization that actually allow the private sector to behave vampirically.

The lack of clarity around trans-related healthcare – specifically, access to hormones and surgery – has existed from the moment such treatment began, in the early twentieth century. Its progress was gradual and uneven, often occurring as the result of the professional inclinations of individual doctors and physicians who treated trans patients. As demand increased, so too did the association of such treatment with mental illness. The power to set the parameters of who could transition, as well as when and how – commonly referred to in trans communities as 'gatekeeping' – gradually became concentrated in the hands of a small number of clinicians (many with a background in psychiatry), who determined whether somebody was 'trans enough' to receive care. From the 1990s onwards, things started to change: worldwide, trans people and progressive medics have pioneered affirmative models, in which the patient's informed agreement to specific treatments – rather than their psychiatric diagnosis – is the key criterion.

Worldwide, that is, except for Britain, where, sadly, large parts of the system remain unreformed, anachronistic and unfit for purpose. The model of trans healthcare in Britain is still built around specialist gender identity clinics, which have long since been phased out in Canada, New Zealand, the US and many European countries and replaced with a more flexible approach. How on earth did Britain slip so badly behind in its duty of care to trans people, with waiting lists that often last years? In order to answer this, we need to look at how we got to this point.

★

Historical accounts of gender-variant people who lived in a social role different from the one assigned to them at birth occur in almost every recorded human culture. Sometimes, they lived their lives with the encouragement and licence of their community, which recognized the existence of a third gender – or even several other genders – beyond man and woman; sometimes, their perceived 'transgression' of gender norms was understood to merit punishment. As early as the seventh to fifth centuries BCE, the Book of Deuteronomy's explicit ban on cross dressing, at Chapter 22, verse 5 ('the woman shall not wear that which pertaineth unto a man, neither shall a man put on a woman's garment: for all that do so are abomination unto the Lord thy God'), formed part of the religious and civil law governing the Israelites. That this 'deviation' needed legislating against suggests that – well – there was something to legislate against, that cross dressing was prevalent enough to generate concern among lawmakers. Even earlier, in the third millennium BCE, the ancient Sumerian goddess Inanna was worshipped by a cult of transvestite priests known as the Gala, who took female names and sang hymns in a dialect associated with femininity. And in third century BCE Rome, the teenage emperor Elagabalus, who reigned from 218–222 CE, appears to have openly displayed his desire to be regarded as a woman. If the classical historians Cassius Dio and Herodian are to be believed, he painted his eyes, plucked out his beard, wore wigs and insisted on being addressed as a queen. Cassius Dio writes that he offered vast sums to any physician who could give him female genitalia. Rituals of body modification and castration were in fact a feature of sects and cults in which adherents led cross-gender lives. In 2002, the remains of a Roman *gala* (a eunuch priest of the goddess Cybele) were found in Catterick, north Yorkshire. She was dressed in women's clothes and jewellery. The *galli* castrated themselves during an ecstatic celebration called the *Dies sanguinis*, or 'Day of Blood'. They bleached their hair and wore makeup. The discovery of the remains in Catterick provides evidence that there were ritually castrated feminine *galli* present in Britain as long ago as 4 CE: the earliest evidence of gender diversity on this island.

Yet 'trans', as we understand the term today, is the product of a more recent conception of gender deviation. The 'transgender' concept was born in the late nineteenth century, when the emerging field of sexology sought to identify, categorize and treat behaviours that suggested sexual and gender deviance. In 1886 the Austro-German psychiatrist Richard von Krafft-Ebing published *Psychopathia Sexualis*, a seminal text that pathologized as psychotic and disturbed behaviours that we might now consider evidence of an LGBTQ+ identity.[12]

A particularly influential idea in early sexology was 'sexual inversion', a phrase used to describe those who were judged to be engaged in sexual and gendered behaviours more properly associated with the opposite sex. This idea obviously didn't distinguish between gay and trans people: a female invert might be a person born female who had sexual desire for women, or a person who dressed and presented in a way more commonly associated with men, or a combination of the two. Nor did it accommodate scientific breakthroughs like the discovery of sex hormones in the late nineteenth century and the realization, in the early 1930s, that members of both sexes produced both oestrogen and testosterone. These discoveries challenged the binary idea of sex based on external genitalia, indicating that 'sex' was a concept less consistent and immutable than it had previously appeared. Furthermore, they seemed to suggest that changing sex was a possibility.[13]

Yet the idea of inversion persisted and became prevalent in medical practice. The same hormone therapies that today are associated with helping trans people – the use of feminizing oestrogen for trans women and masculinizing testosterone for trans men – were used by endocrinologists in the middle decades of the twentieth century in attempts to 'cure' sexual inverts and intersex individuals, by administering hormones to 'remedy' the imbalance which caused their 'disorder'. Homosexual females, for instance, would be treated with oestrogen. Homosexual males were sometimes treated with testosterone and, in some cases, with oestrogen in order to chemically castrate them and prevent them acting on their desires. In the 1950s such hormonal 'cures' for sexual and gender variance diminished (largely because they didn't work), only to be replaced by psychiatric and aversion therapies – the underlying belief in sexual inversion and disorder remained. It must be stressed that the non-consensual, coercive and violent use of hormones to interfere with the bodily integrity of LGBTQ+ people and those born with intersex conditions destroyed countless lives and should be considered a stain on the history of Western medicine. This shared historical experience is also a point of unity for trans people and cisgender lesbians, gays and bisexuals, demonstrating our shared struggle against our pathologizing and mistreatment over the past century and more.

It was Magnus Hirschfeld, a German sexologist and pioneer of more benevolent models of understanding sexual diversity, who first argued for the affirmation of people with variant sexual and gender identities. In 1910 he published *The Transvestites,* a book which drew a distinction between sexuality and gender identity that is taken as read today. Where, before, the sexual inversion model had conflated gendered expression in clothes, manner and so on with sexual orientation, Hirschfeld recognized these as distinct. In 1919, he opened his Institut für Sexualwissenschaft (Institute of Sexology) in Berlin, a private clinic that became a global centre for research on sexuality and gender, and which welcomed 20,000 visitors a year until, in 1933, the Nazis closed it down. It was at the Institute that the modern terminology and treatment of trans people began to emerge. Hirschfeld coined the term 'Transsexualismus' to describe the condition of those who had a strong desire to live as the opposite sex (as opposed to simply cross dressing) and who required hormonal and surgical assistance to do so. His colleague Harry Benjamin would eventually spread the anglicized term 'transsexual' in the English-speaking medical world. Many transvestites and transsexuals lived and worked at Hirschfeld's Institut while receiving treatment from him: in 1931, Hirschfeld performed the world's first full sex-reassignment surgery, on Dora Richter, a 'male-to-female transsexual' (to use more dated language) from rural Germany. His next, even more celebrated, surgery was on the Danish artist Lili Elbe, portrayed by Eddie Redmayne in the 2015 Hollywood biopic *The Danish Girl*.

In Britain, the first two instances of medical treatment for gender dysphoria came in a very different context from the specialist clinical setting of Hirschfeld's practice in Weimar Berlin. The first known case of a British person medically transitioning from one gender to another with the assistance of hormones and surgeries was Michael Dillon, a trans man (or 'female-to-male transsexual'). Born in 1915 into an aristocratic family, from adolescence Dillon consistently presented in a masculine way at school, after which he attended Oxford and became captain of the women's rowing team, attracting tabloid notoriety for his androgynous presentation.[14] In the late 1930s, aware that doctors had successfully developed a testosterone pill, he approached Dr George Foss, who had been experimenting with the use of testosterone in women for excessive menstrual bleeding but whose female patients had also experienced masculinizing effects such as a deeper voice and growth of facial hair.

Foss was nervous but intrigued by Dillon's request, insisting that he see a psychiatrist to confirm he was of sound mind before eventually prescribing him the pills to self-administer. As a science graduate, Dillon possessed the necessary education to give

him an unusual degree of autonomy over his own 'sex change';
throughout, he kept detailed logs of his hormonal transition,
which he subsequently published in 1946 under the title *Self: A
Study in Ethics and Endocrinology*. Despite the word's negative con-
notations, Dillon identified himself as an 'invert' (it is unlikely he
was aware of the newly coined term 'transsexualism'). In order
to protect his identity, he moved to Bristol, where he got a job as
a mechanic, passed as male and was referred to using male pronouns. In 1942, he convinced a surgeon to perform a double
mastectomy, and by 1944 he had had his birth certificate amended
to reflect his new status as male. Given the British media's recent
pained wrangling with the very idea of gender affirmation as a
potential 'slippery slope', the fact that more straightforward
access to medical transition and legal gender recognition was
available during the Second World War than is often the case
today is astonishing. The mainstream media's presumption that
strict 'controls' on transition are and have always been necessary
relies on the suppression, and ignorance, of trans medical and
legal history.

In 1945, Dillon moved to Dublin, to train as a doctor at Trinity
College; there, he underwent several genital reconfiguration surgeries. These were carried out by one of the pioneers of the
emerging field of plastic surgery, Sir Harold Gillies, who during
wartime had performed several surgeries to restore the genitals
of wounded soldiers. The following year, Dillon's publication of
his autobiography brought him to the attention of Roberta Cowell, who would become Britain's first transsexual woman and the
first British person to undergo male-to-female 'sex change' surgery. The two became close friends, and Dillon may have
developed romantic feelings for her, though she declined his
advances. In fact, her first surgery (orchiectomy, that is, castration by removal of the male gonads) was performed by Dillon
himself, despite the fact that he was not yet a licensed physician

and that the operation, then illegal in Britain, had to be conducted in secret. After her orchiectomy, Cowell was later referred to Gillies to complete her reassignment with the construction of a vagina in 1951.

Despite the trailblazing transitions of Cowell and Dillon, it wasn't until the 1960s that transsexualism became a formally recognized diagnosis within the British medical establishment. Cowell had obtained sexual reassignment surgery on a technicality, by managing to get herself inaccurately diagnosed as intersex. Medical support for trans people, however, was still rare. Throughout the 1960s and 1970s, individual trans patients continued to use the ambiguous and contested link between physical intersex traits and the psychological experience of gender dysphoria to get certain doctors to treat them – though, even then, few doctors would. A 1966 study in the *British Medical Journal* found that only '9% of psychiatrists, 6% of GPs, and 3% of surgeons' would agree to actively assist transsexual patients.[15] All of which effectively meant that trans people's lives and destinies were dependent on the whims of a very small number of British doctors. None became more influential – or more notorious – than Dr John Randell, who practised at the very first specialist gender identity clinic, which opened that same year at Charing Cross Hospital in London. The vast majority of British people who medically transitioned between 1960 and 1980 will have had some direct personal contact with John Randell; all will have heard of him. Most British memoirs by well-known trans people – for example those of the travel writer Jan Morris and the transsexual Bond girl and Playboy model Caroline Cossey – mention him. Few speak of him fondly.

Randell was by most accounts an exceptionally controlling individual. He only allowed an estimated 15 per cent of the patients who asked for his help to be put forward for hormones and surgery; moreover, his criteria for allowing medical transition were rooted in his own highly idiosyncratic, patriarchal ideas. He would, for instance, refuse trans women whom he considered too tall, or who would not consider taking up a more feminine profession after transition, to 'pass' as female. 'I think if they are going to be ladies,' he wrote of trans women in 1969, 'they should be lady-like. Conformity . . . is surely what we are looking for.'[16] His view on the nature of gender itself was also clear: 'I do not subscribe to the opinion that a phenotypic male can have a female psyche. Those who profess to have such mental orientations are in fact anatomical males with obsessional beliefs or over-valued ideas that they are female; and therefore, psychiatrically abnormal.' Even when Randell had assisted with transition, patients often found him brusque, even cruel. 'It hasn't made you a woman, you know – you'll always be a man,' he reportedly told one trans woman who thanked him after surgery.[17]

It's worth pausing to consider that the most powerful pioneer of trans healthcare in twentieth-century Britain was a cisgender male psychiatrist who believed neither in the reality of trans people's deeply held identities nor that gender norms were socially constructed ideals that could be relaxed, challenged or abolished. He believed trans people were delusional about the reality of their situation and that at the same time they also needed to be highly competent mimics of gender stereotypes. He did not believe that they should be allowed freedom over their interpretation or expression of gender.

Randell's outlook remains pervasive today; examples of it can be found throughout the dominant public discourse about trans people. 'Nowadays we are all likely to meet people who think they are women, have women's names, and feminine clothes and lots of eyeshadow who seem to us to be some kind of ghastly parody, though it isn't polite to say so,' wrote the feminist author Germaine Greer in 2009. 'Those who "transition" seem to become stereotypical in their appearance – fuck-me shoes and birds-nest hair for the boys; beards, muscles and tattoos for the girls,' the *Guardian* columnist Julie Bindel opined in 2004, encouraging her readers to 'think about a world inhabited just by transsexuals. It would look like the set of *Grease.*' Neither of these analyses is intended to be accurate: they were written to amuse a cisgender readership by confirming their pre-existing prejudices. However, it is important to realize that the framing of trans people as 'parodies' who reinforce stereotypes cruelly disregards the ways in which those same British trans people – whose gender expression, dress, hairstyles, makeup preferences and so on have, it clearly needs to be said, always varied as much as their cisgender counterparts' – have spent the past fifty years being coerced into narrow gender conformity by their doctors, then mocked and derided as too stereotypical and regressive by cis onlookers. If it sounds like a catch-22, it's because it is.

By the early 1990s, some uniformity had been imposed on the British approach to transition-related care for adults: namely, by placing diagnostic emphasis on the patient's account of their own life history and their personal experience of dysphoria, instead of arbitrary criteria arising from the whims of the clinician in question. While by the twenty-first century this change in approach had certainly improved the situation in NHS gender identity services, it hardly precipitated a transformation in clinicians' attitudes. Non-binary trans people in particular still struggled to access care, or had to withhold information in order to fit a more 'acceptable narrative' of simply wishing to transition from male to female, or vice versa. What's more, despite improvements in the past two decades, British trans health providers have retained the same basic route to transition since the 1960s. In the US and in Canada, the gender identity clinic – a centralized institution that holds a monopoly on access to care – slowly gave way to a more flexible model, in which multiple health centres could initiate hormone treatment more quickly on the basis of the patient's informed consent, without any need for a formal process of diagnosis. UK trans people, by contrast, have been left with the gender identity clinic model and, with it, an arcane system for accessing care that now lags behind best practice in many other Western countries.

The crisis in healthcare for trans people in Britain is endemic and requires urgent change, especially given the ways it has been exacerbated further by the temporary cessation of clinical care during the coronavirus pandemic. This is a question not simply of funding, but of the structure and approach of transition-related care. This remains in the hands of a few gender clinics, overseen by consultants with professional backgrounds in mental health, which are increasingly unable to manage their caseloads. Currently, adults in most of the UK who want to access specialist gender identity services need to approach their GP and ask for referral to one of the UK's seven NHS gender identity clinics. The only exception is Wales, which has recently introduced a reformed, modern system. Regardless of where in the UK a person is based, the 2016 parliamentary Inquiry on Trangender Equality found that many GPs were not aware of their responsibility to refer patients to specialist services. Some, indeed, were actively hostile to the idea: the inquiry heard evidence of 'persistent refusal of some General Practitioners to even make referrals to gender identity clinics'.[18] Even when there is willingness, GPs' lack of training on the correct NHS procedure can lead to profound errors in referral processes not seen in other areas of medicine. These include mistakenly referring patients to local mental health services (which is no longer a requirement), and causing delays of several months before the patient can join the correct (and lengthy) waiting lists for gender identity clinics.[19] All of which has left some 24 per cent of trans people saying they receive insufficient support from GPs,[20] compared to 6 per cent of the wider population expressing the same dissatisfaction.[21]

Even when trans people are successfully referred to secondary care, the gender identity clinic assessment process – which requires two separate appointments with a gender clinician (who usually has a professional background in psychiatry) – now involves eye-wateringly long waiting lists. Contrary to NHS guidelines, which recommend eighteen weeks from referral by GPs for a first appointment, as of June 2019, British gender identity clinics were telling trans patients that they had to wait at least two years. The Laurels, the Exeter-based gender clinic for the south-west of England, said it had nearly 2,000 people on its waiting list; this means a patient could expect to wait up to three years for a first appointment. The pandemic lockdowns have only intensified this catastrophic backlog. Given that nearly everyone has to wait until their second appointment to be prescribed hormones, many trans people are looking at a minimum period of three to four years from first speaking to their GP (a step that in itself can take a great deal of courage and time) to a point when they hope to start medical transition.

Moreover, when hormones are recommended, gender clinics do not themselves prescribe. Instead, they direct the person's GP to prescribe. This can bring with it another problem: it is not uncommon for GPs to refuse to prescribe hormones – even with the direction of the gender identity clinic – as they believe prescribing to trans patients is beyond their competence. Further delays can ensue, meaning that some trans people are forced to change their GP to find one willing to prescribe to them.

In addition to hormones, after a second appointment trans women may also be able to obtain eight sessions of laser hair removal for their facial hair. However, given the extreme need to be rid of facial hair to alleviate dysphoria and to blend in as female, waiting times are yet again too long, and not enough sessions are provided (in my own transition I required over twenty-four sessions, which I funded privately, spending thousands of pounds).

These problems stem, in large part, from the structure of gender identity clinics, which are clearly unfit for purpose. In an era when more and more people than ever before feel comfortable to come out as trans, they are, not to put too fine a point on it, swamped.

For those trans people who want surgery on the NHS, there is even longer to wait. Procedures available for trans men and trans-masculine* people include chest surgery (mastectomy and reconstruction of a male chest), hysterectomy and genital surgery. If a trans man wants any of these, clinical guidelines require him to wait more than a year after starting testosterone. Trans women and transfeminine people are typically only offered genital surgery, though in Scotland and Northern Ireland some facial feminization surgeries to reduce the masculine bone structure of the skull are available (in rare cases). Genital reconstruction surgery, known colloquially as 'the op', retains its status in the public mindset as the very core of transition, but it is worth pointing out that for many trans people it is not the most important aspect of their transition. After all, genitals are the part of the body least likely to be seen by others: many trans people consider body shape, facial hair, voice and facial features to be much more important in daily life, allowing their true gender to be recognized by others. Nevertheless, a great many trans people consider this surgery as vital to being able to live comfortably in their body (particularly trans women, 60 per cent of whom will go on to have genital surgery[22]). Current waiting lists, however, mean that most will be waiting for surgery for 5 or more years from initial referral by their GP.

---

* The terms 'transmasculine' and 'transfeminine' are used to describe non-binary people who express their gender through conventionally masculine or feminine aesthetics without identifying as men or women. This may include the use of hormones and surgery.

It's hardly surprising that the wait for surgery is so long. In Britain, there are around six surgeons with the expertise to perform male-to-female genital reconstructions, and two leading surgeons are due to retire in the next five years. 'We need more surgeons,' urologist Phil Thomas told the *Guardian* in 2016. 'The volume that we need to meet the demand is just going through the roof, and NHS England are not keeping up.'[23] Given that referrals for genital surgery have been increasing by 20 per cent every year, the lack of new surgeons creates another roadblock to trans healthcare in the future. Surgery is funded by the NHS but done in private hospitals on private contracts, which increases costs and reduces the likelihood of long-term planning and investment in future surgeons. The 2016 Trans Inquiry report expressed grave and robust concern at the state of transition-related healthcare in the UK.

Yet in the years since the damning conclusions of the Trans Inquiry, nothing has been done to address this crisis. In Britain, there is barely any political will to reform trans healthcare. The Conservative government, never particularly keen on increasing public spending for minorities that don't wield much economic power, instead hoped that reforming the Gender Recognition Act 2004 would be a cheap way to signal its benevolence to the trans community. The trans writer Roz Kaveney described the 2017 gender recognition reform proposals as

a suggested piece of legislation, unlikely to be passed any time soon, which we welcome but which was not high on our shopping list . . . It's a vaguely liberal gesture which the May government favours partly because it doesn't cost anything.[24]

If such a 'shopping list' of trans political priorities existed, the reform of healthcare would be near the top: such reform would have a greater impact on the daily lives of trans people than the ability to change their legal sex, a factor only relevant in limited contexts, such as (formerly) one's pensionable age or one's legal gender at one's wedding ceremony.

The British media is as uninterested as government in the rusted mechanics of trans healthcare. For years, the press's concern with the subject was expressed exclusively in salacious and sometimes demonstrably false stories of 'sex change regret', citing a handful of recurring individual stories such as that of Claudia, a trans-sexual woman interviewed by journalist Julie Bindel in 2003: 'I changed for all the wrong reasons, and then it was too late.' Claudia's personal distress was undoubtedly real, but as a snapshot of trans healthcare it was misleading: hers was a minority experience extrapolated into a general canard about huge numbers of people being irreversibly 'transitioned' too quickly.

In 2014 the *Mirror* reported on Chelsea Attonley, who had decided to surgically reverse a breast augmentation and come off female hormones. The headline and standfirst read: 'Transexual Demands £10,000 NHS Sex Change Op is Reversed, Complaining "It's exhausting being a woman". Chelsea Attonley says she is fed up and wants taxpayers to fund surgery to reverse breast and gender reassignment surgery so she can become a man again.'[25] The story was inaccurate. Attonley had never had surgery on the NHS – her breast augmentation was done privately – and she had never progressed to genital surgery.

Ria Cooper, a trans woman, was described by the *Daily Mail* as 'Britain's youngest sex swap patient', who now wanted to 'reverse her sex change treatment'. In fact, Cooper did not fully de-transition, instead stopping hormone treatment for a few years because of mental illness. She later told *Vice*,

I'd never say that I made the wrong decision in transitioning because I didn't, but I was going through so much. I was doing escorting and then I got attacked by a client. Everything just went wrong for me and that's why I had a breakdown . . . the press will do anything for a story, they chat so much shit.[26]

Decades of stories like these – which depict the vanishingly small number of trans people who regret aspects of their physical transition as either greedy and petulant, or as pathetic, misled victims of a cult – have entirely misinformed the public. Such stories have left many with the impression that medical transition is a questionable practice that occurs too quickly and in which regret is common. The truth is very different. Universal medical consensus is that appropriate medical intervention is highly effective for the alleviation of gender dysphoria. The genital surgery satisfaction rate is at 94 per cent [27] (which throws into relief the reported satisfaction rate for elective cosmetic surgeries among the wider population: as low as 28 per cent, according to one survey). Trans people and clinicians alike also acknowledge – again, pretty much universally – that access to treatment is far, far too slow.

As we've seen, trans medical intervention is not simply a question of process, but of power. In a way, it would be simpler to argue that all that is needed is greater funding and perhaps more NHS gender identity clinics to meet rising demands. But something more fundamental is required: a change in the *culture* of trans healthcare. Trans people's trust that they, their bodies and their identities will be respected in all healthcare settings – from the GP surgery to A&E to specialist oncology or sexual health clinics – is low. This trust dwindles even further in the case of gender identity services, whose practices are still clouded by the ongoing perception of clinicians as 'gatekeepers'. While many modern clinicians refute the idea that they are gatekeeping, the nature of gender identity services – with its continued emphasis on assessment and diagnosis – nevertheless ensures, as the sociologist Ruth Pearce points out, that 'they *do* play this gatekeeping role, thereby exercising power as "gender experts".'[28]

The repeated pre-diagnostic appointments required at UK gender clinics (appointments that can last between thirty and ninety
minutes) focus on the patient's history of gendered feelings and
their relationship with their body, including their sexual experiences, and even involve discussion of sexual fantasies.[29] Trans
patients can also be asked to write a diary or account of their history of gendered feelings and, in one UK clinic, to bring a family
member or friend with them, which can leave trans people feeling they are required to bring a person to 'corroborate' their
account. It is understandable that many find the whole process
disempowering, invalidating and upsetting.

When I was assessed at the adult gender identity clinic in Ham-
mersmith, in London, I was asked extensive and intrusive
questions about my childhood and family background, such as
why my parents divorced and why I didn't have contact with my
father. None of this was relevant to an assessment of whether or
not I had the mental capacity to consent to treatment and to
understand the implications for my body, or whether I was physically suitable to start treatment. It seemed that my private history
was being used to inform adjudication on whether my identity
was real. Yet I felt obliged to answer all the questions in case they
declined to treat me. This fear wasn't unfounded. Though I
believe I was a relatively 'straightforward' case for the gender
identity clinicians who saw me, I was still threatened with delays
or postponement of treatment on two counts. The first was medical. At my initial appointment I was still a smoker who had
struggled to quit despite numerous attempts. I was told that
clinic rules required my having quit for at least three months
before I could be prescribed oestrogen. (This paternalism also
applies to fat trans people, who find themselves instructed to lose
large amounts of weight before being allowed to access surgery.)
The irony was that I was already taking oestrogen: I had paid for
a private clinic prescription eighteen months before. While my

private doctor told me I should be making serious efforts to stop smoking, given the increased likelihood of blood clots in combination with long-term hormone treatment, they recognized that withholding treatment from someone with severe gender dysphoria might well make it harder to break a heavy nicotine addiction than it would be if they were in a better emotional state after commencing treatment. The doctor also acknowledged that refusing access to hormonal transition might have a worse overall impact on a trans person's mental and physical health than allowing them to commence treatment while monitoring them for risks associated with smoking.

Now, while I believe any attempts at coercion by means of refusing treatment are unjust and harmful, I recognize that they came from a solid assessment of medical risk. Yet, years later, I can admit that at my second clinician's appointment I was still smoking but pretended I had complied with the three-month rule in order to progress with my transition. The threats of delayed treatment thereby led to a breakdown in trust between the clinic and me: I was not providing them with all the relevant medical information they needed to monitor me properly.

The second potential reason for delaying was, in my view, more problematic. Though I had changed my name socially and professionally soon after coming out, at my first appointment the clinician asked if I had legally changed my name to 'Shon', and queried whether or not this was a typically female name. I explained that all my friends and family used Shon, which I had been called for many years, and it was the name under which I published as a professional writer. I hadn't yet changed my name legally, I told the clinician, as I hadn't needed to change my passport or driving licence. I was then told that I needed to make the legal change and provide proof. Treatment would be postponed until I had done so – meaning a further delay of at least six months. There was no substantive reason given for this demand.

At the time, I had been on hormones for eighteen months under the care of a private doctor. I had grown breasts and permanently removed my facial hair. The insistence that my legal name be changed before the NHS would take over my treatment seemed punitive. Changing your name by deed poll is free – but, given that a deed poll solemnly declares that you permanently surrender your old name, all documents bearing the birth name (including passports and driving licences) need to be changed, which is expensive. I have since met trans people who wanted to keep their 'unisex' birth names (for example 'Alex'), who told me they experienced pressure to legally adopt a different name because of 'gender clinic rules'. It is in cases like these that Ruth Pearce's observation that clinicians become 'gender experts' starts to resonate: their insistence that trans people adopt a new legal name in many cases requires them to come out in every area of their life before they start hormonal treatment on the NHS. While this might work for many trans people, for others it doesn't. It is not, in my opinion, appropriate for clinicians to impose on people's lives in this way.

There are more egregious examples of this power imbalance between NHS clinicians and patients. As recently as 2018, GPs seeking to refer patients to the Leeds and York Gender Identity Clinic were incorrectly instructed to conduct a physical examination of their patients' genitals,[30] guidance which has now fortunately been removed. Neither international best-practice guidance nor the NHS England specification for gender identity services endorses genital exams as being in any way routine; both explicitly state they cannot be required of patients. However, for some trans people who are told they must endure this invasive inspection (either because of clinician ignorance or intentional abuse of power), this instruction can lead to non-consensual inspection and touching of intimate parts of the body, which may be experienced by the patient as abusive.

The clinician/patient power dynamic is starkly revealed when it comes to surgery. The 'Standards of Care' of the World Professional Association for Transgender Health (WPATH) codified a longstanding historical practice of psychiatrists and other clinicians working in the field of transsexual health, requiring a patient to spend a period of one year living in their 'preferred' gender role, known in the past as the 'real life experience'. UK gender identity clinics require proof that the patient has completed this period in their 'preferred' gender before either genital surgery or chest surgery. While intended to provide patients with the certainty that transition is right for them prior to the irrevocable step of surgery, the 'evidence' that a person has been living as a man or a woman is in many respects subjective. It risks being seen through the filter of clinicians' personally held stereotypes; and, in the case of non-binary people who are trying to be recognized as neither men nor women, or beyond these binary categories, the insistence on living 'in role' as non-binary makes little sense.

In discussing what 'successful' living in the acquired gender may look like, the lead clinician of London's Gender Identity Clinic, Dr James Barrett, writes:

In essence, 'success' amounts to occupation, sexual, relationship and psychological stability [. . .] 'Success' in an occupation is achieved if the patient is treated by most others as if they are of the assumed sex. It is not necessarily that those around the patient believe that they are that sex [. . .] Rather than being believed to be the assumed sex, the goal should be to be taken as and treated as that sex [. . .] Some patients fiercely maintain that they do not care what others think of them, and that their own conviction of their gender is what matters. This position is at odds with the philosophy of a real life experience and if followed seems not to be predictive of a good longer-term outcome.[31]

To translate: trans people wishing to access surgery are tasked with demonstrating to doctors that they are actively seeking (and receiving) acceptance (or at least tolerance) from cisgender people within cisgender-dominated environments. This sense that you need the social consent of others to access surgery can be further intensified for trans people of colour or neurodiverse trans people, such as those with autism.

Racial bias in medicine is hardly something restricted to trans people alone. In the UK, black women are five times more likely to die in childbirth than white women; in the US, a 2016 study revealed that black patients are less likely to be prescribed pain-killers for the same complaints than their white counterparts.[32] Statistics like these suggest that black patients may be taken less seriously, or are perceived to exaggerate their symptoms; both perceptions damage the quality of care they receive. Research suggests that anti-black racism may increase or inten-sify 'gatekeeping' around hormones and surgery for black trans people in clinical settings: black trans women, in particular, have encountered among counsellors prejudiced attitudes that their presentation was 'too masculine' for a woman, which they per-ceived to be grounded in racist perceptions of gender and femininity.[33] It is clear that trans people of colour's experiences of systemic racism in healthcare and surgery are still woefully under-investigated and under-researched and that the accounts of transphobic medical discrimination which receive most trac-tion are likely to be those of white people.

Even where not overtly discriminatory or abusive, the clin-ician/patient relationship remains highly paternalist, in large part because most gender clinicians and surgeons are cisgender men: in this respect, things haven't moved on too much from John Randell. As the trans author Juno Roche recalls of their 2006 gen-ital reconstruction:

Most of the practitioners I encountered during the process – from my family doctor to psychiatrists to surgeons – were men, and it never felt like a safe environment to have those conversations. I didn't feel comfortable talking to cis men, even doctors, about pleasure, because my history of sex work made me guarded.[34]

Male doctors, Roche argues, often see the reconstruction of genitals as being about appearance, forgetting that the genitals are also sex organs designed for the giving and receiving of pleasure. In Roche's own case, they felt some of the clinical attitudes came from ageism and sexism about middle-aged women: 'gatekeepers saw a middle-aged woman who they presumed wouldn't be having sex – because who has sex with middle-aged women, much less middle-aged trans women?'

In particular, Roche argues, the patriarchy inherent in trans medicine manifests for trans women with 'the clinical reality of gender confirmation, which prioritizes depth over sensation, and confirmation over pleasure'. Roche recalls a particularly uncomfortable routine inspection after surgery, called 'the depth test', in which the surgeon checked the depth of the new vagina with his fingers while inattentive to Roche's obvious pain and discomfort, as symbolic of the misogyny woven into standard clinical practice.

Trans healthcare, then, is part of a wider political struggle for bodily autonomy that women, LGBTQ+ people, disabled people and ethnic minorities have all been fighting – a struggle that intensified during the decade of austerity that was the 2010s. This political struggle has primarily focused on trans adults, growing societal awareness of whom has allowed for more robust advocacy and rebuttal of the myths about medical transition. Even transphobes and reactionaries in the media and in politics, uneasy and disapproving though they remain, have come to begrudgingly tolerate adult medical transition as a matter of personal autonomy. After all, as trans people have successfully argued, adults are entitled to do whatever they want with their own bodies.

In the case of children with gender dysphoria, however, the argument becomes more complex. Trans children and young people, while coming out in greater numbers than ever before, cannot speak up for themselves in public life as trans adults do. When I was a teenager in the early 2000s and started to experience acute gender dysphoria with the onset of puberty, I didn't believe it was possible for doctors to help me. I felt – as teenagers so often do – that I was the only person in the world feeling what I was feeling. Yet I also experienced a growing sense that the profound discomfort with my body and the gender role I was being compelled to occupy was not the typical teenage angst of my classmates. I developed an anxiety disorder and withdrew from friendships. As an adult, who ultimately transitioned in her twenties, I imagine that the experience of trans children and teens in the 2020s – particularly those who seek out assistance to begin transition – is remote from my own. While growing up with some similar experiences, we inhabit very different worlds. Neither the fourteen-year-old me, nor any adult around me at the time, would have known about gender dysphoria; now, thanks to greater visibility, the internet and social media, many trans kids can give expression to their feelings more quickly. They also learn of the clinical options for alleviating dysphoria which are available to them at a younger age. For those kids living with severe dysphoria this new openness can be a lifeline. However, this increased awareness among trans young people has created new political problems, myths and – as discussed in the previous chapter – moral panics.

Because of enduring misinformation, it is important to clearly restate the fundamentals of what is meant by 'transition' in relation to children. To emphasize: no trans child in Britain can have genital reconstruction surgery, both because of clinical protocols that establish a minimum age of seventeen for signing-off on surgery, and because no British surgeon would perform it on anyone under the age of eighteen. In the UK, referral for trans surgery can only be made by one of the twelve adult gender identity clinics for over-eighteens. The use of ambiguous and dated terms in media headlines referring to 'sex change children' misleads the public, implying that genital surgery is being carried out on children when it is not. More often than not, when the term 'transition' is used to refer to children and young people, it signifies social transition. When trans young people talk about their own transition, usually they mean using a different name and pronouns from the ones given to them at birth, and adapting their gender presentation to better express themselves, while asking that others (particularly family members, peers and teachers) acknowledge this presentation. If the child in question is pre-pubertal, 'transition' will refer exclusively to these non-medical steps.

Clinically, the first time any medical intervention can be made is with the onset of puberty. In puberty, a child's body starts to produce sex hormones in the amounts required to trigger the development of secondary sex characteristics that typically distinguish cis men and women. While biological puberty is primarily about the ability to reproduce, socially it fixes how a person's gender is perceived.

Unsurprisingly, for children with acute gender dysphoria that has been alleviated by social transition in childhood, the onset of puberty can cause intense distress. After meeting Joe and Kate to discuss their daughter Alex, who has been comfortably and happily living as a girl in the eyes of others for several years already, I could appreciate more clearly how the dramatic shift of puberty could bring with it trauma, reigniting the misery she felt at three years old, when she was depressed and begging her parents to acknowledge she was a girl. It is in cases like these, usually, that medical intervention may be sought: it is possible to arrest a child's puberty through the use of drugs to suppress the release of sex hormones. Puberty blockers have been used since the 1970s to treat precocious puberty, a natural variation that causes some children to start puberty early, but which can cause restricted height in adulthood and result in social stigma, bullying and distress from being visibly 'out of step' with peers. In their more recent use for children with gender dysphoria (in Britain, from the 1990s onwards), blockers are primarily intended to give the child and their family more time to consider their gender identity, as well as their future medical options, without the irreversible changes of puberty taking place. If blockers are administered, there are two possible outcomes. First, as with the procedure for children with precocious puberty, the child ultimately stops taking blockers and their endogenous (what some may call 'natural') puberty begins. Second, the child continues to block their own sex hormones, while beginning to take 'cross sex' hormones (to describe it as doctors would: phenotypic males take oestrogen; phenotypic females take testosterone), in order to begin medical transition by simulating the effects of the 'opposite' puberty.

Not all children who assert a trans identity will want puberty blockers, but wanting them is certainly no guarantee of getting them, not least because there is sustained opposition to their use, both in the UK and globally. In March 2021, Arkansas became the first US state to approve a bill banning doctors from prescribing blockers to any person under eighteen in the state or referring them elsewhere for blockers. Any doctor who does so risks losing their medical licence. Alabama went a step further, proposing a bill that would criminalize any doctor who provided any trans person under the age of nineteen with affirmative healthcare. At the time of writing, a total of sixteen US states are proposing similar bills banning healthcare for trans youth.

Yet, at the time of writing, the UK has arguably matched the US in its ideological warfare on access to blockers. In October 2020, two people – one an adult former patient, Keira Bell, and the other a parent of a current adolescent patient – went to the High Court seeking a judicial review of the Tavistock and Portman NHS Trust, which runs the Gender Identity Development Service (GIDS), the only specialist NHS clinic for children and teenagers with gender identity issues in England and Wales (Scotland has its own). The question was whether under-sixteens should be prescribed puberty blockers by doctors, or whether a court should decide on a case-by-case basis. The arguments of the claimants rested on whether any teenager could have the competence to consent to treatment. Keira Bell was a twenty-three-year-old woman who had been referred for puberty blockers by GIDS when she was sixteen, before progressing on to testosterone at seventeen and chest reconstruction surgery at twenty in order to live as a man. Her lawyers told the court she had come to regret her decision and 'detransitioned' in her early twenties. They argued that she and, by extension, other teenagers did not have the capacity to consent to puberty-blocking treatment.

To the astonishment of many trans health advocates, the High Court ruled in Bell's favour. It ruled that referring any child under the age of sixteen for blockers would require express legal permission from the court. No other medical treatment given to teens in Britain demands this interventionist approach. In coming to its decision that blockers should be treated in this unique way, the court pointed to evidence that nearly all children who go on blockers progress to cross-sex hormones at a later stage. As a result, it deduced that blockers, despite being reversible themselves, function as a kind of 'gateway drug' to later, more irreversible treatments. Consequently, in order for a court to grant permission for the prescription of blockers, it must be persuaded that the child in question has the capacity to understand not just what suppressing their puberty means in the here and now, but an understanding of how future cross-sex hormones and even future surgeries may affect the rest of their life. This judgment puts England and Wales out of step with international approaches to trans adolescent health, and struck many in the trans community as a decision influenced by a bias: that transition is something to be averted wherever possible, and that the regret of Keira Bell about irreversible changes she made as an adult trumped the distress of trans youth living with dysphoria. Again, there is a parallel with individuals who regret having abortions being used as a principle by which to judge access to abortion for all. It comes as no surprise, then, that Bell's solicitor, Paul Conrathe, is a lawyer with a long history of taking anti-abortion cases. In 2001 Conrathe, working with the single-issue anti-abortion party Pro-Life Alliance, sought an injunction on behalf of Stephen Hone to force his ex-girlfriend to continue an unwanted pregnancy. That this is the man successfully arguing for the legal review of a different kind of bodily autonomy should give us pause for thought.

In the immediate aftermath of the Bell decision, NHS England suspended all new referrals for puberty blockers for any GIDS patient under the age of sixteen: in effect, a blanket ban. At the time of writing it remains in place for all new patients. A glimmer of hope for partially reversing this extreme position came in a subsequent High Court judgment in March 2021. It was a case brought by the mother of a fifteen-year-old trans girl. The mother applied to the court for a declaration that she had the ability in law to consent on behalf of her child to treatment to suppress puberty. The judgment found in the mother's favour: as with other medical treatments for children under English law, a child's parents can consent to puberty blockers on their child's behalf where the child themselves may lack the competence to consent. While an important legal principle, the longer term practical effect of this for actual patients is far from clear. In April 2021, NHS England announced that a new independent review group would be created to help determine if existing GIDS patients under sixteen should be able to continue treatment but that the blanket ban would remain for new patients. Whatever GIDS' policy, it is clear that only trans children with parental support may once again be able to access treatment; those without parents onside cannot. While this is an undesirable distinction in terms of trans children's own right to access care, it was always the case in reality. While, in theory, a GP could refer a child to GIDS without parental involvement, it is in practice impossible for a child who does not have the support of their parents to be seen by GIDS, and only those with supportive parents have ever had a real chance of accessing blockers. The Bell decision itself is due to be appealed at the time of writing, and whether access to blockers will be similarly challenged in Scotland or Northern Ireland is uncertain. An independent review of gender identity services for young people in England, chaired by a former president of the Royal College of Paediatrics and Child Health, Dr Hilary Cass, was announced in September 2020, and its findings are yet to emerge. It is clear that the legal status of trans youth healthcare is an ongoing maelstrom unlikely to be settled in the immediate future.

Current waiting times for a first appointment at GIDS are over two years. The GIDS assessment process for referral, and the waiting times involved in commencing treatment once referred, mean roughly another year will elapse before those teenagers approved for blockers start taking them. Three years from first referral to starting treatment is a long time in an adolescent's life. Yet, medically, to be at their most effective in suppressing the development of secondary sex characteristics, blockers should be started at the outset of puberty, or what paediatricians call 'Tanner Stage 2' (at 'Tanner Stage 1' the child's sex characteristics are entirely prepubertal). The precise timing of this optimum stage of course varies from child to child; typically it occurs at any time between the ages of nine and twelve. In cases of precocious puberty, blockers are usually first adminis-tered to children under the age of eight without any need for court oversight. As a result, international consensus outside the UK is that it is not clinically prudent to specify a blanket mini-mum age for blockers in cases of gender dysphoria.

Prior to the Bell case, less than half of patients under GIDS' care were prescribed blockers, while figures shown to the court in 2020 indicated that, in the year 2019–20, just ninety-five people under the age of sixteen started using blockers and only twenty-two under the age of thirteen. According to GIDS' published figures, in the financial year 2018–19 it received 2,406 new refer-rals; of these, only 230 (9.6 per cent) were aged ten or under at the time they were referred. This means that, even before the Bell case, over 90 per cent of children who were referred to GIDS had no practical chance of ever starting blockers before their puberty began anyway. The vast majority of new referrals to GIDS in 2018–19 were teenagers between the ages of thirteen and sixteen. Given the three-year waiting time, this means those aged thirteen will be eligible for blockers at sixteen. The sixteen-year-olds will already be adults.

The reality, then, is this: the number of children receiving timely medical intervention was vanishingly small even before the legal challenge to its use in December 2020; the UK's approach to puberty-suppressing treatment is highly conservative com-pared to other Western countries; and the waiting times, already almost unendurably long, are getting worse, with no plan in place to bring them under control.

As all this indicates, the voices that have been lost in the legal and media battles over Britain's trans children and young people are those of the young patients themselves. Even as a trans adult working in the media, I have often been asked to comment on an experience that is not my own when discussing young people's access to medical treatment.

In order to better understand what it's like for teens trying to access care, I attend a 16–25 trans youth group in south Wales. There I meet Henry, an eighteen-year-old trans man who has just started taking testosterone. Henry first started to come out six years previously, in Year 8, first 'as bi or gay and then a year later I came out as trans to friends. Around the same time, I told my Head of Year, because I was having problems with anxiety at the time, so I'd go to her.' Henry says that while casually homophobic language was always in the background at school, he never felt personally targeted.

'It was actually surprisingly easy. I was expecting so many comments or questions, and nobody asked me a thing. The school said we'll just change the name more or less immediately. My friends got all the questions because everyone was too afraid to ask me.'

Eventually, he told his mum. 'She was surprised, she thought I was just going to say I was gay,' he says. 'It took a while to get on board. But she was never transphobic. She was just like "I'm going to take some time to understand this."'

Henry always knew he wanted to medically transition and had already been encouraged to see his GP by a teacher who was supporting him: 'She said, "Go to the doctor, because there's no harm in doing that. You don't have to make any decisions." I'm actually really glad she told me to do that, otherwise I would have put it off for years.'

Henry was fourteen when his GP made the initial referral; his first appointment with a GIDS clinician came over a year later. He went with his mum to see the clinician. 'They were pretty basic questions – When did you realize you were trans? When did you come out? How is your mental health?' Henry says. His mum was asked questions about his childhood too. Six months later, now sixteen, Henry had a second appointment in London with two clinicians. This time, he and his mum were interviewed separately.

At first, the clinicians went over the same ground, asking him the same basic questions. Then, Henry says, they asked him to describe his experiences of gender. Henry found this line of questioning difficult. 'There were questions about gender that I find really hard to describe. Because even though I'm a trans man, I find it really hard to describe my gender without resorting to stereotypes that I don't fit because I'm not particularly masculine.'

Henry found the process emotionally exhausting – but, he says, the clinicians were always 'nice' and personable in their manner towards him. 'I'd say "I don't know why I'm trans and I can't explain what gender is." So they would try to get on board with me and change their question and say, "Well, how would you explain it?" but I still struggled.'

Sometimes, in subsequent interviews at the London clinic, Henry's frustration would spill into anger, especially with the knowledge that he would have to be on blockers for at least a year before starting cross-sex hormone treatment. 'I was quite angry a lot in my time there, because I knew that I'd be put on blockers first and I thought "I'm answering all these questions that are really difficult and I'm not going to get any support [in the form of accessing testosterone]." So, I got quite annoyed with them a lot of the time. And they could tell.'

The process was so long and drawn out that Henry knew that, by the time he was finally able to take blockers, it would be too late. Typically, patients have between three and six GIDS appointments. Henry struggles to remember how many he had in total but recalls he had at least four. These recurring appointments often involved Henry having to describe his dysphoria, which he found really hard. 'It's really personal and I don't know these people. It brought it all up and now all my problems are in the front of my head, and you're not giving me any support with it. It's still going to be years until I start treatment and now I'm hyper aware of everything.' Henry tells me that he would cry a lot in appointments and would often 'shut down' part way through the clinicians' questioning.

Henry's frustration was not just down to the difficulty of the clinical approach in his face-to-face sessions with GIDS staff, but the nature of the medical protocols themselves. Aged sixteen, he still hadn't been referred for blockers, and many of the irreversible pubertal changes to his body had already occurred. 'I would ask, "What is this [puberty blockers] going to do for me?"' he recalls, 'and they would say something like, "Oh, you might benefit from a year with no hormones in your body." I just thought, "No, that's not going to be helpful."'

The reality was that, by this point, Henry had been living as a boy day in day out for several years. He felt the clinicians at GIDS lagged far behind – and that neither individuals nor the system were concerned to catch up. It was, he says, especially difficult to see the other boys around him mature through male puberty while he was still waiting for medical intervention: 'I just felt like I was stuck because of some arbitrary rules that don't actually make any sense. It felt,' he continues, 'like this wasn't for the benefit of trans people. It's for cis people who feel uncomfortable with the idea of trans teenagers going through the puberty they want at the age other kids go through puberty.'

In their assessments, GIDS staff use a psychodynamic approach: they attempt to investigate a person's early life experience to understand what drives them, including at an unconscious level. Their training often incorporates the therapeutic models and language of attachment disorders, symbolism and dream theory derived from the work of Carl Jung and the child psychoanalyst Melanie Klein, a disciple of Sigmund Freud. This was evident in the interviews with Henry's mum, who was asked to provide an account of his birth. She found this line of questioning baffling and, despite being told there were no wrong answers, was like Henry unsure of the reasoning behind many of the questions. This is another consequence of the traditional psychodynamic method. Seeking to diagnose, the clinician does not always prioritize explaining the purpose of their questions to the patient.

By the time Henry was referred for blood tests and bone tests to start on puberty blockers he was seventeen and a half. Three years had passed since his initial referral. He was advised to transfer on to the waiting list for the adult gender identity clinic, with the likelihood of an appointment soon after his eighteenth birthday. Henry's frustration and distress is evident: 'GIDS,' he tells me, 'is not fit for purpose for people who are aged sixteen or seventeen.'

A few months after turning eighteen, Henry was seen at the adult Gender Identity Clinic in west London. This was, he thinks, at least the sixth appointment with a clinician in which he had to answer the same questions he'd been answering for years. At the end of the appointment, the clinician said he should have yet another appointment before starting hormones and Henry broke down.

'She wasn't very understanding,' Henry says of the clinician. 'She was like, "Why are you crying like this?" and I said, "Because I'm so disappointed." In the end my mum came in and explained everything. Even then, the clinician answered, "I don't get why you're still upset." I don't think they can be very understanding sometimes of how emotional and how draining it can be, and how much emphasis people put on these appointments. It means so much to people.'

Finally, the clinician was convinced to recommend Henry for testosterone there and then. When I speak to him, he's been taking it for two and a half months – not quite long enough for the most prominent changes, such as his voice deepening, to begin. It has been nearly five years since his first visit to his GP: a long and emotionally exhausting process.

Henry fits the type of younger trans person that is the source of the most intense media scrutiny: a teenager, assigned female at birth, who came out as trans after initially indicating he might be bi or a lesbian. There is intensifying critical media attention on referrals to GIDS of people assigned female at birth who identify as male or non-binary. In 2009–10 the number of new referrals from this group was forty; in 2017–18 it had risen to 1,806. Whereas young people transitioning from male to female were once the largest group, now two thirds of GIDS patients were born female. This is a trend reflected worldwide, and it has caused significant speculation. Though the root cause is unknown, the general explanation offered by trans communities – that it is a result of increased visibility, acceptance and openness about trans people and gender variance in society – is met with widespread media scepticism.

Many commentators in the conservative British press have a different theory: that coming out as trans has become a social contagion among teenage lesbians and girls with autism, who are either seeking to escape the misogyny that comes with developing an adult female body, or who are ashamed and distressed by homophobia. In September 2018, responding to a welter of press coverage on this issue, the then Women and Equalities Minister Penny Mordaunt MP announced an inquiry into the increase in the number of 'girls' seeking support with their gender identity (the inquiry was later quietly shelved when Mordaunt was sacked in a cabinet reshuffle by Boris Johnson). Evidence for such a social contagion is spurious and based on the subjective and hostile impressions of commentators. The following observation – by the *Times* columnist Janice Turner, writing in November 2017 – is typical:

The LGBT community will not countenance that a huge spike in transitioning girls is – like anorexia or self-harm – a social contagion, because this counters a central pillar of trans doctrine that gender is 'innate'.[35]

I ask Henry what he makes of this narrative. 'Oh I've had that so much online. It's so frustrating,' he responds. 'If you talk to a teenage girl that had anorexia or body dysmorphia and then hear a trans man talk about their experience you realize they are so different.' The crucial difference being, of course, that anorexia can cause you to starve yourself, in some cases to death, whereas medically transitioning does not kill you, it alleviates psychological pain.

Henry says the conflation of being trans with anorexia or self-harm doesn't help those trans people who actually do struggle with these things: 'A lot of trans people do suffer from eating disorders because of that link with wanting to change your body. I think dysphoria can sometimes cause an eating disorder – but it's not the other way around. I think trans people with eating disorders do need that extra support. Not just being told they're not actually trans. Some trans people have mental illnesses that aren't connected to being trans at all, and I think it really harms those people.'

A lot of his trans friends are autistic, Henry tells me. But, he adds, the press-fuelled idea that autistic people are mistaken about their gender is similarly harmful. 'It's so ableist and insulting that autistic people can't make decisions or know themselves – being stereotyped does nothing but harm actual trans people.'

Henry thinks that, ironically, the negativity of the media narratives around healthcare for young trans men is due to the way this group is routinely infantilized, which he believes is connected to sexism. 'Me and my trans guy friends definitely get treated as a lot younger [than we actually are]. There's this whole question of whether trans guys experience sexism. I think a lot of us do, because we're still seen and treated as women. There are a lot of sexist stereotypes which I think are still applied to me.'

Henry's subtle analysis of the gendered ways in which he sees himself versus how society sees him resists the simplistic story that he's just a lesbian trying to escape homophobia and misogyny. In fact, Henry says, he's unclear of his precise sexual identity because his teenage years have not involved romantic relationships. 'I don't know yet if I'm just uninterested or if it was because I was struggling with untreated dysphoria.'

Back in 2013, the medical ethics expert Simona Giordano published a clinical, ethical and legal review of treatment for children with gender dysphoria, in which she concluded that, 'omitting to treat, or deferring treatment, is not a morally neutral option.'[36] What she means by this is clear: there is a correlation between the deeply entrenched revulsion at transgender lives and bodies in many parts of the media and society, and the current restrictions around treatment for trans children, as experienced by the likes of Henry. Yet affirmative healthcare around the world recognizes that we have a responsibility to help young people living with dysphoria – and that there are serious ethical consequences for making their experiences not easier but more difficult. As Giordano put it in a 2020 paper:

Puberty blockers are not 'novel' treatment. They were recommended by prominent bodies of medical opinion in the UK and internationally over two decades ago and have thus been part of standard medical treatment for many years.[37]

To put it another way, there's no earthly reason why puberty blockers should not be made available to trans teenagers for the alleviation of gender dysphoria. As with any drug, patients on blockers should be monitored, and research into any and all side effects is to be welcomed so that patients are better informed about every aspect of their treatment. However, the current political panic about trans teens' clinical treatment in Britain is neither scientific nor focused on outcomes; it is purely ideological.

So what can be done? With the current saturation of waiting lists, the obvious next step would be for a coalition of progressives – ranging from families of trans teens and well-disposed clinicians, to LGBTQ+ organizations, feminists and politicians – to loudly and publicly champion affirmative trans healthcare, and to fight for a wider range of treatment options. The monopoly currently held by a single London clinic (staffed by psychologists rather than paediatricians) over access to care for all English and Welsh under-eighteens must be challenged. All trans patients in the UK, whether child or adult, deserve more options and more flexible models of care. This may include local GPs taking on a bigger role in providing access to blockers and hormone treatments; or the opening of localized services such as NHS community trans health clinics, similar to walk-in sexual health clinics, which involve trans people in their governance and day-to-day management. The psychiatric model of assessment and diagnosis must end, and be replaced with multiple options for elective therapy and counselling for those who want it. This approach is already common in other countries. Here, it is due to be trialled in small pilot schemes in London and Manchester. In the 2020s, timely access to transition-related healthcare will be the most pressing issue facing trans communities in Britain.

Of course, not every aspect of trans health is about transition. Related to – but distinct from – transition healthcare are the issues of sexual health, fertility and mental health: all areas in which trans people experience unique challenges in mainstream services due to clinician ignorance or prejudice. This has given rise to alternative services, run by and for trans people with the support of affirmative clinical staff. In London, 56T and CliniQ are two specialist walk-in clinics providing sexual health advice and care to trans people, both operating one evening a week in Soho and Camberwell respectively. Both trans men who have sex with men and trans women who have sex with men are in higher risk categories for certain sexual health issues, including HIV. Though the data on Britain is scant, worldwide 19 per cent of trans women are estimated to be living with HIV; globally, trans women are forty-nine times more likely to be HIV positive than the general population.[38] This risk increases for BAME trans women and/or sex workers, who make up a significant proportion of the trans population. The data on trans men and non-binary people living with HIV is extremely poor. As a result, non-stigmatizing sexual health support from clinicians who are aware of and affirm trans people's identities and bodies is crucial, both for the purposes of specific research and for trans health. Sadly, outside London the kind of Rolls-Royce service offered by these trans-run outreach services is non-existent. Trans people find themselves having to access sexual health services that can misgender them, misunderstand their experiences and stigmatize their sexual behaviour.

Trans-run sexual health and wellbeing services like 56T and CliniQ offer a vision of how more holistic trans healthcare could be administered in Britain. Both also provide counselling and, though they have not thus far been able to prescribe hormones, have the capacity to administer necessary injections as part of hormone treatment for patients whose GPs are less cooperative. Increasing the breadth of these kinds of services beyond sexual health to mental and transition-related health, outside London, would be one step towards dismantling the oppressive structures trans people have experienced for almost a century in their interactions with the medical establishment.

Fertility is one of the key areas in which trans people have, in the UK and around the world, been subject to the greatest medical injustice. In the early 1970s, Sweden became the first country in the world to allow trans people to change their legal sex. However, it simultaneously enforced a strict policy of compulsory sterilization, on the grounds that such people were mentally ill and unfit to care for children: eugenics, pure and simple. The Swedish courts finally overturned this foul policy in 2012 – but, in the intervening forty years, the practice had spread to many other European countries, including France, Belgium, Bulgaria, Cyprus, the Czech Republic, Finland, Greece, Latvia, Lithuania, Luxembourg, Romania, Slovakia and Slovenia. Astonishingly, all were signatories to the European Convention on Human Rights when they enshrined this coercive violation of trans people's bodies. The United Nations has recognized the mandatory sterilization requirement to be a form of torture, cruel, inhuman or degrading treatment, and the Council of Europe has, in the past decade, finally established that member states must abolish this requirement: in 2017, the European Court of Human Rights ruled that coerced sterilization violates trans people's right to privacy and family life.[39] Yet sterilization of trans people is still demanded in many countries around the world, including Japan.

In the UK, sterilization has thankfully never been a legal requirement. However, it has been – and remains – the indirect result of the refusal to fund trans fertility treatment by local NHS Clinical Commissioning Groups. Hormone treatment tends to reduce patients' fertility – and sometimes eradicates it altogether; consequently, when a trans person is about to be prescribed hormone therapy, they are told to preserve their fertility before they begin. Though research on the permanence of infertility is scarce, trans patients are told to assume that after a few months on hormones they will be permanently sterile. Some trans people also undergo surgeries involving the removal or transformation of various reproductive organs, for example hysterectomy (removal of the uterus), orchiectomy (removal of the testicles), genital reconstruction surgery, and so on.

Gamete storage, otherwise known as freezing one's sperm or eggs, is expensive. It costs several thousand pounds up front and several hundred pounds every year thereafter in 'rent' for the clinic's storage of the cells until they are used. Coming in the midst of the upheaval and expense of transitioning, such a cost is out of all but the richest trans people's reach – unless, that is, it's available on the NHS. The availability of free fertility treatment for British trans people, though, is a postcode lottery. While there is a clear funding approach for other patients who may be rendered infertile (such as those undergoing chemotherapy), the approach to transition-related fertility treatment is highly inconsistent. Like many other trans people, I gave up my own fertility for ever while still in my twenties, because I could not access gamete storage on the NHS and could not afford to pursue it privately. While in my case this was an easy decision (I thought that I would prefer adoption if I were to ever want a family), for many trans people it is a devastating ultimatum: live longer with your dysphoria or give up your dreams of biological children. In many cases, transition and being a genetic parent are made incompatible in Britain. But it doesn't have to be that way.

The assumption that it is acceptable for trans people to be coerced by law – or, as in Britain, by economic circumstance – into being sterile goes to the heart of the way trans bodies have been constructed, understood, maligned and contained by those with an ethical duty to treat us, and by society at large. 'Trans people were never meant to reproduce!' the British trans woman Aoife Bale says ironically in an essay on trans fertility in a zine published by the Trans Health Collective:

We were a sick aberration, a dead branch on the tree of society that needed to be cut to avoid sucking up any more nutrients from the healthy parts – but with a method that would avoid leaving an ugly blunt stump ruining the view.[40]

Trans healthcare must be revolutionized urgently: it was created not to help us but to conceal that which is unpalatable to cisgender people and to erase the implications of our existence for the rest of society. That is why we were not permitted families in so many cultures and why authoritarian governments always attack our access to care. Yet in this we are not unique. Cisgender women, disabled people, fat people, black people, HIV-positive people and trans people are all groups that experience high degrees of medical discrimination and abuse, historically and currently. Our struggle is, then, a shared one – and it should not be left to us alone. In the wake of the coronavirus pandemic especially, the 2020s and beyond will see us all struggle in a new era of recession and growing social conservatism about who deserves healthcare investment. This is a daunting, frightening time, but solidarity between all of us who are pushed to the margins may yield new health activist movements and resistance.

3.

Class Struggle

In December 2017, the London Central Employment Tribunal heard a discrimination case brought by a former Primark employee, Alexandra de Souza E Souza. De Souza, who was trans, claimed constructive dismissal against the retailer after enduring systematic bullying and harassment at work. One of de Souza's supervisors repeatedly referred to her by her (male) birth name, in front of colleagues and customers – a name she had not used for sixteen years and which was only visible on her passport. A fellow retail assistant sprayed perfume on her until she coughed, saying de Souza smelt of urine 'like a men's toilet' and had a 'deep, man's voice'. Another colleague told an electrician that he could enter the ladies' toilets as there were 'no ladies in there', when she knew de Souza was present and could hear her. One member of staff called her 'a joke'; another said she would pray for de Souza because she had 'evil inside her'. De Souza's complaints to the company were ignored; grievance procedures weren't followed. Finding in favour of de Souza, the tribunal agreed that this contributed to a culture of harassment that had caused 'very severe' injury to de Souza's feelings and that she was 'bullied out of a job'.[1]

Lack of financial access to justice and limited awareness of one's legal rights means that the experiences of low-paid trans workers like Alexandra de Souza rarely make it to tribunal. In most cases of workplace bullying, one of two things happens: the trans worker simply leaves their job, probably through stress;

or they stay and endure mistreatment out of financial necessity. The available evidence indicates that if a person is in work and not hiding the fact that they are trans, they're at substantial risk of workplace harassment, which can range from procedural injustice to verbal taunts and physical violence. The last of these is all too real a possibility. A recent Stonewall report provides a sobering statistic: one in eight British trans people have been physically attacked at work.[2]

In general, trans people are more likely to have lower incomes and to experience poverty than the wider population. A 2015 EU report found that trans people living in the EU were more likely than their cisgender counterparts to be in the bottom 25 per cent of earners.[3] In the UK, as many as one in three employers say they would be less likely to hire a trans person.[4] Though trans unemployment is not monitored in the UK, studies show it is certainly much higher than the national average;[5] in its near neighbour Ireland, trans unemployment is running at 50 per cent.[6] Half of all trans people who do manage to find employment have to hide the fact they are trans:[7] either they are closeted and unable to come out and transition, or they transitioned some years ago and are able to hide their history (though unchangeable physical traits mean only some trans people can do this).

Prejudice persists. It is not just a personal affront, but an economic reality that shapes and limits trans lives. According to the British Social Attitudes survey, British people are much more transphobic than they think they are. While 82 per cent of people say they are not prejudiced against transgender people 'at all', only 41 per cent of Britons believe trans people should 'definitely' be able to teach kids, and only 43 per cent agree that trans people should be allowed to become police officers.[8] This often-unconscious prejudice makes employers less likely to hire a trans person. That the general population does not trust trans people's involvement in the fields of teaching and policing is telling.

Both professions require trust and authority; both are seen by large sections of the population as the bedrock of an ordered, prosperous and civilized society, either in their upholding of the rule of law and preventing crime, or in their education of society's youth. Given the way in which LGBTQ+ people have historically been portrayed as a threat to children or as seducers of the young, this lack of trust in trans teachers strikes a depressingly familiar note. The damaging effects of this kind of suspicion on trans people themselves are clear from the tragic case of Lucy Meadows, the trans schoolteacher we met in the Introduction who took her own life in 2013 after becoming the focus of a media frenzy.

Historically, transition meant financial ruin, even for those who were better off to begin with. Jenny-Anne Bishop, a seventy-year-old British trans woman who has been prominent in community-led activism in north Wales, estimates that 'over the years, I reckon in lost salary, seniority, and pension interruptions I have lost at least £250,000, just for being trans.'[9] Like many trans people of her generation, Bishop experienced financial difficulty in the years when direct discrimination in employment was legal: 'I'd been out in the [trans] community from the early seventies, but every time work found out I was trans in my private life it wasn't long before I was fired or made redundant.'

In the UK, trans people have had some degree of protection from discrimination since 1999, when new regulations covering gender reassignment were introduced under the Sex Discrimination Act 1975. This has since been superseded by the Equality Act of 2010, which contains more robust protections. Under the Equality Act, any person who takes steps to reassign their gender or is perceived to have done so is protected from discrimination on that basis. It means that you cannot refuse to hire a person for being trans, fire them for being trans or refuse them goods or services for being trans. These protections also extend to family members and partners of trans people who are discriminated against because of their connection to the relevant trans person. While legislative protections are crucial, and their presence should not be taken for granted (only twenty-two US states currently protect trans people in employment, for example), they alone cannot change the underlying prejudices. As Jenny-Anne Bishop recalls: 'Even after the gender reassignment regulations were added, particularly in the private sector, there was always a way found to get rid of you.'[10]

Even if a trans person is in secure employment with a formal contract, the legal costs of seeking advice and taking a case to tribunal are likely to be prohibitive. Since 2010, successive Conservative governments have cut legal aid, and for employment discrimination cases both a merits test (that is, is the case likely to succeed?) and a means test are applied before legal aid is granted.

A trans person's ability to rely on their legal protections is dependent on the broader landscape of workers' rights. The employers most at liberty to discriminate against trans people will be those offering low-paid jobs with precarious conditions – such as zero-hours contracts, where, rather than being formally dismissed, the worker can simply be offered no further work. Working-class or 'unskilled' trans people are particularly likely to occupy such roles. Indeed, the first time I ever met a trans woman (to my knowledge) was in 2007 when, as a student, I worked during the summer vacation in one of the many call centres in my hometown of Bristol. It was cold calling: a truly thankless and poorly paid job on a zero-hours contract, where toilet breaks were timed and, if deemed over-long, flagged to a manager who sternly told you to go more quickly in future. The office demographic was unlike anywhere else I have worked, in that two minority groups were over-represented: visibly trans women, and women from Bristol's Somali community. (A customer service role in which you didn't have to face the customer in a wig or a hijab was doubtless a common attraction for both groups, who are also over-represented in Bristol's hate-crime statistics.[11])

The experience of being trans is shaped by social class. While there are middle-class trans people, the vast majority are working class – just as the vast majority of the total population is working class. Trans workers are often employed in lower paid and more precarious jobs, with a high risk of discrimination and bullying in the workplace. As a result, trans political struggle is part of a wider class struggle.

Despite this, trans politics is commonly misrepresented as coddled, bourgeois and anti-working class. In 2013 the controversial British columnist and feminist Julie Burchill rushed to the defence of her friend the *Guardian* columnist Suzanne Moore, with a piece in the *Observer*. Shortly before, some trans people and their supporters had challenged Moore on Twitter following her misjudged quip about 'Brazilian transsexuals' in a piece on feminism and anger for the *New Statesman*. Burchill's defence of Moore consisted of berating what she described as the vocal, authoritarian and monolithic 'transgender lobby' for having the temerity to lecture a working-class female writer – Moore – on her privilege. This gave way to a tirade against trans people which was so vitriolic and hateful that the *Observer* retracted it, removed it from its online servers and published a grovelling apology for running it. 'Shims, shemales, whatever you're calling yourselves these days – don't threaten or bully us lowly natural-born women, I warn you,' Burchill blustered. 'We may not have as many lovely big swinging PhDs as you, but we've experienced a lifetime of PMT and sexual harassment.'[12]

For those open-mouthed at the sheer ugliness of Burchill's language, it might be easy to miss her portrayal of trans women waving around PhDs: a caricature designed to cast trans people as products of privilege and obscure gender discourse, divorced from the bodily and economic reality of working-class woman-hood. Burchill's polemic rests on a conceit – entirely unfounded, as it turns out – that sets 'working-class people' on one side of a divide and 'trans people' on the other. As Burchill's misguided justification puts it, she and Moore are 'part of the minority of women of working-class origin to make it in what used to be called Fleet Street and I think this partly contributes to the stand-off with the trannies . . . We know that everything we have we got for ourselves. We have no family money, no safety net.' This implication – that trans people can be dismissed as wealthy children of privilege – rides roughshod over the evidence, which clearly shows that trans people are in fact more likely than the general population to live in poverty.

After the *Observer* pulled Burchill's piece from the internet, Suzanne Moore wrote her own column on the furore. Despite its grudging attempt at a placatory tone (it was entitled 'I Don't Care if You were Born a Woman or Became One'), it reaches for precisely the same false dichotomy and specious argument as Burchill's invective: 'transphobia' is a pointless concept, a friv-olous and largely meaningless distraction used to perpetuate infighting among progressives over irrelevant linguistics. 'In Ice-land, they put bankers in prison for fraud. Here, we give them knighthoods. So to be told that I hate transgender people feels a little . . . irrelevant.' Trans people's struggle against inequality, unlike that of cisgender women, strikes Moore as petty: 'other people's genital arrangements are less interesting to me than the breakdown of the social contract.'[13] Which is a pretty ill-considered argument, overlooking the fact that the widespread and prurient preoccupation with the 'genital arrangements' of trans people is so often a source of violence against them and that it has a huge and degrading impact on their very place in the 'social contract' of capitalism.

The idea that trans activism, rather than being the struggle of an oppressed group who suffer – among many other problems – a severe economic disadvantage, is the navel-gazing 'ideology' of an entitled cultural elite is common on both sides of the political spectrum. Transphobes on right and left alike rely on rhetorically separating trans people from the broader working class, their efforts bolstered by a sustained critique of millennial 'identity politics'. Similarly, the media generally gives house room to trans people's political arguments only in a select few contexts, in which the actors are more likely to be middle class: the commentariat's obsession with the question of no-platforming on university campuses being an obvious example.

In the wake of Donald Trump's November 2016 presidential win, US conservatives and centrists alike speculated that the hitherto minor gains made by trans people might be responsible for his rise. 'The legitimation of identity politics by the Democrats has finally come back to bite them,' thundered Charles Krauthammer in the *Washington Post*, arguing that, 'Trump managed to read, then mobilize, the white working class,' who felt left behind, while minorities like 'the relatively tiny population of transgender people, receive benefits, special attention and cultural approbation.'[14] It was an argument picked up in *The New York Times*: 'how to explain to the average [i.e. male, white, working-class] voter the supposed moral urgency of giving college students the right to choose the designated gender pronouns to be used when addressing them?'[15] speculated Mark Lilla, before revealing his own bias against trans people: 'How not to laugh along with those voters at the story of a University of Michigan prankster who wrote in "His Majesty"?' The same implication – that trans rights caused Trump – was made most explicit in a joke made by comedian Colin Jost on *Saturday Night Live*: 'The dating app Tinder announced a new feature this week which gives users thirty-seven different gender identity options,' Jost quipped. 'It's called, "Why Democrats lost the election".'[16]

From the hostile feminism of Burchill and Moore in Britain to the jibes of male comedians in the US, the instinct to separate trans people from any meaningful economic and political struggle is a refusal of solidarity. Paradoxically, it also harms the very causes these liberal commentators support, by providing ammunition to the political right. On the right, trans people are simultaneously – and, again, paradoxically – framed as a powerful and dogmatic cultural elite and as infantile, pathetic 'snowflakes' who revel in their fragility and sensitivity. The rightwing blogger Milo Yiannopoulos, the conservative commentator Ben Shapiro, and Toronto University's controversial professor of psychology and popular author Jordan Peterson have all positioned themselves to conservative audiences, with varying degrees of success, as free speech libertarians speaking truth to power. This 'power', in their minds, comes from an elite mandating political correctness or 'compelled speech' (for which read: referring to transgender people with the pronouns they have expressly asked others to use, which Peterson has described as ceding 'linguistic territory to post-modernist neo-Marxists [sic]').[17] In the UK, this reactionary framing of trans politics as the product of a powerful lobby is mirrored in publications like *Spiked*, whose editor Brendan O'Neill regularly inveighs against trans people. In July 2017, O'Neill pronounced as 'Orwellian' the proposed reforms to the UK's Gender Recognition Act:

> It's madness. And most people know it's madness. Ask any normal, decent member of the public if Dave, 32, born a boy, still in possession of a penis, and a five o'clock shadow on a rough weekend, is a man or a woman, and I bet you they will say: 'Man'.[18]

O'Neill goes on to argue that, 'The authoritarian implications of the government-backed trans agenda are chilling.'

The consistent and methodical insistence that there are 'ordinary working-class people' to whom trans people can be opposed as a distinct mystery or active menace has been a powerful and effective tool in allowing trans people's political demands to be ridiculed or dismissed. It also obscures the reams of evidence that in Britain, as around the world, the vast majority of trans people are working class. To be trans is an experience bound up with economic struggle. There cannot be one without the other.

While for most trans people their gender identity will usually negatively affect their income, for the minority of wealthy trans people there are many aspects of societal transphobia they can simply pay to escape. If you are a middle-class, educated trans person with a university degree who speaks with Received Pronunciation, you will very probably continue to benefit from the favourable bias shown towards people of your class background, irrespective of your gender identity. In terms of your social transition many bureaucratic processes – changing documents, medical records and gender markers, and dealing with doctors and employers – will be made immeasurably easier if you are from the same class as the relevant gatekeepers. In the same way, you are more likely to be aware of your rights or able to solicit effective advice.

'High net worth' trans people are rare. In 2014, the richest woman CEO in America was sixty-five-year-old Martine Rothblatt, a trans woman who transitioned at the age of forty. By her own account, the substantial riches she had amassed in her career prior to coming out (that is, while being treated by society as a man, rather than a trans woman) insulated her from many of the most devastating effects of transphobia. Of course, Rothblatt still faced the stigma and shame of transphobia in her family life and no doubt in many areas of her professional life – but, even so, she had the means to effect a social, legal and medical transition more quickly and smoothly than poorer counterparts, and with far fewer economic consequences. In the UK, Pips Bunce – a gender-fluid director at Credit Suisse – made headlines in 2018 after ranking in the *Financial Times* and HERoes 'Champions of Women in Business' list of 'Top Female Executives'. Born and raised as male, Bunce has a non-binary identity, presenting as a conventional businessman, Phillip, some days and as a woman, Pippa or 'Pips', on others. Much of the mainstream media coverage was hostile and focused on whether Bunce, who does not permanently live as female, ought to have been featured on a list for women business leaders. Yet, for many trans people, the more frustrating issue regarding the coverage had to do with the question of class: that Bunce's high-powered career as a banker misrepresented the financial realities of many trans people. Like Rothblatt, Bunce has recognized their own advantage:

> I was fortunate that I'm quite senior, I'm a director . . . I'm very established . . . I have a pass card that has photos of me as both Pippa and Phil on it. That took many, many months to get in place but at least I know that, for subsequent people, this will be another obstacle already sorted.[19]

Comparing the wealthy trans individual fighting to obtain a dual pass to access their offices at an international investment bank with the experiences of Alexandra de Souza in Primark, the gulf in psychological and financial harm experienced is stark. What's more, with Bunce's economic privilege comes political influence: in May 2018, they spoke at a parliamentary event on trans equality hosted by the Conservative Minister for Women and Equalities, Maria Miller MP. Not only has Bunce been able to negotiate institutional barriers in their own workplace, but their high-status job also grants them the ear of legislators.

Wealthier trans people can also use their resources to conform to societal gender norms, thereby further reducing the risk of transphobia. Sometimes referred to in trans communities as 'passing' or 'blending', it is generally acknowledged that, the more a trans person meets society's expectations of what a man or woman should look like, the more likely they are to be hired – and, even more crucially, the more likely to avoid street harassment. A 2017 Stonewall report found that two in five British trans people adjust the way they dress because they fear discrimination or harassment; the same number avoid certain streets in their local area for the same reason.[20] These two statistics are connected: many trans people feel compelled to change either their appearance or their negotiation of public space because of the threat of violence.

If they choose the former, hierarchies of class and ethnicity strongly influence the standards of appearance they are required to meet. Gendered appearance is not only indivisible from social class and economic means; it's also racialized. A working-class black trans woman's ability to meet society's requirements of acceptable femininity and avoid violence involves negotiating with female beauty industries that are often as racist as they are financially exclusive. As such, the likes of Open Barbers, a dedicated hairdressing salon for trans customers in London, is a vital form of community activism. As Tobi Adebajo, a Nigerian non-binary person and hairdresser at the salon, explains:

> It boils down to money. A lot of trans people are poor. We need to consider their safety in coming to the salon and once they get to the salon too. Many of my clients don't feel safe without their hair being done. That's completely legit y'know. This world is mad transphobic. Getting their hair done properly helps them face that world.[21]

Adebajo's point applies especially to women or other trans people who wish to have a more conventionally feminine gender expression: body and facial hair removal, hairstyling, makeup and clothing are all expensive enterprises. At the extreme end of this spectrum are cosmetic feminization surgeries, which in Europe are usually private and cost an average of £20,000.

Where some aspects of trans healthcare, including surgery, are available on the NHS, accessing this care often relies on the patient proving their ability to 'function' as a worker in capitalist society, as discussed in Chapter 2: the year-long period of living in your 'preferred' gender role (the 'Real Life Experience'), completion of which is compulsory for genital surgery (previously, you had to have completed it to be prescribed hormones). Until 2011, moreover, clinician guidance specified that the way to ascertain whether the trans person had sufficiently completed their Real Life Experience was by assessing their ability to 'maintain full or part-time employment, function as a student or to function in community-based volunteer activity'. Such guidelines continue to be influential.

This creates a double bind for many trans people: they can struggle to access transition-related treatment without functioning as a worker – but they are also likely to be discriminated against and struggle as a worker because of their lack of transition-related treatment. This catch-22 historically led to the common experience of seeing visibly trans people volunteering in charity shops to satisfy these onerous conditions.

A key tenet of the drive by trans people towards 'visibility' in mainstream media in the past decade has been the belief that, the greater amount of more accurate media coverage, the more chance trans people have of encouraging empathy in the wider population. This, it is hoped, will make people want to treat trans individuals better both in daily life and in policy.

This strategy hasn't worked – or, at least, it hasn't worked sufficiently to materially improve the lives of the majority of trans people. The problem is that it involves a rose-tinted view of the media, which is imagined as some kind of benevolent megaphone, which amplifies our voices, uncovers truth and educates.

This is an apolitical understanding of the raison d'être of the media in a capitalist society, which – as for any other industry – is first and foremost to make money. To this end, much of the mainstream media exists to entertain people, for which purposes it clings to tried and tested formulas and conventions, to avoid any risk to its revenue streams. In the case of trans people, it tends to focus less on what wider society might recognize as familiar about our experience, instead foregrounding what makes us different, peculiar, titillating, aggravating or freakish. Cisgender people, media bosses conclude, do not want to watch a news item about a trans call-centre worker talking about his poor pay and how his shift patterns make medical appointments difficult – because it is depressing and, arguably, familiar to many low-paid non-trans people with medical conditions of their own. People do, however (or so the reasoning goes), want to watch a late-night Channel 4 documentary in which a trans woman gets large breast implants or has her browbone shaved down. Such documentaries have been a regular occurrence on British television since the 1979 BBC2 documentary *A Change of Sex,* with more recent examples including Channel 4's *Embarrassing Bodies* series, the *Born in the Wrong Body* season and *What Makes a Woman*, featuring the trans model Munroe Bergdorf. Trans bodies when objectified are entertainment; trans bodies when at work in the service of profit are not.

I have experienced this directly. When I began working regularly as a freelance journalist and columnist, I had not long been 'out' publicly as a trans woman. Like many in the afterglow of coming out, I was self-righteous, zealous and painfully opinionated about how I could make a difference in the media discussion surrounding trans people. The online media cycle and the so-called 'gig economy' – in which freelance writers and journalists work job to job based on whatever pitches editors decide to take, with no guaranteed income – favours short, first-person opinion pieces with a hook to current news items and a quick turnaround. The jobs that paid better, and were more professionally satisfying, were longer features in which I would interview subjects and present different voices, with thorough analysis on a particular social issue. Yet I found these pieces (particularly on trans issues, which were judged as 'niche') generally harder to get accepted by publications. If accepted, they took longer to prepare for publication, meaning payment was often delayed.

I also discovered that there was no shortage of online editors keen to read first-hand essays about my personal experiences. Suggested topics included, among other things: how I came out to my family; what makes me a woman; how makeup helped me discover my true identity (it didn't); what dating is like as a trans person; how did having sex compare after I started taking oestrogen to what it was like before I transitioned; are the men who date trans women gay or straight; did Germaine Greer have a point that I was not a 'real' woman; and so on. The theme was clear and consistent: I could earn the most money in the least amount of time from either mining intimate details of my private life or responding combatively to something negative people with bigger platforms than me had said about trans people. Oversharing or being adversarial in the first person are still the main options for the professional trans writer who wishes to write about trans issues. I often obliged because I needed the money and wanted to ingratiate myself with publications to get future work.

Seen solely through the lens of visibility politics, it is indisputable that I was in a position of prestige and privilege: for a trans woman to have a platform and voice in the media at all is still a rarity. It is also undeniable that I achieved this because of my education, class background and media connections. None of this, however, detracts from the fact that my position as a worker was weak and that the publications held most of the power in the negotiations. This imbalance not only affected my career, it affected and arguably distorted the type of representation trans people received from me as a result. First, media working conditions favoured someone from my background writing in the first person over less advantaged trans people – normalizing a white, middle-class, professional and non-disabled trans experience as the default, when it is, statistically, the exception. Second, it made me feel financially pressured to engage in exhausting levels of candour and emotional labour when dealing with the inevitable hostility and degrading comments that resulted online. I also felt an enormous weight of responsibility to fellow trans people to be a spokesperson for a large and diverse community.

On reflection, I suppose none of this should have come as a surprise, given that the British media is owned, controlled and staffed by an extremely small cohort of middle- and upper-middle-class people. A few statistics illustrate the point. Whereas 7 per cent of the British population are privately educated, in 2016 51 per cent of Britain's top journalists went to private school, with just 19 per cent having attended a state school(unlike nearly 90 per cent of the population). The same is true of other powerful institutions, like parliamentary politics and the upper echelons of the law. Logically, then, people working in the media are likely to move in the same social networks as those from similar backgrounds across 'the Establishment' and, as a result, are more inclined to defer to and collude with these systems of power. Preserving the economic and political status quo is integral to the mission of many of the institutions setting media agendas.

Given this media ecosystem, the only way for social-justice movements to gain favourable traction in the media is to present themselves in a palatable, de-politicized way that does not threaten the status quo. It requires the liberal amplification of the (approved) trans individual and their personal freedom or 'rights', without reference to structural politics. All this looks superficially progressive.

Yet without a broader movement in solidarity with other groups, it is inevitable that wealthier trans people will effectively become the oppressors of their poorer and dispossessed siblings.

Not long after Alexandra de Souza won her discrimination case against Primark, the company became a 'diversity champion' for Stonewall. Stonewall's diversity champion scheme is a good-practice forum for employers who wish to commit to greater inclusion for their LGBTQ+ employees. In return for a membership fee, the charity offers training, conferences and resources to companies to help them comply with their legal duties and to go beyond simple policy compliance to create a more inclusive workplace. While the scheme, and Stonewall's work in supporting large organizations more generally, has undoubtedly had a significant positive effect on the lives of many trans people in Britain, this model of isolated top-down change raises a number of political problems. An optimist might argue that Primark decided to collaborate with Stonewall to learn from its mistakes and to ensure there would be no future mistreatment of LGBTQ+ employees. A cynic might counter that the case was extremely bad PR for the company: its bosses perhaps felt that the social cachet of Stonewall's diversity-champion schemes would help to rehabilitate the brand's image.

'Pinkwashing' is a term sometimes used to describe this process, by which corporations and brands try to veil unethical practices or boardroom avarice by publicly claiming to support LGBTQ+ rights. Yet even if corporate cynicism is the motivating factor, surely if it can be successfully harnessed by LGBTQ+ organizations to improve conditions for some trans workers, then the net effect is positive? The problem is that such day-to-day improvements in some workplaces, beneficial though they may be, are piecemeal, isolated and entirely dependent on the discretion of individual employers. The bigger picture at a societal level remains unaltered – particularly, the ongoing problems that remain for the most vulnerable trans people – and no amount of employer-led diversity schemes can provide any progressive, structural solution to the oppression endured by trans workers. This must be said: corporate diversity schemes can never guarantee the safety, dignity and prosperity of the transgender worker – or, indeed, any worker – in the way that a strong and robust trade union movement and a properly funded welfare state can.

The voluntary, discretionary nature of corporate diversity is especially apparent with regard to trans people. Most employers in Britain are not partners of Stonewall; most do not pay for regular training on trans inclusion – indeed, the vast majority are unwilling or unable to pay the stipend required to join diversity and inclusion schemes. Those trans workers who benefit from the training offered by LGBTQ+ and trans charities are likely to be working for large companies with HR departments or for public-sector bodies: by definition, therefore, those workers already fall into the category of the more socially enfranchised.

The poet and activist Nat Raha deftly outlines another reason why the emphasis on corporate diversity falls short:

> white-collar trans liberalism will enable the success of those trans lives deemed acceptable to an expanding multicultural society, in which businesses understand diversity as good practice and trans subjects as highly productive workers.[22]

In a capitalist society, the most effective way to convince employers of the need to change working practices – anything from changing the office layout, to using different video conferencing software, to respecting and protecting the dignity of a transgender employee – is the argument that such changes will increase efficiency and productivity. Trans workers, by this logic, ought to be afforded dignity and acceptance because those who feel accepted will be better workers. This, indeed, is an argument made explicitly at events like the annual *Economist*-sponsored 'Pride and Prejudice' conference. From 2016 to 2019 the conference held annual events in London, New York and Hong Kong, and played host to some of the largest and wealthiest employers on the global corporate stage. It billed itself to prospective attendees as 'a global LGBT conference and initiative that will catalyse a fresh debate on the economic and human costs of discrimination against the LGBT community',[23] and had sessions and workshops with titles such as 'Redefining the business case for LGBT inclusion'. According to *The Economist*, LGBT rights are a cause all companies should support.

Which is fine as far as it goes. The problem is, it doesn't go very far – deliberately so. While this sort of liberal agenda is presented as emancipatory, it creates boundaries of acceptability: trans people and their political demands are acceptable only insofar as accepting them allows better participation in the capitalist system. This, as the writer and performance artist Ray Filar says, divides liberation movements: 'The suit wearers come in, then they take over. It happened to women's liberation, to the gay liberation front, to the anti-AIDS movement, to black power.' Filar suggests that this development leads to more 'palatable' trans people pulling the ladder up behind them and leaving their less acceptable comrades behind.

> Movements are taken out of the hands of the radical, angry, non-respectable, non-conforming people who did the years of unrewarded hard graft to make it all happen, then gradually they are overrun by small-minded career activists out to make a name for themselves.[24]

In other words, social justice movements that cede their ability to decide priorities and direction to wealthy corporations and media outlets also grant those groups the right to determine which political demands are acceptable and which are not. The transfeminist writer Sylvia McCheyne believes that, while this form of liberal activism may help some trans causes like research and awareness,

> it still relies primarily on a vision of liberation that is catered towards the dominant white audience, whilst paying lip service to the likes of intersectionality. Essentially, it's trying to create a capitalist approach to trans 'liberation', or for those who are worthy of such under capitalism.[25]

Liberation cannot be left to charities and NGOs. The LGBTQ+, trans and feminist charity sectors all have severe limitations, both in the UK and globally. Stonewall, where I worked as a Trans Engagement Officer for four years, operates as a parliamentary lobbying organization that is also 'nonpartisan': that is to say, neither the organization nor any of its employees can publicly criticize political parties in a way that might suggest partiality. This is to some extent due to its way of working, which relies on the cultivation of right-wing gay men and lesbians for influence in an era of continuous Conservative governments; and because David Cameron's Conservative government used legislation to gag charities from political campaigning around elections. (You can see why: most charities would, given half the chance, have criticized his government's punitive austerity policies.)

By their nature, charities exist to plug holes in social welfare. Sometimes, their language and approach imagines that prejudices like transphobia occur in a vacuum, or are old-fashioned prejudices bequeathed to us by a past generation, rather than being a direct product of the way our society operates in the here and now. While in Britain the sector has achieved much to be celebrated, particularly in work with trans youth, they are always firefighting in a building that actually needs to be rebuilt. There are, of course, some other immediate problems with the current structures and cultures of most LGBTQ+ organizations. Stonewall, for example, has few people of colour and no trans people in any senior positions; its board of trustees was entirely cisgender for several years until the appointment of a trans woman in 2021. Generally, trans people remain confined to lower-paid, more precarious roles even in the organizations that campaign for our welfare. In particular, Black and Asian trans communities in Britain remain completely under-represented in LGBTQ+ sector organizations; these are the same communities experiencing the brunt of systemic anti-LGBTQ+ oppression in the UK. Trust in NGOs is often very low among trans people and communities of colour, who are rightly critical of these organizations' uncritical proximity to, for example, policing and the Home Office, despite the entrenched racism of both institutions (something to which I return in later chapters).

Nor are corporate and media 'partners' who profess allegiance to LGBTQ+ people consistent. *The Economist*, host of the 'Pride and Prejudice' conference, actually opposed the much-needed reform to the Gender Recognition Act in an extremely hostile leader published in October 2018.[26] The reforms in question, as we have seen, are not particularly radical; indeed, they are already in place in several European countries, including Ireland, Norway, Denmark, Sweden, Malta and Portugal. Gender recognition reform has the approval of every major UK LGBTQ+ and trans organization, follows the guidance of EU regulations, and implements the recommendations of the Yogyakarta Principles (a document published by a convention of human rights groups that provides international guidance on LGBTQ+ rights). Politically, it has, at one time or another, been supported by the manifesto of every major party in Britain, and has been approved by the democratic voice of the trade union movement. Despite all this, despite the relative conservatism of the proposals and the magazine's previous acknowledgement of the importance of the rights of trans people in a fair and liberal society, *The Economist* and its editors quickly dismissed the political demands of the mainstream trans movement when they did not approve of a less medicalized approach to legal gender recognition.

A corporate approach to trans liberation also ignores the fact that some trans people experience multiple disadvantages. There is insufficient research on the ways in which race and disability impact British trans people's employment prospects, but it is clear that not being white (trans people of colour are more likely to experience workplace discrimination than their white counterparts) or having a disability is more likely to mean a trans person is impoverished. For the most vulnerable, these multiple oppressions combine and place them not only at the greatest risk of violence and poverty but also far from the advocacy and professional lobbying of LGBTQ+ organizations. It is the global prevalence of these challenges that means the vast majority of the world's working trans people are still engaged in one industry above all others: the sex industry.

4.

Sex Sells

I regularly encounter the vague assertion that trans people were simply invisible or unknown to the general population until some time around 2013, the trans equivalent of Philip Larkin's 1963. This was not my experience growing up in the early 2000s. During this period, trans people were very much present in our collective consciousness. But they were almost always represented as caricatures and in lewd gags. In particular, the 'trans hooker' or prostitute was something of a cultural archetype for trans women who appeared, usually as a source of comedy (except in crime drama, where they appeared as a dead murder victim), throughout pop culture. When used in comedy, the jokes were always the same: a straight man engaged her services, always mistakenly, before being sexually embarrassed by the 'hilarious' truth. In the opening eight minutes of the hit 2003 British romantic comedy *Love Actually*, a groom and his best man are introduced as characters in the following exchange at the wedding ceremony:

PETER: No surprises?
MARK: No surprises.
PETER: Not like the stag night?
MARK: Unlike the stag night.
PETER: Do you admit the Brazilian prostitutes were a
    mistake?
MARK: I do.

PETER: And it would have been much better if they'd not turned out
   to be men?
MARK: That is true.[1]

In another British comedy, *Bridget Jones: The Edge of Reason*, a
similar joke relies on Hugh Grant's character recounting his
experience with a Thai escort: 'I spent the night with a gorgeous
Thai girl . . . who turned out to be a gorgeous Thai boy.'[2] US
network television regularly fell back on the same tropes. In the
series finale of the third season of *Sex and the City*, lead character
Samantha Jones is kept awake by the black and Latina trans sex
workers ('Samantha's friendly neighborhood pre-op transsexual
hookers',[3] Carrie Bradshaw tells us) who hustle outside her apartment window in New York's Meatpacking District. 'I am paying
a fortune to live in a neighborhood that's trendy by day and
tranny by night!' Samantha shouts over breakfast with her (similarly affluent, white and cisgender women) friends as they share
laughs about the transsexuals. These trans women have 'boobs
on top and balls down below' to lure their kerb-crawling clients –
described as 'pseudo-straight men from New Jersey'. Clearly, the
existence of trans sex workers selling services to men has been
common knowledge for a long time. The jokes even seem to realize that trans women of colour are often the ones who do such
work.

Globally, trans people are over-represented among sex workers. In Britain, trans people are less than 1 per cent of the
population but make up 4 per cent of sex workers.[4] And people's
awareness of trans sex workers is not limited to fiction. If our
definition of sex work includes pornography and online cam
work, as well as escorting and street work, streaming and sales
figures indicate that erotica featuring trans performers has a
healthy and ever-growing market. Its primary consumers are
heterosexual-identified men, who are an eyebrow-raising 455 per

cent more likely than women to search for trans pornography online.[5] In January 2018, annual streaming statistics published by the online porn streaming service PornHub indicated that searches for their transgender porn category had increased by 36 per cent worldwide, and the category was in the top ten most popular in countries including Argentina and Russia.[6] While the majority of trans sex workers are trans women, other trans people – including transmasculine and non-binary trans people, who do not identify as women – will nevertheless market themselves as 'women' to clients.

Less commonly known to those outside trans communities is the specialist market for trans men who sell sex and make 'FTM'* (female-to-male) porn. As one trans male sex worker puts it:

> I think not a lot of people know about trans guy sex workers, in part because there's not heaps of porn with us in it. There's lots of cis man porn, cis women porn, and trans women porn (though for the latter it comes under much different tags that aren't so . . . tasteful) so that's what people think of, I think. People's desires are very fluid and flexible, so of course there are people who want to book us.[7]

The ongoing growth of trans porn, watched by hundreds of thousands worldwide, suggests that for a notable proportion of men with internet access, the first – or, indeed, the only – time they knowingly see a transgender person, that person will be a

---

* Trans pornography tends to describe the performers using standardized industry language tailored to its (largely male) audience rather than language used by trans communities themselves. Porn featuring trans women tends to describe the performer as a 'shemale' or 'tranny'. Porn featuring trans men tends to be marketed as 'FTM' (female-to-male), which is borrowed from an older medical description. Many trans people would not use these terms and consider them offensive outside of the context of sex work.

sex worker. This makes trans sex workers more visible than their siblings in other occupations, even though they usually receive the least institutional representation at policy level or in LGBTQ+ workers' movements. Despite the extreme ways in which their bodies are mythologized, fetishized and denigrated by our culture, trans sex workers, compared to other kinds of trans worker, enjoy the least solidarity and have the least political attention paid to the reality of their lives. This disparity only increases when the trans sex worker is also a migrant and a person of colour.

The wide dissemination and consumption of trans sex workers' labour for pleasure does not appear to translate into any reduction of transphobic prejudice in society. In fact, the two seem to be almost entirely distinct. Nowhere is this better demonstrated than in August 2018 news reports that the right-wing conspiracy theorist and founder of *InfoWars*, Alex Jones, whose homophobic and transphobic rants had led to the removal of his videos from YouTube for hate speech, had allegedly been caught watching trans porn. According to the reports, Jones inadvertently allowed open tabs on his phone's internet browser to be caught on camera. Viewers noticed that one of the open tabs began 'Naughty tbabe Marissa Mi . . . ', apparently referring to the Australian trans porn performer and escort Marissa Minx. Jones was criticized and derided on social media for his 'hypocrisy' – being a consumer of trans porn while using his platform to spew hate against trans people.

Jones later denied that he had opened the page himself (he blamed it on an unwanted pop-up) and claimed that he has never watched trans porn. We should nonetheless consider his critics' suggestion that the alleged behaviour amounted to 'hypocrisy': that hatred of a group precludes sexual desire for them.

This charge misses the point entirely. In a society that is both patriarchal and capitalist, men's misogyny towards women sits comfortably alongside their desire to extract women's sexual labour. This does not change because the woman is trans. In fact, given the political invisibility of most trans women, it may be intensified. To put it plainly, many of the men who purchase the services of trans sex workers will be the same men who argue for the oppression of all trans people and all sex workers. They will be the same men who preach hate and incite violence against them and the same men who, in some cases, personally use physical violence against them.

It is no coincidence that trans sex workers are often at the forefront of LGBTQ+ community organizing and activism across the globe, particularly in countries where LGBTQ+ rights are opposed by the state. At times, the two collide. On 28 June 2015, the LGBTQ+ Pride parade in Istanbul, Turkey, descended into violent carnage. As thousands of people arrived to march through the city, police used pepper spray on protesters, opened fire on them with rubber bullets, and hosed them off their feet with water cannons. The transgender activist Ruzgar Buski told CNN that the state's vicious crackdown on the Pride parade, a feature of LGBTQ+ life in Istanbul for thirteen years, was due to the recent failure of Turkey's president, Recep Tayyip Erdoğan, to secure enough votes for single party rule.[8] Erdoğan's attack on LGBTQ+ people was a cynical, populist move designed to appeal to his conservative base and intimidate other minorities. As often happens, one press photo came to symbolize the resistance against police brutality for Turkey's LGBTQ+ community. That image was of twenty-two-year-old transgender woman Hande Kader in a tearful rage with police officers. Young and passionate, Kader was a sex worker and activist who had shouted at the journalists who took the photographs that ultimately made her a high-profile advocate in her community: 'You take pictures, but you do not publish them. No one is hearing our voices.'[9]

On 12 August 2016, just over a year after she rose to fame at

Istanbul Pride, the remains of Hande Kader were found by a roadside in Zekeriyaköy, a secluded neighbourhood that is home to many of Istanbul's business elite. Kader had been raped repeatedly before being stabbed to death in a frenzied attack. Her body was then set alight. In the speculation that followed her murder, one theory had it that she may have been killed by a gang rather than a lone murderer. According to eyewitnesses, she was last seen getting into a client's car. The killer has never been found and no one has been charged, so we may never know if Kader was killed by a misogynist client, or in a specific and intentional act of political retribution for her public advocacy for LGBTQ+ rights. Either way, her trans status and her work on the street combined to make her especially vulnerable, and directly led to her horrific death at the age of twenty-three. In a sense, they are impossible to separate when analysing the extreme violence under which Kader, and many like her, have lived.

Hande Kader's fate is disturbingly commonplace. I mentioned that, in the past, when pop culture wasn't mocking trans sex workers, television shows like *Law and Order: SVU* were depicting them as murder victims. There's a reason for this. Globally, trans sex workers make up 62 per cent of all trans murder victims, where the victim's profession is known. In Europe, this rises to 88 per cent. According to a report on trans sex workers published by Transgender Europe (TGEU), forty-four trans women, the majority of whom were sex workers, were murdered in Turkey between 2008 and 2017.[10] While Turkey has the highest trans murder rate in Europe, in France, Italy, Portugal and Spain – the countries to which most trans and gender-diverse people from Africa and Central and South America migrate – 69 per cent of reported trans murder victims were migrants. Most were selling sex.[11] Even in Britain – where, fortunately, the trans murder rate is one of the lowest in Europe – three of the nine trans homicides between 2008 and 2020 were sex workers: Vanessa Santillan, Andrea Waddell and

Destiny Lauren. On 20 November every year, British LGBTQ+ communities, organizations and societies commemorate the trans people lost to violence around the world. I support the event and have myself attended these vigils – though I feel some discomfort that they are led by middle-class, white trans people who do not do sex work. Overwhelmingly, it is not financially comfortable trans people, with a platform in the community, who are vulnerable to the fatal violence endured by our sisters. (There is a valuable discussion to be had about properly paying tribute to these murdered people without co-opting their experience or obscuring the role of sex-work violence and anti-migrant racism in their deaths.)

Nor are most murders of trans people the result of random 'hate crime' from strangers. The victims are usually trans women, and the killers are men who desire sex with them. A 2018 analysis of murder statistics in the sex worker industry reported that, 'In a . . . study of sex workers in London, cis-gendered female sex workers' mortality was recorded as 12 times higher than for women from the general population, and murder was identified as one of the leading causes of death'; and this is as true of trans women as cis women.[12] Trans sex workers around the world are often at most risk from the very same men to whom they sell their services. This is not some puzzling 'hypocrisy', but a horrifying and sometimes deadly reality. It should also be an urgent wake-up call for society and workers' movements to better protect and support trans sex workers. Trans people's increased likelihood of experiencing family rejection and homelessness, combined with substantial healthcare costs and a struggle to secure other forms of employment, means that many engage in the stigmatized work of selling sex. And, as we have already seen, trans sex workers experience unique and severe forms of vulnerability and violence. Therefore, the issue of sex-worker rights and safety must be at the heart of the trans liberation movement.

*

The political connection between gender-variant people and prostitution goes back many centuries. According to an entry in the Plea and Memoranda Rolls for the City of London in December 1394, a transvestite prostitute in women's attire was arrested in Cheapside for 'committing that detestable, unmentionable and ignominious vice' (a sex act, we can safely assume) with a man, John Britby. Born as John Rykener but also known as Eleanor, the prostitute – still dressed as a woman while giving the name Eleanor to officials – was interrogated by the mayor of London. The account of proceedings includes a lurid account of Rykener's life and sexual history. Rykener described being first dressed as a woman at the Bishopsgate house of a woman named Elizabeth Brouderer, an embroiderer who moonlighted as a brothel madam by training her female apprentices and her own daughter to sell sex. Rykener told the court that, despite Rykener having been born male, Brouderer gave Eleanor the same lessons in sex with men. The intention may have been to use the deception around Rykener's sex to blackmail clients: Rykener's interrogation reveals a client list that included several priests and friars, one of whom paid with a gold ring for sex. While the court record (written in Latin) says that Rykener described these male clients as *ignotos* ('unsuspecting'), it isn't fully clear whether they ultimately became aware of Rykener's sex and continued regardless. John Britby, the Yorkshireman arrested for procuring Rykener's services, claimed to have been looking for a woman. In this respect not much in the discourse has changed between the fourteenth century and the jokes in *Love Actually*. Both Rykener and Britby agreed that Britby propositioned Rykener, who named a price. The document provides no indication whether Rykener was convicted or punished.[13]

Though the inquisition of John/Eleanor Rykener is the only English legal case dealing with same-sex intercourse or cross-dressing in the late medieval period, similar cases recur throughout

British legal history. Indeed, police and legal records relating to cases against prostitutes paint the best historical picture of people living either fully or part-time as another gender in Britain. Commercial sex between a male customer and a male prostitute who has adopted a female name and dresses in female attire was a common feature of eighteenth-century 'molly houses' ('moll' being contemporary slang for both a gay man and a woman selling sex). On 5 October 1728, reporting a police raid on one such house, the *Weekly Journal* described how

> On Sunday Night last a Constable with proper Assistants, searched the House of Jonathan Muff, alias Miss Muff, in Black-Lyon Yard, near Whitechapel Church, where they apprehended nine male Ladies.[14]

There were up to thirty known molly houses in England during the eighteenth century, which, given the size of population, indicates an extensive subculture of this kind of sex work. By the nineteenth century, it was common for men dressed in female attire to be arrested on the same public-order grounds as prostitutes, or for 'inciting others to commit unnatural offences', even when they had not been engaged in sex work.

This historical connection between gender-variant people and sex work means that the history of their respective resistance movements – demanding less state oppression, less stigma and better conditions – are also interlinked: a phenomenon which had become particularly visible by the second half of the twentieth century. In the US, the trans and gender nonconforming people who led the Stonewall riots of 1969, like Sylvia Rivera, were street sex workers. By 1973, Rivera felt the emerging gay liberation movement was already forgetting trans and gender-nonconforming 'hustlers' in its quest for respectability. In a memorable speech, during which she was booed by the crowd at

New York City's Christopher Street Liberation Day Rally, she chastised those 'men and women that belong to a white, middle-class, white club' for seeking rights for themselves without considering the conditions of queer sex workers. These people, whom she describes as 'our gay brothers and your gay sisters in jail', had been left behind – and the new gay rights movement did not 'do a goddamn thing' for them:

> Have you ever been beaten up and raped and jailed? Now think about it. They've been beaten up and raped after they've had to spend much of their money . . . and try to get their sex changes. The women have tried to fight for their sex changes or to become women . . . I have been to jail. I have been raped. And beaten. Many times! By men, heterosexual men that do not belong in the homosexual shelter. But, do you do anything for me? No.

As in Rivera's time, trans sex workers today – especially those who are migrants and/or people of colour – span several political groups who lack political and economic power, and for this reason are regularly treated as dispensable. Yet some of the most famous trans people in the world are open about being former sex workers. These include the American writer Janet Mock, who discusses her experience in the sex industry in her memoir *Redefining Realness*. The world's first out transsexual Member of Parliament, Georgina Beyer, was open about her past as a sex worker before her election to New Zealand's parliament in 1999; she campaigned on New Zealand's sex work decriminalization law, passed in 2003. In the UK, the writer and campaigner Paris Lees has also been vocal about her past experiences as a sex worker, in 2016 dedicating her honorary doctorate to sex workers.

A 2017 survey of trans sex workers in five different European countries (Georgia, Poland, Serbia, Spain and Sweden) gives a sense of how marginalized a group they are. Close to 70 per cent of those who had engaged in sex work in the previous twelve months decided to do so primarily to earn a living; almost 40 per cent stated that their main reason was that they lacked other opportunities.[15] As the British feminist authors and sex-worker activists Juno Mac and Molly Smith reflect:

> The high prevalence of marginalized people in prostitution is seen as evidence for its predatory strangeness, but in reality, it reflects the normalized, systemic failures of mainstream society.[16]

Staff at the Outside Project, the UK's first LGBTQ+ homeless shelter (which we visited in the first chapter), acknowledge that many of their trans residents who have lived on the streets are sex workers. Tim Sigsworth, chief executive at homeless charity akt, confirms this for the homeless trans youth he works with, who often do survival sex work in return for money or shelter.

Yet, in a transphobic society, sex work can provide some important non-monetary advantages. Trans people often find working among other trans people to be a source of support: sex work can provide a community that gives them a sense of belonging and family, offering networking and mentorship from other, often older, trans people about transition, health and socializing.[17]

What would liberation mean for trans sex workers? Well, it could start with focusing above all else on the safety of the worker. This emphasis can be controversial in some feminist debates led and shaped by women who are not trans and who are not sex workers. In British feminism, the only divide perhaps more acute and bitter than that over trans people (which I will discuss further in Chapter 7) is the divide over sex work. The arguments involved are complex – they can and have warranted whole books themselves – but there are some key conceptual disagreements about the treatment of sex work under the law.

Broadly, the divide is between, on the one hand, sex-worker-led collectives and their feminist allies, who tend to focus on sex work as an issue of safety and labour rights, and who consequently want sex work to be decriminalized; and, on the other, those feminists whose prime concern is an analysis of prostitution as the ultimate expression of patriarchy, male violence and exploitation of women.[18] Our ire, the second group argue, must be aimed at the male client ('punter'). Sometimes, it also highlights the managers ('pimps') found in certain types of sex work. Above all, anti-prostitution feminism argues, men's demand for the right to purchase sex should be condemned and criminalized. Given the extreme violence to which trans people, particularly trans women, who do sex work are subject worldwide, it seems tempting for trans politics to join with this condemnation of male violence and, consequently, with the condemnation of men who purchase sex. It is true that many sectors of the sex industry, from pornography to street sex work to managed brothels, rely on the exploitation of trans sex workers' financial and social vulnerability by cisgender men for profit. Yet the converse argument – for pro-sex-worker trans politics – isn't intended as a moral absolution of the client or unethical industry practices; it isn't concerned with morality at all. Rather, it recognizes that trans sex workers exist in a society in which money is necessary for survival, and that sex work is one of a limited number of options available to the marginalized in this society – and so, regardless of any condemnation or criminalization of clients, trans sex workers will still *need* to sell sex. Accepting this reality turns the focus from 'ending demand' for sexual services, to harm-reduction for the worker.

It is on this basis that full decriminalization of sex work in all its forms must be a central tenet of the movement for trans rights, just as it is the unanimous central demand for sex-worker groups around the world including, for example, SWARM in the

UK, SWAI in Ireland, Strass and Acceptess-T in France, OTRAS in Spain and, beyond Europe, Empower in Thailand, SANGRAM in India and KESWA in Kenya. Decriminalization is also the policy position of major human rights organizations such as Amnesty International and the World Health Organization (which supports decriminalization as the best way to reduce HIV and other sexual health problems among those who sell sex).

But what does decriminalization mean? In England, Wales and Scotland, selling sex is ostensibly decriminalized, but 'brothel-keeping' – which can simply mean more than one sex worker working indoors together for safety – soliciting, loitering, incitement, kerb-crawling and third-party management are all illegal. This has the effect of forcing sex workers to work alone, when indoors, and makes all street sex workers vulnerable to arrest, thereby removing vital ways in which they can protect themselves. This legal model largely means that a client does not commit any crime under the law – but it also means sex workers may be subject to repeat policing, such as raids and arrests, and seizure of their earnings. In the case of migrant sex workers, contact with police can lead to deportation. This is a particular travesty in the case of migrant trans sex workers, who have typically left home countries where being trans may incur imprisonment, rape or death. It also prevents sex workers who have been trafficked into the UK for the purpose of sexual exploitation from seeking help. In April 2018, *Pink News* reported that the government intended to deport 'Tanya' (a pseudonym), a Thai trans woman who had been detained at Yarl's Wood detention centre. Tanya had been smuggled into the UK in 2014 by a gang and was indentured as a 'ladyboy' escort. After escaping the gang, she had tried to rebuild her life but was detained and, after successful intervention by activists, narrowly escaped deportation. Criminalization of sex work harms sex workers.

Full decriminalization, in contrast, is a model that overturns all criminal laws and administrative or civil orders that aim to punish sex work. This model removes all laws on prostitution and decriminalizes the client, the sex worker and all ancillary occupations, from drivers to management. Instead, sex work becomes a matter of labour law (though the laws on sexual assault, rape, coercion and exploitation that apply in all contexts beyond sex work of course still apply). Decriminalization also removes the police from their current position as the prime regulators of the sex industry.[19] It is important to stress that decriminalization is not the same as legalization, a system seen in countries such as Germany, in which, as writer Ray Filar notes, 'prostitutes are forced to sign a register and are subject to invasive health tests, creating a still-illegal underground economy for those who are not willing to do so.'[20]

There is an alternative model proposed by certain feminists, who argue that sex work is de facto always violence against women and ought to be ended by stopping demand. They are typically called either 'prostitution abolitionist' feminists or (more pejoratively) 'carceral' feminists (in reference to their call for the use of policing and prisons). Their alternative is a legal model that criminalizes the client while aiming to help the sex worker to leave sex work if they wish. Usually referred to as the 'Swedish' or the 'Nordic' model (Sweden was the first country to adopt such laws), this legal approach is now also used both in France and Ireland (north and south). But sex-worker organizations in both countries argue that this legislation has made them less safe – and the concerns are especially acute among trans sex workers. In France at the time of writing, two trans sex workers have been killed since the country's adoption of the Nordic model in 2016. The first was a Peruvian trans woman, Vanesa Campos, who in trying to prevent a gang of armed men from robbing her client was shot dead in August 2018 in the Bois de Boulogne, a city park in Paris. In a statement released after her death, the Parisian sex-worker union blamed France's criminalization of sex work for Campos' vulnerability to violence:

> This phenomenon of gangs of men targeting female sex workers is currently developing throughout the Île de France (Paris) region. The sex workers who try to organize and defend themselves and chase them are then attacked separately. Today we mourn this loss and feel as usual abandoned. The murders of trans women sex workers are not rare. This is a recurring phenomenon and we regularly try to alert public opinion and the authorities to this violence. Unfortunately, as always, we find ourselves alone.[21]

Hundreds of protesters turned out to march for sex-worker rights in response to the murder. They argued that France's 2016 criminalization of men buying sex had forced French sex workers – especially migrants and trans workers like Vanesa – to operate in more secluded areas to avoid police detection, in turn jeopardizing their safety. In February 2020, a second migrant trans sex worker, Jessica Sarmiento, was intentionally run over by a car in the same area of Paris.

The purchase of sex was made illegal in the Republic of Ireland in 2017. By 2019, the Sex Workers Alliance Ireland (SWAI) was already raising concerns about the new law. There had been ten cases in inner-city Dublin that year in which trans sex workers were attacked by men posing as clients; in many cases the victims were Brazilian trans women. In order to understand better why SWAI felt the change in the law contributed to this increased risk for sex workers, in March 2020 I spoke to Addy Berry, an SWAI representative. Addy is Irish, trans, and a sex worker based in Dublin. Aged almost fifty, Addy says they have done sex work of various kinds, on and off, since their teens. 'It's basically client criminalization,' they say of the new law, 'but all they've done is increase stigma towards sex workers' – 'which I think,' they add meaningfully, 'is what it was designed to do.'

The definition of 'sexual services' in the legislation is exceedingly broad. Something merely has to be deemed sexual in nature for it to be criminal: a dominatrix who does not have sex with her clients could fall within its scope. Addy believes that the patriarchal nature of Irish society means that, even now, stigma has never really attached to clients, remaining instead with sex workers, something reflected in prosecutions under the new law:

> There's been a few instances where clients have been prosecuted, mainly in Northern Ireland [SWAI advocates for sex workers in the Irish Republic and Northern Ireland]. Occasionally a client will get prosecuted in the south – but it's something like almost sixty sex workers prosecuted compared to two clients.

This is an imbalance Addy witnesses directly as part of the outreach programmes SWAI does on the streets, for those selling sex outdoors. Addy argues that the Nordic-model legislation fails to consider the uneven approach of police on the ground:

> When I'm on outreach, I tend to see two police officers per sex worker. And they're flashing their lights to scare off the clients because, frankly, a lot of the cops are clients themselves.

In stating that the police are not neutral authorities, Addy voices the feeling of many sex-worker groups. Criminalization assumes that the police, who are established as the de facto regulators, are a separate group from clients. In reality, police violence and male violence (including sexual assault) are intertwined. Police abuse, as far as Addy is concerned, is relatively common: 'I've definitely spoken with people in the west where the Gardaí [police] are insisting on sexual favours in exchange for not punishing the worker.'

Addy recalls a July 2015 case in which an Eastern European sex worker accused an officer of raping her, following a police raid at her apartment for 'brothel-keeping' under Ireland's earlier, pre-2017, prostitution law. The officer in question said he had merely had consensual sex with the sex worker. Prosecutors declined to bring charges against him; he received a small fine for breach of professional discipline. [22]

Even when police are not abusive, says Addy, their enforcement of the law often shows little regard for the economic imperative that drives street sex workers.

> They're coming up to the workers – who are completely decriminalized – and telling them, 'You're wasting your time out tonight, love, you may as well go on home', which of course they can't, because that doesn't mean their rent is free now. It just means that they're moving to less well-lit areas and less familiar areas, or they're jumping into cars with less negotiation time, and it's increasing the opportunity for something bad to happen.

Without tackling the systemic causes that have driven people, particularly trans people, into sex work in the first place, criminalization of the purchase of sex only serves to further disempower the worker. It entrenches an already unequal transaction, because the client knows lack of custom and fewer options to work safely only make the worker more desperate. 'This is basically emboldening the clients,' Addy says. 'I haven't talked to one person who feels that now the workers have more power . . . the clients are demanding unprotected sex and workers are being forced to consider it.'

Anybody associated with sex work now risks criminalization: Addy themself, doing sex work indoors as a dominatrix, was evicted from the premises by a landlord who feared prosecution. Eviction of sex workers is now common:

> When it comes to homes, even when a worker is working by herself, the police will then contact the landlord and threaten him with third party law. So he's forced to evict her, which happened to me and it's happened to other workers.

The consequences of not being able to work in a safe place alongside friends are very clear:

> I've spoken to a trans sex worker who was raped, basically because of being forced to work alone. They were afraid to contact law enforcement for fear of making their situation worse.

Addy tells me that the 2017 attacks on Brazilian trans women in Dublin – largely brushed under the carpet by the authorities – were an extreme example of a wider community hostility towards these workers in Dublin:

> There have been scenes of mob violence where the neighbours have noticed that there's trans Brazilian workers working out of a house and have turned into the stereotypical angry mob outside, smashing the windows.

Migrant trans sex workers under a Nordic system do not benefit from the purported lack of criminalization its advocates suggest. Any contact with police puts workers at risk of being handed over to the immigration authorities and effectively imprisoned in a detention centre or deported – which can deter migrant sex workers, including those who have been trafficked and exploited, from seeking help if subjected to violence. Indeed, while the Nordic model is commonly positioned as a feminist solution to male violence, sex-worker activists argue that its adoption by Western governments is less about eliminating male violence than it is about a broader agenda to restrict migration.

But it doesn't have to be this way. New Zealand decriminalized prostitution in 2003. The positive impact was marked: by 2007, 90 per cent of New Zealand street sex workers felt they had employment rights, 96 per cent that they had legal rights. Indoors, sex workers can work together in groups for safety. Managers are subject to labour laws similar to those governing other occupations and workplaces. Managed sex workers are protected from sexual harassment at work: one New Zealand sex worker won a sexual harassment case against her manager in 2014 and, in December 2020, the New Zealand human rights commission confirmed that a sex worker had won a landmark six-figure payout as part of a settlement after filing a sexual harassment complaint against a business owner. 'Context is everything,' the tribunal said. 'Even in a brothel, language with a sexual dimension can be used inappropriately in suggestive, oppressive or abusive circumstances.'

Under labour law, sex workers in New Zealand also have a right to adequate breaks between shifts and a right to be provided with safer-sex materials such as condoms.[23] Removing the fear of criminal consequences and the threat of policing empowers sex workers to conduct their work safely. The decriminalized context in New Zealand also strengthens sex workers' ability to organize and campaign: the sex-worker-led New Zealand Prostitutes' Collective (NZPC) campaigned for decriminalization prior to 2003 and has since developed into a strong, government-funded organization that is well respected as an authority on sex-work issues. The New Zealand model is to be recommended, but it still, naturally, has significant flaws, particularly in the case of migrant sex workers. Migrants on temporary permits are banned from doing sex work and can be deported if they are found to be working in the industry. This risk, and the accompanying fear of being deported, makes migrant workers more vulnerable to exploitation. Decriminalization should be a universal demand for all, whether with residency documents or without.

Here, it's important to reiterate that decriminalization is distinct from legalization, in which the state takes an active role in legislating or licensing around a permitted sex industry (as in Amsterdam). In a society in which poverty and transphobia still force trans people into sex work, decriminalization is the only way to reduce harm. It must become a key demand, not only of sex-worker groups and human rights charities, but also of feminist and LGBTQ+ organizations in allegiance with trans sex workers.

Like much else in our globalized world, the sex industry is today reliant on technology and the internet. Throughout the 2010s, the US saw growing legislative antipathy towards online platforms that host sex workers' ads. This culminated in the Fight Online Sex Trafficking Act and the Stop Enabling Sex Traffickers Act ('FOSTA/SESTA'), passed by the House of Representatives and the Senate respectively in 2018. These Acts criminalize sites that host content linked to sex 'trafficking'. The term 'trafficking' was used disingenuously by legislators; the laws were drafted broadly, so as to cover all sex-industry advertising, support sites and community organizing. Sites like the Craigslist personals and Backpage.com, which allowed sex workers to identify dangerous clients, have been removed as a result. 'We're monumentally fucked,'[24] said Ceyenne Doroshow, a black trans woman, former sex worker, and the founder and executive director of the NYC-based group Gays and Lesbians Living in a Transgender Society (GLITS).

Trans sex workers speaking to *Vice* in 2018 explained that the legislation on trans sex workers created a climate of desperation that pimps and managers were feeding off, offering their services in connecting workers to clients. Sonja, twenty-seven, a disabled trans woman, spoke about how FOSTA/SESTA prevented her from advertising and screening clients, and reduced her to dire financial straits: 'I tried to go back to clients that had sexually abused me or crossed my boundaries out of desperation for money . . . including one who had directly sexually assaulted me.'[25]

While the endangering of sex workers, trans or otherwise, is the most damaging result of FOSTA/SESTA, the curbing of sex workers' ability to work is the motivation for a wider conservative attack on LGBTQ+ digital content generally. At the time of writing, YouTube has de-monetized LGBTQ+ videos, and Instagram has been restricting LGBTQ+ content as NSFW (Not Safe for Work – that is, inappropriate content). Owing to FOSTA/SESTA, Facebook has recently announced changes to its policies that are so broad as to ban all 'sexual slang, sexual roles, and fetishes', and, as of 2018, Tumblr has banned all 'adult content'. Given that most social networking sites are hosted in the US, British sex workers are also affected. State censorship of trans sex workers' labour directly affects the workers who lose their livelihoods. It also impacts the wider LGBTQ+ community, who use these online forums to form communities and find sexual health information.

Sex-worker unions and organizations, like all trade unions, are a vital tool for protecting the labour and livelihood of the most vulnerable trans workers. Yet it is highly likely that, as more legal rights are won for trans people in the 'respectable' employment market, middle-class trans people will be induced to abandon trans sex workers. The latter, it will be implied, taint the trans movement by association or reinforce the negative stereotypes of *Love Actually* and *Sex and the City*. In Ireland, the major trans organization lobbying for legal rights is Trans Equality Network Ireland (TENI), the equivalent of UK charities like Stonewall

and Gendered Intelligence. Addy, though, says forthrightly that
TENI and similar organizations are silent when it comes to
defending trans sex workers:

> I have friends at TENI, but I can't recall a time I personally
> remember TENI speaking up for sex workers. I tend to have a bit
> of a musketeer attitude – all for one and one for all – but they
> [mainstream organizations] are in a difficult place, because there's
> some respectability politics involved.

Addy thinks LGBTQ+ organizations and charities worry
about their credibility with the public if they take on too many
issues:

> Amongst sex workers, the general level of mental health is not
> great, and amongst trans people mental health is not great, and
> so people will point to people who are part of both groups and
> say, 'You can't listen to them, they're crazy.'

All of which emphasizes why the labour rights of trans sex
workers are synonymous with those in the sex industry as a
whole: these rights must be a key demand of any radical liberation movements for LGBTQ+ people and for women. One
of the first groups to suffer immediate financial harm during the
Covid-19 pandemic were sex workers, for whom organizations
like SWARM (a UK sex-worker advocacy group) immediately
set up a hardship fund. A more caring community for trans sex
workers could involve better fundraising efforts for sex-worker
advocacy groups, and larger more 'respectable' LGBTQ+ organizations beginning to share resources and power with sex-worker
organizations. More fundamentally, sex-work advocacy ought to
form part of the policy of large trade unions and LGBTQ+
advocacy organizations in the UK. Charities like Stonewall

publicly declaring a pro-decriminalization stance is a first step, but these organization must also support sex-worker-led groups to conduct their own work. Sex workers and trans campaigners have been the first to recognize their shared interests and the importance of solidarity in a hostile society where they lack visibility and power. As their organizing principle goes: 'Nothing about us, without us'.

5.

The State

I don't think we would be where we are today – encouraging ever
larger numbers of people to think within an abolitionist frame – had
not the trans community taught us that it is possible to effectively
challenge that which is considered the very foundation of our sense
of normalcy. So if it is possible to challenge the gender binary, then
we can certainly, effectively, resist prisons, and jails, and police.

Angela Davis, June 2020[1]

On 30 March 2020, the Hungarian parliament enacted a law
granting the prime minister, Viktor Orbán, power to govern by
decree: the law had no time limit. Supposedly made in response
to the Covid-19 crisis then engulfing the world, it legally removed
all checks and balances on Orbán's ultra-conservative government (with the exception of Hungary's Constitutional Court,
which in any case has been stuffed with Orbán-supporting
judges since his election in 2010). This power grab alarmed commentators across Europe, who saw it as a classic example of a
tactic employed by countless authoritarian regimes, using a crisis as a means to expand executive power and stifle democratic
opposition. The emergency powers, moreover, were not ad hoc.
They marked the culmination of years of Orbán's Fidesz party
suppressing press freedom and the independence of the judiciary
and central bank.

The day after it was handed these new powers, the Hungarian government released a draft law, Article 33 of which proposed amending the Registry Act, which regulates the registration of births and the issue of identity documents. The article's wording intended to replace the word 'nem', which in Hungarian can mean both 'sex' and 'gender', with the word 'születési nem' ('birth sex'), defining it as 'biological sex based on primary sex characteristics and chromosomes'. This seemingly small alteration would have massive consequences for Hungary's trans community. It meant that, once recorded, birth sex could not be amended on any birth certificate or identification document. The government's reasoning was explicit: 'Given that completely changing one's biological sex is impossible, it is necessary to lay it down in law that it cannot be changed in the civil registry either.' The move was universally condemned by human-rights and LGBTQ+ groups in Hungary and across Europe as not only illegal under the European Convention on Human Rights, and a contradiction of the case law of Hungary's own Constitutional Court, but as a malicious targeting of trans people's ability to operate safely as citizens in society.

Its malevolence aside, Hungary's Article 33 spoke volumes for the government's political priorities: why on earth would any government faced with coordinating its medical and economic response to a major pandemic concern itself with curtailing the civil liberties of trans people? Simply put, it shows the extent to which trans people have in many countries become a lightning rod in a 'culture war' between left and right.

Trans people are emblematic of wider, conceptual concerns about the autonomy of the individual in society. Their rejection of dominant, ancient and deep-seated ideas about the connection between biological characteristics and identity causes a dilemma for the nation state: whether to acknowledge and give credence to the individual's assertion of their own identity in law and in culture; or to mandate that it, the state, is the final authority on identity, and to assert its power over the individual – by force if necessary. Attacking the very concept of trans people by imposing rigid and immutable definitions of sex and gender, as Orbán's Fidesz party has done, is the latest iteration of the way national governments embrace totalitarian ideology. After all, attacking trans people has been a part of fascist practice since the destruction of Magnus Hirschfeld's Berlin Institute of Sexology back in 1933 by Nazi youth brigades.

Given this long history of state violence and suppression, I want to examine the relationship between trans people and mechanisms of state power: in particular, I want to consider the relationship between trans people and the police, trans people and the prison system, and trans people and the immigration system, particularly in the UK. But first, let's take a look at the United States military. It is not only in dictatorships like Orbán's that this state-sponsored violence flourishes. In fact, one of the clearest recent examples of how trans people have been framed as enemies of the state comes, perhaps unsurprisingly, from the federal government of the United States during the Trump presidency.

On 26 July 2017 Donald Trump tweeted:

> After consultation with my Generals and military experts, please be advised that the United States Government will not accept or allow . . . Transgender individuals to serve in any capacity in the U.S. Military. Our military must be focused on decisive and overwhelming . . . victory and cannot be burdened with the tremendous medical costs and disruption that transgender in the military would entail.

The ensuing ban on trans people in the American military reinstated an earlier policy, in place since the 1960s, which the

Obama administration had lifted in 2016. It was one of a string of anti-trans policies that Trump enacted in his first two years in office, including rejecting guidance for federal schools that trans students be allowed to use restrooms in accordance with their gender identity. Trump's justification for the trans military ban was the 'burden' of tremendous medical costs the Pentagon would have to bear in funding the healthcare of trans service personnel. This wasn't even a coherent justification on the face of it: not all trans people will transition medically while in service and many transitioned years before entering the military. Yet the ban affected anyone who was trans whether currently medically transitioning or not. Trump's emphasis on the uniquely burdensome cost of trans healthcare was also quickly debunked. Compared to the other types of healthcare required by active service personnel and veterans, the costs of trans healthcare pales into insignificance. (One statistic that gained popularity in the media in the wake of Trump's announcement was that the Pentagon spends five times more on Viagra than transgender health.[2])

Among the trans community, the trans military ban was met with different reactions. For some, the ban denied trans people the right to honour their country by service. These voices included current and former trans soldiers, such as the campaigner Charlotte Clymer, who argued that trans people had a proud history of fighting for their country. 'There are thousands of openly transgender service members – trained professionals, some of the best and brightest our military has to offer – serving right now, many of them in combat zones,' she said in a televised address for *CBS News*, adding that 'they continue to meet the highest standards of excellence.' Both in her address and on Twitter, Clymer frequently and disparagingly referred to Trump's own avoidance of service in the Vietnam War, referring to him as a 'draft dodger'. There was no evidence, so this argument went, that trans people were any less capable of military service than any other US citizens, and, given that military service was an expression of patriotism, singling out trans people in this way was in itself unpatriotic.

For those more critical of the US military and the global projection of US power generally, these pro-military criticisms of the ban were dubious. As a socialist and anti-imperialist, I find it difficult to accept that service in the military of a Western power is inherently honourable (or indeed that it should be a civil right at all). So, I found myself caught between sympathy for those trans military service personnel whose healthcare was now threatened, who were now living in fear of unemployment and even harassment because of the way their president had marked them out as fundamentally unequal, and my supreme discomfort at having to argue that, well, a trans soldier was just as good as a cis soldier at invading other countries and killing human beings. Liberal arguments by fellow trans people tended to focus on the importance of re-inclusion within the present military system as an end goal; others (among whom I count myself) were reluctant to strive for inclusion within a system we find repugnant.

This is an argument (and a dilemma) trans people as a political group have inherited from the gay and lesbian movement, when in the 2000s the right to join the armed forces became a central goal of gay rights campaigns, alongside equal marriage. It drew similar criticism from queer academics and activists, who argued that the gay liberation movement was being de-fanged of its radical and revolutionary potential for society as a whole, and instead being subsumed into capitalism and Western imperialism.

In those years, to be perceived as gay-friendly was fast becoming a way for governments and the white-majority citizenship of countries in Europe and north America to present themselves as exceptional in contrast to other cultures and racial groups. As the academic Jasbir Puar puts it: ' "acceptance" and "tolerance" for gay and lesbian subjects have become a barometer by which the right to and capacity for national sovereignty is evaluated.'[3] In other words, integration of the 'right kind' of LGBTQ+ citizen (white, documented, non-criminal, sexually respectable) has become a way for imperialist Western powers to maintain their dominance and confirm their credentials as the ultimate arbiters on human rights and justice for the rest of the world – which explains why both gay and trans soldiers are such popular mascots for mainstream LGBTQ+ campaigns and equality awards. British examples include James Wharton, the first openly gay soldier to appear on the cover of *Soldier Magazine* – the official monthly publication of the British Army – and Hannah Graf, who, after transitioning in 2013, would go on to become the highest-ranking trans person in the British Army. Named 'Trans Role Model of the Year 2019' by Stonewall, Graf was awarded an MBE in the same year. Through the visibility of such figures in public life, the concept of the military is reinforced as the ultimate example of participation in and contribution to the life and prosperity of the nation.

We can critique this unabashed jingoism, yet it provides a chilling insight into Trump's prioritizing of a ban on trans people in the military. The ban heralded a paradigm shift away from this socially liberal approach of Western governments. In stating that trans healthcare is uniquely unworthy of state support and ought to be regarded as distinct from all other types of healthcare, it harnessed the symbolic power of the military to signal that trans people are considered a burden to the state and a liability to the nation. As with Orbán's elimination of legal gender recognition, such debasement of one minority group is inherently fascist, even as it occurs within a democracy and a problematic military system. This is why – despite my criticisms of US foreign policy – I still found myself condemning the ban. It was eventually lifted by the newly elected President Biden within days of his inauguration in January 2021, signalling a reversion to the liberal approach of inclusion and assimilation about which I remain deeply sceptical. Nevertheless, it still needs to be emphasized: trans people are not a burden to society or to the state. It ought to be the state's obligation to support trans people, not the other way around.

Up to now, this book has looked primarily at trans people's struggle to secure the necessary conditions for a happy life and participation in the community: family and friends, health and money. However, examining the relationship of trans people to the state forces us to ask two big questions about how the existence of trans people challenges the way we organize ourselves as a society. To what extent must trans people bend themselves to fit the way our society is ordered at present? To what extent do the challenges trans people present to lawmakers expose fundamental flaws in the entire system?

As trans people start to become a more normalized idea for some societies, there are signs that the state is assuming the position of authority once held by medical gatekeepers, in its fresh attempt to set, define and control the boundaries of what it means to be acceptably trans under capitalism. This is particularly apparent in the national conflict over the reform to the UK's Gender Recognition Act, where vocal opposition to giving the individual full freedom to change their gender on legal documents without any external tests or conditions suggests a wider reluctance for the state to relinquish its dominion over trans lives.

Any consideration of the relationship between trans people and the state in the UK must begin with policing. As trans people start to become more visible, and more accepted, in society, so the police's purported role as the defenders of trans people against bigotry and violence continues to evolve. Since 2007, violence, verbal abuse and the harassment of trans people (something regularly experienced by pretty much all trans people, myself included) has fallen within the scope of 'hate crime' law. In England and Wales, 'hate crime' describes a range of criminal offences in which the perpetrator is motivated by hostility or demonstrates hostility towards the victim's disability, race, religion, sexual orientation or transgender identity. Breaking your neighbour's window because they parked their car across your drive is criminal damage; breaking your neighbour's window because they are a trans man is also a hate crime.

Calling a criminal activity a 'hate crime' helps to flag it to prosecutors as more serious. Evidence of a transphobic motivation for a crime will make it more likely that a prosecution is required in the public interest, and it will be considered an aggravating factor for the purposes of sentencing: prosecutors may request, and magistrates or judges may ultimately impose, a heavier sentence than that which the same crime would normally receive in different circumstances. Hostile behaviours towards another person which are motivated by hate, but which are not in and of themselves criminal offences, may be recorded by police as hate incidents. Trans people experience high rates of hate crime: according to Stonewall research conducted in 2017, 41 per cent of trans people had experienced a hate crime or incident in the previous year.[4] What's more, the problem is getting worse: police records show a huge increase in reported hate crime against trans people over the past few years. In June 2019 a Freedom of Information request by the BBC showed that the number of anti-trans hate crimes recorded by police forces in England, Scotland and Wales had risen by 81 per cent: 1,944 crimes were recorded across thirty-six forces in the financial year 2018–19, up from 1,073 in 2016–17.[5]

The Home Office ascribes this increase in figures largely to better rates of reporting rather than a surge in hate crime itself. Police involvement in documenting and responding to transphobic harassment and violence has increased, because of a concerted effort both within police forces and mainstream

LGBTQ+ organizations to advance policing as the best remedy for transphobia in the community. This approach usually emphasizes the importance of training police on LGBTQ+ issues and encouraging LGBTQ+ police officers within the force to be out about their identities at work. For example, in its 2017 *LGBT in Britain* report, Stonewall explicitly recommends training for 'all police officers and frontline staff to ensure they can identify and record transphobic hate crimes, better support victims and bring perpetrators to justice'.[6] Mermaids, the UK charity supporting parents and families of trans children, trains police forces on trans inclusion.

Perhaps inevitably, this closer relationship between trans groups and police forces has drawn media criticism – and has even mobilized protest groups who believe that the police are unduly favouring trans people and closing down free speech. 'Under its vociferous pressure, local and central government, universities, the NHS, and even the police, are hell-bent on silencing anyone who might dare offend the trans-Taliban,' wrote the commentator Julie Bindel in October 2018.[7]

While the idea that a shadowy trans lobby or 'Taliban' has achieved institutional capture of the police is delusional conspiracy theory, part of the creation of a 'folk devil' in moral panics, there are legitimate criticisms to be made of a trans movement that becomes too ideologically and politically invested in policing. In order to understand why there is an inescapable conflict between full trans liberation and the institutional power of the police, we need to recall the historical antagonism between the two. As we've seen, almost all historical records we have of gender-variant people who seem to closely align with what we would today call trans experience are criminal records, related to the punishment of sexual deviance. This isn't a coincidence.

Modern policing was founded in the nineteenth century, the same period in which our contemporary understanding of sexuality was being constructed. As the trans writer Juliet Jacques argues,

> London's swift industrialization allowed unprecedented numbers to flee their villages for the capital's anonymity. The population grew too fast for the law to keep up, and previously suppressed behaviours flourished: amid concerns about rising divorce, prostitution and cross-dressing, widely seen as the visible face of sodomy, the Metropolitan Police was established in 1829.[8]

This new way of controlling the unruly urban population's behaviour included policing masculinity itself, and led to arrests of men in 'female attire'. There are accounts of women dressed in men's clothing, too; though, as Jacques argues, this was generally dismissed as a deception in order to obtain work normally restricted to men, a purely economic choice. Male transvestitism, however, was presumed to be motivated by sex and deviance. One notorious case came in 1870, with the arrest of Ernest 'Stella' Boulton and Frederick 'Fanny' Park, two cross-dressers who performed as a glamorous double act on the British stage. Boulton and Park were national celebrities: their arrest outside the Strand Theatre drew hundreds of curious onlookers to Bow Street Police Court. With cross-dressing not an offence in itself, the pair were instead arrested on suspicion of homosexual offences, something to be confirmed by an intimate – and, we can assume, painful – police examination to determine whether or not they had had anal sex. The examination proved inconclusive and the sodomy charge was dropped. In the end the pair were tried only for 'conspiring to incite others to commit unnatural offences'. Their lawyers successfully argued that their cross-dressing and female personas in public were simply an extension of their stage characters. The judge begrudgingly agreed and freed them: in his summing up, he lamented the fact that there existed no laws criminalizing Boulton and Park's gender abnormality (though he did condemn the unwarranted rectal examination the pair had endured).

The cruel and violating treatment Boulton and Park suffered at the hands of the police is a ghastly milestone in a grim history that continued through the twentieth century. Even supposedly progressive legislation brought with it new opportunities for police harassment. The partial decriminalization of male homosexuality in private homes in 1967 is falsely remembered as the beginning of a new era, when in fact it led to even more energetic policing for anyone suspected of engaging in homosexual acts in public. Long after Boulton and Park's ordeal, appearing to be dressed in the 'wrong' clothes for one's gender continued to attract unwanted police attention.

Things have since changed for the better. The present rapprochement between the police and some elements of the trans movement is some twenty years old. It began with a change in police attitudes towards gay men and lesbians in the 1990s, following the 1990 foundation of the Gay Police Association (GPA) by Constable James Bradley. This was a network of gay and lesbian officers who gradually sought to change the homophobic culture in elements of the force; one huge landmark was being allowed to march in uniform at the 2003 London Pride. Gradually, as trans communities in Britain became more politically organized, more gay and lesbian organizations became 'LGBT'; the same happened with the GPA. Closing in 2013, it was replaced two years later by the National LGBT Police Network (except in Scotland, where the GPA remains). In recent years, this network has worked more closely with trans groups: a guide on hate crime was produced in 2015, and in 2018 it released a 'National Trans Toolkit' for all police officers, on trans awareness, terminology and how to assist officers transitioning at work. That

year, too, the Metropolitan Police said it employed fourteen officers who voluntarily declared themselves to be trans.

At first glance, this seems to be a straightforward trajectory of
progress and growing acceptance of trans people by the police,
and vice versa. But there are legitimate reasons for caution. The
first is a matter of efficacy: the question of whether, on a practical level, the police are the people to create a less transphobic
society. Hate crimes against trans people continue to go significantly under-reported: most trans people – 79 per cent – don't
report their experiences to the police,[9] either because they don't
feel they can or because it's not worth doing so. Tellingly, though
the number of transphobic hate crimes reported to police *is*
increasing, the number of cases being solved and resulting in a
charge is not: most hate-crime cases are closed without resolu-
tion. Even more worryingly, in the UK most transphobic hate
crimes are committed by young people. BBC Freedom of Information requests show that, in the years 2014 to 2017, most suspects
in anti-trans hate crimes were young people, with many suspects
being teenage or even younger.[10] Figures for the same years show
that seventy children aged under thirteen – including some
younger than seven – were reported to police for homophobic or
transphobic hate crimes. This seems valid cause to question
whether the current approach towards hate crime is the right
one. There is an issue in tackling violence, especially by young
people, with the police force – itself another source of violence.
Reliance on policing to solve transphobic hatred among teenagers and young adults, instead of questioning the underlying
causes of their hate, is what some radical activists call 'carceral
logic': a punishment mentality, which is more concerned with
being seen to punish violence with greater force than with working towards the creation of a less violent society. Preventing a
culture from developing in which hatred towards trans people is

normalized is much more likely to reduce harm than the ineffective use of hate-crime legislation and police powers.

The second cause for concern is the state monopoly on violence as embodied by the police, an institution that until very recently was universally hostile to trans people. There remain signs of this residual hostility today. In June 2017, a trans woman in Bristol won substantial damages against Avon and Somerset Police. She claimed male officers forced her to strip naked and refused her requests that only female officers be present as she undressed. 'All of a sudden they grabbed me again, pulled me to the floor. There were male officers removing my clothes on the floor,'[11] she told the LGBTQ+ newspaper *Gay Star News*. She had been arrested when she tried to hang herself in hospital after the mental health team refused to admit her. Police charged her with criminal damage and took her into custody in an extremely vulnerable state, then attacked her. After her bra and trousers were forcibly removed, she was pepper-sprayed in the eyes; officers also reportedly asked the woman if she was a 'Mr or Mrs today' and repeatedly referred to her as 'he', despite her identity documents clearly stating she was female. CCTV footage corroborated the woman's account and the police subsequently admitted to assault and discrimination. Examples like this make many trans people extremely suspicious of police forces' attempts to position themselves as allies and friends to the trans community.

At Glasgow Pride in summer 2017, some trans protesters didn't think the police should be celebrated in the parade as allies. In a counter-protest, a small group of trans young people attempted to bring the official Pride march to a halt by lying down in front of it. According to *Gay Star News*,

Some of them carried anti-police messages. They were objecting to the fact Scottish officers were at the front of the parade, marching just behind a Scottish band. They shouted out: 'No pride in the police'.[12]

Police tried to move the group on by force: they were pinned face down to the ground by officers and handcuffed. Several were arrested, though ultimately released without charge. Nevertheless, the use of excessive force against peaceful protesters at Pride, which originated as a queer protest against oppressive policing, seemed to underscore many radical and left-wing suspicions about the price trans communities pay for giving police forces such a central position in their politics. Any protection and allegiance the police offer, Glasgow Pride showed, is dependent on satisfactory cooperation with the state – any dissent may still be punished with violence. Such episodes serve as a reminder that, ultimately, the new-found relationship between the police and trans people in the twenty-first century is based on supplication, not solidarity.

The idea that the British state and its police forces will help to secure freedom for all trans people also presumes whiteness and complicity with white supremacy. The British police are institutionally racist and hostile to communities of colour, including trans people of colour. Black Britons are forty times more likely to be stopped and searched by police in England and Wales than white Britons;[13] BAME people are twice as likely as white people to die in custody. Trans people of colour, therefore, exist at a crossroads of historic police hostility towards trans people and ongoing police brutality visited upon communities of colour.

In both the US and the UK, black trans people have been integral to organizing within the Black Lives Matter movement, resisting and demonstrating against police violence. More recently, black trans activists have engaged leftist movements over the issue of defunding the police and working towards a police-free state. With the police killing of cis black man George

Floyd in the US on 25 May 2020 prompting a new, worldwide wave of Black Lives Matter demonstrations, black trans activists also tried to raise awareness of the police murder of the black trans man, Tony McDade, in the US two days later. 'Nobody is protecting us, and our lives are being routinely put in danger – to be black and trans is to live on the edge of life – knowing at any moment it can be snatched from you,' the trans Black Lives Matter organizer Melz Owusu wrote in the wake of McDade's killing.[14] Where black trans people are murdered by aggressors who are not part of the police, police forces continue to misgender and disrespect them in reports and investigations after their death. All of which underscores that white trans people cannot claim a liberation for ourselves which depends on passively accepting the continued violent policing of our black and brown peers.

There is a presumption of whiteness within the British trans movement and its over-familiar relationship to the state and its police. This allows white trans people to overlook race-related issues, such as mental health. An astonishing one in four incidents of the use of police force result from an individual's mental health issues – and, as we've already seen, we live in a society where both trans people and people of colour receive inadequate care and are disproportionately likely to experience acute mental health issues. Put these two factors together, and it is understandable that a white trans person's suspicion of the police may become for a trans person of colour outright distrust, even fear. In 1984, the writer James Baldwin talked about the different expectations of white gay people and black gay people in a racist society. His words can be applied equally to trans people:

A black gay person who is a sexual conundrum to society is already, long before the question of sexuality comes into it, menaced and marked because he's black or she's black. The sexual question comes after the question of color; it's simply one more aspect of the danger in which all black people live. I think white gay people feel cheated because they were born, in principle, into a society in which they were supposed to be safe. The anomaly of their sexuality puts them in danger, unexpectedly . . . There's an element, it has always seemed to me, of bewilderment and complaint.[15]

While Baldwin's argument isn't specifically about policing, police brutality would certainly be one of the many ways black people and other people of colour are 'menaced and marked' by racism in ways that white people, including white trans people, are usually not. For those left-wing activists in the queer and trans movement who believe anti-racism is fundamental to their politics, this fact alone makes any form of partnership with police forces unconscionable. Other trans activists, in contrast, consider a more friendly line of communication between trans communities and the police to be a practical necessity. While I have some sympathy for the pragmatic defence of cooperating with police where no alternative is possible, this is a rather different issue from uniformed police marching at Pride, winning 'LGBT diversity awards' or being praised merely for acting in a slightly less oppressive manner towards the 'right kinds' of trans people. Even if some aspects of day-to-day interaction between individual trans people and individual officers in local communities can be improved by greater awareness of trans issues within the police, full reconciliation between trans liberation and policing is impossible, because the police still function as the arm of a larger machine of criminal justice that cannot now and will never easily accommodate many trans people.

Nowhere is this more apparent than in the prison system. Trans people are much more likely to be victims of crime, particularly violent crime, than to be perpetrators. This fact directly contradicts media tropes depicting the trans population, particularly trans women, as especially deviant and dangerous. Trans women are all too used to being framed as predators, stalkers or perverts. The cross-dressing psycho killer has been a recurrent subject of Hollywood thrillers since the golden age of film. Most people in Britain are aware of the basic plot of Hitchcock's 1960 film *Psycho*, in which the gender-troubled and matricidal Norman Bates keeps his mother's decomposing corpse in a fruit cellar and assumes her identity as an alternative personality. The cross-dressing Norman then stalks and kills innocent young women. Three decades later, *Silence of the Lambs* won every major Academy Award. Regularly listed as among the most influential films of all time, it centres on a serial killer of women who (falsely, we are told) claims to be a transsexual woman and then kidnaps women to remove their skins to wear as a coat. Not exactly subtle – but, as the critics say, the film is influential. The unstable transsexual or transvestite killer recurs in other popular horror classics including *The Texas Chainsaw Massacre* series and the 1980 film *Dressed to Kill*. It is not that these films have always explicitly encouraged audiences to see real-life trans people as killers, but they have established tropes which conflate trans people – especially in this case, trans women (or anyone perceived as male while in women's clothes) – with predation, stalking, sexual fetishism, violent misogyny and obsession.

It's not just horror films. In February 2017, the *Sun* – the UK's bestselling newspaper – ran the headline: 'Soham Murderer's "New Name"'. This was a reference to the notorious killer Ian Huntley, who in 2002 abducted and murdered two ten-year-old girls, Jessica Chapman and Holly Wells, in the Cambridgeshire town of Soham: a news story that horrified the nation. Fifteen years later, the *Sun* reported, Huntley was buying makeup and using a female name at the all-male high-security Frankland prison. The story had originated in another tabloid, the *Daily*

Star; other British newspapers were quick to pick it up, repeating and embellishing the details. Huntley apparently liked to wear a blonde wig and asked to be called 'Nicola' (the same name as the mother of one of his victims), while demanding that prison bosses respect his new gender. The subliminal connection between trans people and child murder was bound to be emotive. Even the *Guardian*, Britain's left-leaning broadsheet, regurgitated the story in a column by Hadley Freeman, referring to Huntley's supposed desire to change gender, with the headline: 'Identity is the Issue of Our Age: So Why Can't We Talk More Honestly about Trans Women?'

Yet the entire story was false. Two years later, at Huntley's request, the *Daily Star* eventually published a small correction, stating that Huntley 'does not own a wig, has never asked to be addressed by any name other than his own and that there has never been a plan for him to change his gender identity'.

Undeterred, in April 2020 the *Sun* ran another headline: 'Female Prison Officers Raped by Inmates Who Self-Identify as Trans, ex-Tory Minister Rory Stewart Claims'. The story repeated another false claim, made in an interview with *GQ* magazine by the London mayoral candidate and former prisons minister Rory Stewart. Despite the alarming headline, the *Sun*'s own piece included a caveat, eight paragraphs into the report: 'A Prison Service spokesperson said: "We have no record of this happening. Strict safeguards are in place to manage transgender prisoners while protecting our staff and other inmates."'[16] In 2017, a website called Trans Crime UK appeared online: its tagline was 'Documenting crimes committed by transgender individuals in the UK'. The site collates every conviction of a trans person since 2014. The purpose of the site was to emphasize a link between trans people and violent criminality in order to pressure the government to drop reforms to the Gender Recognition Act. It remains live at the time of writing.

Naturally, as with any social group, some trans people do commit crimes. 'Crime' itself is a broad conceptual category used by the state to describe breaking laws. Criminality is sometimes distinct from questions of ethics or harm, despite the fact that we are encouraged to see them as one and the same. History provides countless examples of laws that were unjust and caused harm, which it was ethical to break. Some types of crime – for example those connected to drugs, sex work or poverty (for example shoplifting) – will sometimes appear in higher rates among marginalized groups, including trans people. This does not mean, however, that minority groups harbour an inherent criminality that threatens physical, emotional or sexual harm to the wider population.

As members of a commonly marginalized group, then, trans people can and do have contact with the criminal justice system: both for the kinds of crime that arise from being marginalized and, occasionally, for crimes that present danger and harm to others. When they end up in the prison system, trans people experience some of the worst treatment and outcomes.

Discussions of prisoners, including trans prisoners, as a category often generalize and omit the seriousness of the offence or levels of violence for which the person has been imprisoned. At the time of writing, the Ministry of Justice counted 163 trans prisoners in England and Wales out of a total prison population of 82,634 (or 0.2 per cent). The actual number is likely to be higher, both because this number excludes prisoners who have changed their legal gender and birth certificate, and because it relies on the prisoner having presented themselves to prison authorities as trans – something which tends to be done only by those serving long sentences. Even allowing room in these figures, however, the amount of trans people in prison is minuscule – not that you would know that from the media coverage.

Coverage of trans people in prison tends to focus on one issue:

where in the prison system trans women prisoners are placed. This is because it centres cisgender people's unease with the idea of trans women in general and particularly the idea of them sharing space with cis women. Since its inception two centuries ago, the modern prison system in Britain (as elsewhere around the world) operated on strict sex segregation – typically based on external genitals – of all prisoners into male and female estates. This division was modified for the first time in Britain after the passage of the Equality Act 2010. New guidance in 2011 stated that a trans man who had changed his birth certificate and legal gender prior to his imprisonment (by undergoing the process outlined in the Gender Recognition Act 2004 to obtain a Gender Recognition Certificate) should be placed in the male estate. The same was also true of a trans woman who had changed her legal gender, *except* where placing her in the women's estate would pose a security risk to other female prisoners. The criteria were still quite narrow – most trans people do not obtain a Gender Recognition Certificate – but there was, nonetheless, a recognition that trans people complicated a binary system of incarceration.

The policy softened further in 2016, in part because of the high-profile imprisonment of Tara Hudson, a young trans woman who spent six weeks in jail the previous year after she admitted head-butting a barman. Though on hormone treatment since her teens, Hudson did not have a Gender Recognition Certificate. Her appearance – which undoubtedly helped her cause with the public – was very conventionally feminine in photographs. Hudson was initially sent to HMP Bristol, a men's prison, for seven days, before a campaign by her family and an online petition signed by 150,000 people put pressure on the Ministry of Justice, who moved her to a women's prison, Eastwood Park. Hudson later said that during her brief period in a men's prison she suffered sexual assault and found the prison's atmosphere intimidating, hostile, degrading and humiliating. The deaths by suicide of two trans women prisoners, Joanne Latham and Vikki Thompson, in men's prisons within the space of a few weeks in late 2015 also shifted public attitudes. Beyond Britain, the greater media spotlight on trans issues in the mid 2010s created correspondingly greater sympathy for the plight of trans prisoners. One such was the world's most famous trans prisoner, American whistle-blower Chelsea Manning, who was held in solitary confinement at a men's prison and frequently denied resources to begin her external transition, treatment which was widely perceived as an act of torture. The conversation was changing.

From 2016, in England and Wales, trans prisoners without legal gender recognition had the right to apply to a Local Transgender Case Board: officials who would look at the individual circumstances and decide if a request to move estates could be granted. Their decision was based on criteria such as degree of physical transition, years lived in their acquired gender and offending history. The guidance, however, only considered trans men and women. Non-binary people would continue to be housed by sex assigned at birth. At the time of writing, no recorded trans men have used this facility to move to the men's estate, while the majority of recorded trans women (119 out 130) are held in men's prisons. Only eleven trans women without legal gender recognition are held in women's prisons in England, and seven in Scotland. It bears re-emphasizing that this is a vanishingly small number in relation to the amount of media coverage this issue has received.

There is a common myth that all trans women in prison desire to be held in or moved to the women's estate. For many, this isn't true. There are far fewer women's prisons in the UK than men's (and none at all in Wales). As a result, relocation could mean being moved further away from your family and community on the outside. Some trans women will prefer the familiarity of a male prison they have been housed in for many years to an unknown female prison; some will have support networks and friends in the male estate. For some, it may even be a question of having sexual relationships: 'Why would I want to go to a women's prison?' trans woman Sarah Jane Baker told *Dazed* in a November 2019 interview, 'I like men! I'd never get a shag!'[17]

Whether they want to move estates or not, it's usually a question of the lesser of two evils: trans prisoners suffer greatly, regardless of which prison they're in. In the same interview, Baker, the longest-serving trans prisoner in UK history, described years of daily abuse by other inmates. Asked what her lowest point in men's prison was, she answered: 'Getting raped in the prison showers by five people'.[18] In May 2020, the BBC reported that, in the previous year, eleven trans women housed in male prisons had been sexually assaulted. Not only are trans women many, many times more likely to be victims of sexual assault in prison than to perpetrate it, they are sexually assaulted at a higher rate than either cis men or cis women prisoners.[19]

Prison authorities in both the male and female estates fail to manage the care of trans prisoners effectively. One problem is the inappropriate use of vulnerable-prisoner wings: trans people are placed on separate wings for their own protection because of the risk of violence from other prisoners, which simply increases their isolation. In a 2017 report on the health and social care needs of trans people in the criminal justice system, several healthcare professionals working in prisons stated that the use of vulnerable-prisoner wings endangers trans people. According to one such professional: 'The regime punishes people because it can't adequately meet their needs, for example, placing them in segregation.'[20] In 2020, the Independent Monitoring Board (IMB), the UK prison watchdog, found that a small number of high-risk trans women prisoners were left segregated for more than six weeks before being transferred elsewhere, something it described as inhumane treatment.[21]

One 'solution' to the problem of trans women's extreme lack of safety in the men's estate, commonly touted by those media commentators with little knowledge of the prison system, is separate 'trans wings' in which trans prisoners can be housed together. In fact, an attempt at a separate trans wing has been made. The first opened in 2019 at HMP Downview, a women's prison in Surrey, where three trans women, judged to represent an elevated physical or sexual risk to fellow prisoners, were placed in a high-security unit. Within a year, the IMB found that the trans wing had been set up too quickly and failed to provide proper activities (such as exercise or library access) for its inmates. One prisoner in the unit had harmed herself thirty-five times in three months. The reality is that, when it comes to trans prisoners who are a high risk to other inmates, failed attempts at accommodation within the prison system harm them further and dehumanize them by keeping them isolated, rather than respecting their human rights.

Historically, the challenges facing trans and gender nonconforming prisoners were disregarded as distasteful by mainstream LGBTQ+ political campaigns. This goes back to the inception of the modern LGBTQ+ movement. In 1973, as we have seen, Sylvia Rivera chastised the crowd at an early Gay Pride event for having forgotten trans people in prison, and in modern Britain this longstanding reluctance to discuss, compassionately, the actual conditions in which trans prisoners live persists. Sometimes, it is not as simple as bourgeois respectability: the discomfort can stem from the few instances in which trans people have perpetrated actual harm, in particular acts of sexual violence that reinforce transphobic tropes. The rare instances in which a sexual predator is also trans is weaponized to derail campaigns for the rights of trans people on the outside, the reform of the process for legal gender recognition being a key example: the issue of trans prisoners 'gaining access' to cis women by easily changing their legal gender was a key argument for dropping the entire reform. In 2018, some sixty prisoners in England and Wales convicted of a sexual offence were recorded as having declared themselves trans. The rhetorical importance given to this small cohort can be exhausting for the 200,000–500,000 trans people in Britain who fear being tainted – and denied civil rights – by association.

This is something I can empathize with. In 2018, a trans prisoner named Karen White was convicted of sexually assaulting two female inmates while held on remand for other offences in HMP New Hall, a women's prison in Wakefield. White had previously raped two other women while living as male, and had admitted to sexual desire for children. Passing sentence, Judge Christopher Batty said: 'You are a predator and highly manipulative and, in my view, you are a danger. You represent a significant risk of serious harm to children, to women and to the general public.' That a sadistic and manipulative predator like White was given unfettered access to assault inmates when her history was known was a grave failing on the part of the authorities, who were responsible for keeping her victims safe.

When the story of White's conviction broke, I was phoned by a reporter at a British newspaper asking if I would provide a comment for her story on White. Her rationale for contacting me was that I was trans – no more, no less. I was incensed. That I should be called for comment on a case that at the time I knew little about, simply because White and I were both trans, seemed to imply that, in advocating for less medical gatekeeping in the gender recognition process, I was personally enabling a violent serial rapist. 'Assuming I have a soundbite for this is astonishing,' I remember saying to the reporter; 'would you ring up older white men working in the media asking for a response on Jimmy Saville?'

Some trans people's instinctive reaction to the likes of Karen White is to draw a distinction between 'real' trans people on one side and, on the other, predators pretending to be trans to gain access to victims. I understand the temptation to establish this distinction for the purpose of laws and rights – but I also think it's a largely untenable position. Arguing that every unsavoury or abusive person claiming a trans identity is not 'really' trans by virtue of that fact is logically incoherent and risky. It shows bigots that successfully repressing trans people is easily achieved: you need only accuse them of being sexual predators or violent thugs to delegitimize their identities.

Human rights, broadly speaking, are inalienable. Every human being has the right to autonomy over how they define their gender and to some appropriate expression of it. Appropriate expression does not mean locking up vulnerable people with known rapists, and to argue that it does is a sleight of hand used by reactionaries. It might, however, mean still allowing someone the means to medically transition, to change their name and gender marker on documents and to have authorities use their requested pronouns, regardless of their crime. Naturally, this topic is emotive. If a person who committed acts of sexual violence against women or children while being perceived by their victims as a man subsequently transitions, there will be a great many people who refuse to accept that that person is now a woman. It is easy to understand why. Similarly, one can see why many victims of rape and families of murdered people wish the perpetrator could be executed – and many of us would not condemn the strength or sincerity of such feelings. Nevertheless, as a society we understand that we should not have a death penalty because it would violate human dignity. Similarly, we cannot have a society in which a general principle of respect for trans people's autonomy to determine their own gender socially, legally and medically is only given in return for good behaviour. There are no easy ways out.

In the Karen White case, it was the Local Transgender Case Board (that is, the prison authorities) who failed to implement their own guidance properly: given the obvious facts available to them about her offending pattern, White's abuse of two vulnerable prisoners should never have been allowed to happen. In this sense, the gravity of White's own violence towards her fellow prisoners should not be considered independently from the grave and endemic sexual and physical violence incubated and perpetuated by the existence of the prison system itself. Given that trans people are much more likely to be victims of violence than they are perpetrators, trans prisoners and vulnerable cis prisoners have far more in common than media narratives would have you think. To truly make all prisoners safer and reduce harm we must move beyond narratives which see transphobia as a bug in the system to be resolved and start to understand that the system itself is broken. I believe that trying to adapt the present prison system for trans people, while leaving that system otherwise intact, is an abdication of moral responsibility. Trans campaigners, activists and allies should be bolder and move towards explicitly anti-prison politics.

Prisons do not work. Despite the fact that the UK prison population has risen by 69 per cent in the last thirty years, giving us the highest imprisonment rate in western Europe, there has been no corresponding reduction in violent crime. The homicide rate is the highest it has been for ten years. Killings of sixteen- to twenty-four-year-olds are at an all-time high. One in five UK women aged sixteen and over have been sexually assaulted, and the conviction rate for rape remains staggeringly low. Neither do prisons work to rehabilitate offenders: nearly half of released adults (48 per cent) are reconvicted within one year; for those serving sentences of less than twelve months this increases to 64 per cent.

Community sentences are better than prison sentences for re-offending rates. What's more, most people imprisoned in the UK – 69 per cent – have not committed a violent offence, and 82 per cent of women in prison are non-violent offenders.

Prisons operate as containment facilities for a growing mental health crisis: 26 per cent of women and 16 per cent of men said they had received treatment for a mental health problem in the year before they were imprisoned; 25 per cent of women and 15 per cent of men in prison reported symptoms indicative of psychosis (the rate of these symptoms among the general public is about 4 per cent).[22] As with police stop-and-search, prison populations are the result of institutional and systemic racism: over a quarter of the prison population are from a minority ethnic group, and research has found a clear association between ethnic group and the odds of receiving a custodial sentence. Black people are 53 per cent and Asian people 55 per cent more likely than white people to be sent to prison for an indictable offence at the Crown Court.[23]

It's important to emphasize that many of the vulnerabilities experienced by trans prisoners are part of a dismal bigger picture for all prisoners. Self-inflicted deaths in prison and self-harm have reached record levels in the past decade. The Covid-19 pandemic exposed, like never before, the supreme risk to both prisoner and public health caused by the UK's current levels of incarceration, and resulted in prisoners being inhumanely confined to their cells for months on end to control the spread of the virus. While anti-trans voices in media and politics depict trans female prisoners in the women's population as a unique risk to their fellow inmates, they ignore the endemic culture of sexual violence within prisons. Sexual abuse of prisoners is widespread: prison rape is under-reported, but even recorded sexual assaults have quadrupled since 2012. This includes sexual assault of inmates by staff:

between 2013 and 2018 a total of sixty-four staff working at prisons in England and Wales were disciplined for inappropriate relationships with a prisoner.[24] In December 2018, Iain Cocks, a male prison officer at HMP New Hall, was convicted of two counts of misconduct in a public office for an exploitative consensual relationship with one prisoner and one count of sexual assault of another prisoner. This was the same women's prison in which Karen White had committed sexual offences against inmates, a year previously; she was sentenced a few months before Cocks. Yet while the Karen White case was used as the basis for many comment pieces in the media on keeping 'men' (trans women) out of women's prisons, and in campaign messaging against gender recognition laws, it's notable that the Cocks case did not translate into the same feminist arguments against the presence of male guards in female prisons.

There is often, too, a callous disregard in these arguments for the high levels of sexual violence against men in prison. Sexual violence affects many male prisoners, but particularly gay or bisexual male prisoners (or those perceived as such). Male prison rape is normalized and accepted in our culture and is even a source of humour. That violence in prison is often a punishment for 'weak' or failed masculinity means that prisons for men often foster a culture of hypermasculinity, thereby reinforcing the harms of gender for men, women and non-binary people alike. Those who campaign for the safety of vulnerable cisgender women in prison are absolutely correct to do so – but if the sole solution proposed to this is a binary prison system based on genitalia, then the problem of violence is not actually being resolved.

Prisons are human misery factories that increase violence and dehumanization and fail in almost every positive role we are commonly told they fulfil beyond punishment, such as deterrence and rehabilitation. The cruelty they produce is also for profit: fourteen of the UK's prisons, containing one fifth of the total prison population, are owned and run by private firms. Even public prisons in Britain are a huge source of revenue for the private sector, with companies being awarded multi-million-pound contracts to provide services like maintenance, cleaning, food and materials, as well as ancillary services such as transporting people between courts and prisons. Private companies also exploit prisoner labour. Prisoners who work have no rights to unionize and no minimum wage. No health and safety legislation applies to them. If they refuse to work, they can have 'privileges', like visits or time outside of cells, taken away. As of 2017–18, 10,200 prisoners are working for external companies in the public prison estate; a further 2,100 are working in private prisons – for a total of 17 million hours per annum.[25] A normal wage for a prisoner is as little as £6 for a five-day working week.

There's a lot of money to be made from incarcerating people. This is why there is huge political will from Conservative governments to continue expanding what the academic and activist Angela Davis calls the *prison industrial complex*: a nefarious alliance between government, business and media to continue to feed a system of surveillance, detention and imprisonment that suppresses or masks deeper wounds in society like poverty or mental health problems – and generates capital. In 2016, David Cameron's Conservative government announced plans for one of the biggest prison-building programmes in generations: the construction of six new 'mega prisons', plus five new 'community prisons' for women. While ostensibly the intention is to create more capacity and reduce overcrowding, almost every prison expansion in history has resulted in an increased prison population. It is no wonder that the most popular solution to the 'problem' of trans prisoners is building dedicated trans prisons. Italy opened the world's first trans prison in 2010, with more than thirty trans prisoners locked up in a former women's prison at Pozzale, near Florence. Most are inside for drug-related offences and prostitution. In 2018 it emerged, in a consultation document released as part of the Scottish government's review of the Gender Recognition Act, that the Scottish government was considering building a new prison to house non-binary trans people. The mechanism of the prison industrial complex is clear: as it builds more cages it also finds more people to put in them. By logical extension, then, the normalization of 'the trans prison' will only lead to more trans people being incarcerated.

It is for this reason that the ultimate liberation and wellbeing of all trans people, right down to the most vulnerable, depends on moving towards a world with no prisons at all. Prison abolitionism does not have much mainstream presence in the UK, where – despite all the evidence to the contrary – there is an entrenched belief that we still need prisons. Yet, as Angela Davis argues, the abolition of both slavery and capital punishment were both once viewed as similarly outlandish.

What would replace prisons? The prison is a blunt instrument which attempts to control a range of violent hierarchies and social ills: alternatives need to engage with the complexity that carceral justice lacks. To quote Davis,

> rather than try to imagine one single alternative to the existing system of incarceration, we might envision an array of alternatives that will require radical transformations of many aspects of our society. Alternatives that fail to address racism, male dominance, homophobia, class bias, and other structures of domination will not, in the final analysis, lead to decarceration [ending the practice of imprisoning people] and will not advance the goal of abolition.[26]

Working towards abolition means, over time, building a society in which prisons are not needed. This vision is far removed from the caricature of abolitionist theory, which imagines we simply want to release all prisoners immediately, with no alternative. One roadmap to abolition is outlined in *Instead of Prisons: A Handbook for Abolitionists*, a 1976 work by Fay Honey Knopp that has since informed many radical movements.[27] It proposes five basic stages our society could move through to diminish the function and power of prisons in our society: five stages, I'd argue, that feminists, human-rights organizations and all LGBTQ+ activists might usefully incorporate into their politics and which I adapt here for the purposes of my argument.

First, a moratorium on new prison construction, cutting off the financial resources of the prison system and, instead of expanding it, shrinking it. Trans and LGBTQ+ campaigners, along with feminist organizations and human-rights charities, would all explicitly take a position against *any* new prisons and lobby against any specific guidance for the management of trans prisoners that justified opening new prisons, units or wings. This would include less emphasis on prison sentences and other criminal justice punishments being the way to resolve transphobic hate and violence.

Second, decarceration: releasing prisoners who are not a risk to others. Decarceration became a mainstream talking point, briefly, during the first lockdowns of the Covid-19 pandemic. When it became clear that overcrowded prisons could present a public health risk for the spread of the coronavirus, a proposed solution was to release all non-violent prisoners with immediate effect (though most suggestions did not intend the decarceration to be permanent once the pandemic was overcome). The pandemic aside, the sheer number of prisoners who are in prison for non-violent offences and who are not a danger to others, particularly women and children/ juvenile offenders and those in prison for drug offences, means that large releases are possible and necessary.

Third, excarceration, or decriminalizing behaviours which swell prison populations (including trans prison populations), such as ending the failed war on drugs and decriminalizing drug use, decriminalizing sex work, decriminalizing poverty (that is, welfare fraud) offences.

Fourth, restraint of the few (using the least restrictive and most humane option for the shortest period of time). This is for the minuscule numbers of those offenders whose behaviour is genuinely dangerous to others, i.e. the violent, sadistic or predatory repeat offenders who are used to justify the entire prison system's existence. This approach recognizes, however, that violence and danger is a product of our society, not simply of monstrous individuals, and that it is still a huge failing to have to respond to violence with force and caging.

Fifth, building a caring community, in which support services are privileged over punitive options. This will be the most difficult stage under present political conditions, in which we are socialized to believe that punishment and vengeance are both effective and helpful. In the case of trans prisoners, some of this community care may involve: teaching children about gender difference and creating accountability for transphobic bullying; proper housing provision for homeless youth; a proper welfare system; drug and alcohol projects and mental health services; and seeing the proper funding of early intervention and crisis services as part of 'LGBT rights' alongside legal equalities.

Full liberation for vulnerable and marginalized populations, which includes trans people as well as people of colour and mentally ill people (and the many who fall into all three of these groups), will depend on refusing the terms of the present discussion, which accepts a society fixated on punishment as normal and unchangeable. This seems a big ask in our current climate, with little hope of achievement in the foreseeable future. Yet such large-scale, transformative visions – utopian though they may seem – can and do inform practical activism which builds solidarity with people on the inside. At the grassroots level, this ethos informs the work of some collectives and groups in Britain: the Bent Bars project, for instance, brings together LGBTQ+ prisoners with LGBTQ+ penpals, with the aim of developing stronger connections between LGBTQ+ communities on both sides of the prison walls. With prisoners being routinely marginalized, including in the trans and feminist movements, we urgently need to find new ways of bringing them into our movements and amplifying their voices.

It's clear that we need to turn away from a society in which imprisonment for criminal offences is seen as the solution of first resort. Yet the shocking reality is that Britain also regularly locks up people who have committed no offence under law whatsoever. The difference is that those incarcerated are migrants, and we call the cage a 'detention centre' instead of a prison. Among their number are trans migrants, who flee persecution in their home countries and seek asylum in the UK, only to receive appalling treatment at the hands of the British state. In 2015 (the most recent year for which such figures are available), according to a Home Office response to Freedom of Information requests, there were five inmates in detention centres whom the Home Office recognized as being trans. Over the previous three years, twenty-one inmates recorded as being trans had been held in immigration removal centres. Given the Home Office's relatively narrow definition of trans, which will have most likely centred on trans men and women who have undergone some medical process, the actual number will very likely be higher.

On a bright July morning, I go to meet Dr S. Chelvan, an internationally renowned barrister and legal expert on refugee and human-rights claims based on sexual, or gender, identity and expression. As we sit in his London chambers, Chelvan tells me that there are fewer than twenty asylum cases relating to trans people in the UK in a given year. He explains that the UK's draconian and callous approach reached its nadir in the years 2004 to 2010, under the New Labour governments of Tony Blair and Gordon Brown, during which time individuals who claimed asylum in the UK on account of their sexual orientation or gender identity were not considered to be in need of international protection if it would be 'reasonable' to expect them to be 'discreet' on return to their home country. The British government's expectation that any aspect of queer identity could simply be concealed in order for the claimant to avoid persecution, all to avoid the need for Britain to accept a queer asylum seeker, was a travesty. Fortunately, this argument was eventually ruled null and void by the Supreme Court in 2010, since which time there have been successful appeals against Home Office attempts to deport trans asylum seekers. In one 2016 case, a thirty-three-year-old Singaporean trans woman living in the UK won the right to remain, after two immigration judges found that she would face persecution in her home country for failure to undertake eight years of compulsory military service as a man under Singaporean law.

While in some cases the legal system could provide an avenue for trans asylum seekers, during the 2010s the system still largely treated LGBTQ+ asylum seekers with scepticism. This view was exacerbated by the 'hostile environment' policy of successive Conservative governments, which fanned a general anti-migrant sentiment. Until a successful legal challenge in 2015, many people arriving in the UK to claim asylum were immediately detained, locked up in high-security immigration detention centres while their claims were processed under the Detained Fast Track or 'DFT'. LGBTQ+ people were often detained on the DFT, which, though it processed claims at an accelerated rate, rarely found in favour of the claimant: the Home Office refused an astonishing 99 per cent of claims for those placed on it.

With one of the largest detention estates in Europe – a total of nine immigration removal centres in which people are held against their will – the UK detains more migrants and asylum seekers than the vast majority of other countries. Moreover, it is the only European country which detains asylum seekers indefinitely. Research published by Stonewall and the UK Lesbian and Gay Immigration Group (UKLGIG) in 2016 revealed that trans asylum seekers face particular threats of violence in detention. Often already traumatized by mistreatment in the countries they fled, they are routinely held in centres which do not match their gender identity, and where the healthcare staff are not equipped or qualified to respond to the needs of trans people. This results in many detainees abruptly having to stop medication, which in turn causes physical and mental distress. As one trans asylum seeker from India told researchers, they were misunderstood by staff and feared for their safety. One problem, they related, concerned the communal showers. 'Obviously, I can't go to the shower and people are watching me. If they see me, I would be in big trouble. I couldn't use the shower. For fifteen days I couldn't use the shower. That was really bad.'[28] There were instances of asylum seekers' hormones being confiscated; and of staff exhibiting discriminatory treatment, such as the intentional misgendering of detainees.

As with prisons in general, the pattern of brutality towards trans asylum seekers in detention is part of a wider problem affecting gay people and cisgender women. Yarl's Wood, a detention centre mostly inhabited by adult women, has drawn widespread criticism from across the political and media establishments (which are not typically known for radical anti-carceral politics). The centre has been hit by repeated scandals, from staff locking detainees inside during a fire, to several allegations of sexual abuse, to detainees going on hunger strike against their treatment. In 2018 the then shadow Home Secretary, Diane Abbott, stated that, if elected, a Labour government would have closed Yarl's Wood.

The treatment of trans asylum seekers and prisoners in Britain is a complex and depressing challenge. But a shared call for the abolition of prisons and the immediate closure of all immigration removal centres is one way that trans activists, cisgender feminists and LGBTQ+ campaigners could come together, in order to challenge the mechanisms of state oppression against some of the most vulnerable in our communities, both here and around the world. In recent years, companies like British Airways, who assist the government with deporting LGBTQ+ asylum seekers on their flights, have been allowed to sponsor LGBTQ+ events like Brighton Pride: it is this normalization of the system of detention and deportation in community spaces that needs to be challenged, without exception. Much more has to be demanded of those involved in assisting state oppression. Britain should be a country whose borders are open to all who are fleeing persecution. It also should be a country where trans people are not subjected to violence by the British state itself, through brutal misuse of policing and prisons. Trans communities and our allies here and everywhere should fight for our siblings who face state violence and systemic transphobia in all its forms.

6.

Kissing Cousins: The T in LGBT

The 2018 Pride in London parade took place on a sweltering Saturday in July. Undeterred by the heatwave, massive crowds gathered in the capital's streets to watch the parade of brightly decorated open-air floats, which were led by the first Muslim mayor of London, Sadiq Khan, in a vibrant display of London's ease with diversity and multiculturalism; and, indeed, mainstream LGBTQ+ politics' discomfiting ease with corporate sponsorship – the logos on floats ranged from banks with poor ethical practices and arms manufacturers supplying homophobic regimes, to airlines which have deported LGBTQ+ asylum seekers to regimes that want them dead.

As the parade set off, a group of about ten women, slipping past security staff with ease, joined the front of the march. Carrying a large yellow banner which read 'Trans Activism Erases Lesbians', members of the group brandished smaller signs with slogans such as 'Get the L Out' and distributed leaflets proclaiming that lesbians were being coerced to sleep with men in the name of 'transgender ideology'. One of the women told a reporter for *Pink News*, 'We want to get the L out of Pride: a man cannot be a lesbian, a person with a penis cannot be a lesbian.'[1] When Pride staff attempted to move the women on, they lay down in the street, obstructing the parade's progress. Unable to resolve the situation, staff eventually gave up, and allowed the women to continue marching at the front so that the parade could continue.

The sight of the largest Pride march in Europe being led by counter-protesters openly making statements such as 'Men are saying they are trans, they are lesbians and they pressure lesbians to have sex with them'[2] sent shockwaves through trans communities in the UK and around the world. Apart from astonishment at how easily a huge, corporate-sponsored and policed Pride could be disrupted, what most people found shocking was that the protesters were lesbians – people who might be assumed to be on the side of those marching. But the women's motivation for their counter-protest was clear: they believe that trans women pose an existential risk to lesbians.

The forty-six years of Pride marches in Britain have attracted plenty of counter-protests, usually organized by religious conservatives or street fascists – but never before by people who themselves had an identity that sits within the LGBTQ+ umbrella. At the core of this celebration of diversity, something had clearly gone badly wrong. Pride in London later released a statement apologizing for allowing the protesters to lead the march, a decision which had caused so much distress to trans people and their allies, blaming its failure to act on the hot weather.

Following the protest, the idea of a rift between different factions of the LGBTQ+ coalition over the question of trans politics – and even the right of trans people to membership of that movement – garnered characteristically eager coverage in the right-wing press. On 4 October that year, *The Times* published a letter criticizing the charity Stonewall for its uncompromising approach to transgender rights. The letter had been organized by Jonny Best, a gay man, and signed by seventeen people, including the singer Alison Moyet. Most of the signatories identified as lesbian, gay or bisexual. Two of the signatories were self-described 'male-to-female' transsexuals who agreed that Stonewall's inclusive approach was wrong. In an accompanying article, headlined

'Stonewall "backing transgender bullies" ', the *Times* writer Lucy Bannerman reported that, 'leading members of the lesbian, gay, transsexual and intersex community have started a petition urging the charity to rethink its transgender policy, saying that they are fed up with its refusal to recognize other viewpoints.' The reality was that the letter was signed by a very small group of people, but the *Times*' amplification of it lent weight to a – not entirely unfounded – sense that trans rights were, for some in the LGBTQ+ community, a point of serious division.

This media narrative fuelled a longstanding tension: not only over the exact nature of the relationship between trans people and LGB people, but about the merit of the traditional 'LGBT' abbreviation (which for the purpose of this chapter I will use instead of the more expansive but less established term 'LGBTQ+'). Many straight and cisgender people can find it difficult to grasp why lesbians, gay men, bisexual people and trans people are all grouped together under the banner of 'LGBT'; at times, it's equally confusing for some who come under that banner. 'It is all a bit of an unholy alliance,' as the lesbian feminist Julie Bindel described the situation: 'we have been put in a room together and told to play nicely.'[3]

The trans writer Juliet Jacques traces these differences as far back as the 1970s: discussing one 'split' between gay organizations and transsexual and transvestite groups during that decade, Jacques argues that, as the difference between gender identity and sexuality became clearer, 'the common ground eroded.'[4] She also believes that 'there was already some antagonism, with each side worried that association with the other would make their cause seem less acceptable in a conservative society, especially given the complexities of their historical relationship.'[5] This sense of mutual discomfort was echoed by the trans writer Paris Lees in 2015, when it was announced that Stonewall would begin campaigning on trans issues. 'There is bigotry on both sides,'

Lees said. 'You get trans people saying, "I'm not homosexual you know, I've got a medical condition," and gay people going on about "cross dressers and perverts".'[6] If the relationship between trans people and their cisgender LGB siblings can be fraught, why is it that they are all grouped together? And if their experiences are often quite different, what political advantages are there to solidarity and a shared movement?

One crucial reason why LGBT people have cause to organize together politically is that, even though we see ourselves as distinct tribes, the rest of society has tended to conflate us. Or as one trans person succinctly put it: we are all beaten up by the same people.[7] This shared oppression, both historic and current, drives – indeed, necessitates – solidarity between lesbians, gay men, bi people and trans people. In an era of growing right-wing populism in the United States and the UK alike, accompanied by an alarming rise in visible street fascism, there is more need than ever for unity across the four different letters (as well as queer, asexual, intersex and other groups). It is in the interests of those who hate us all for us to be at war with one another; it is no coincidence that the Murdoch media and the American Christian right are very keen to support LGB people who oppose trans liberation.

It may seem paradoxical that in a period where civil rights for LGBT people seem to be at unique risk – a time in which Boris Johnson, a man who once called gay men 'tank-topped bum boys' and equated gay marriage with bestiality, can be prime minister – there has never been more media representation for LGBT people or more companies happy to insist they support us. This is not out of the sheer kindness of corporate hearts. Brands have recognized that the rainbow flag lends them the goodwill of people who care about social justice. Corporations can purport to be part of a movement with countercultural and liberationist roots, package that movement as 'aspirational' for marketing purposes, and in doing so denude it of all the politics that threaten the capitalist status quo and sell it back to those who can afford it. The idea that conspicuous consumption is a route to sexual and gender freedom has been effective in allowing the LGBT movement's muscles to atrophy. In a godless age, there are new ways to give the masses their opium.

The effect of both division and consumerism is to encourage individual identity over and above commonality. A person's sense of their own identity is certainly important for psychological wellbeing – but as a political end point it leads to solipsism and detachment from others. From this perspective, identity is understood as a set of immutable and finite categories with particular criteria for membership. Yet the political justification for the LGBT coalition must begin with something different: the overlapping and occasionally muddled history that all four letters share. Sometimes, gay and trans people are reluctant to admit how entwined we have been and remain, despite our attempts to educate the rest of society about how we're different. The reality is that the labels we cling to as clear and consistent definitions of identity are still extremely new, and the language around gender and sexuality is still evolving rapidly. Throughout this book, I have stressed the need for caution when categorizing people from the past – such as the Roman emperor Elagabalus or the cross-dressing prostitutes of the molly houses of seventeenth-century London – as 'transgender'. This is because, as we've seen, the emergence of 'trans' (originally 'transsexuals' and 'transvestites') as a way of understanding gender diversity only emerged in the twentieth century as a response to the earlier concept of sexual inversion. The same is true of homosexual or bisexual identities, which make little sense as labels to describe a type of *person* before the late nineteenth century; previously, variation in human sexuality was instead considered in terms of deviant or unnatural *acts*. Sexology categorized deviant behaviour, without the strict distinction between gender identity and sexual orientation that is so central to modern LGBT politics. The relatively recent creation of discrete lesbian, gay, bi and trans identity brackets usually precludes us from looking at historical figures and definitively placing them neatly into these boxes.

Yet there can be a strong impulse by LGBT people today to understand people in the past through the lens of our own language, and to sketch the lives of these historical figures with the conceptual tools available to us in the present. For example, Anne Lister, a Yorkshire landowner from Halifax whose life spanned the late eighteenth and early nineteenth centuries, is often described as a lesbian, sometimes 'the first modern lesbian'. Lister's story was preserved by her vivid diaries, including details of her sexual affairs with women, which she wrote about in code. Lister's passionate and exclusive desire for other women is explicit: 'I love and only love the fairer sex and thus beloved by them in turn, my heart revolts from any love but theirs,' she wrote in one diary entry.[8] Her relationship with another wealthy woman named Ann Walker, with whom she took communion in 1834 (an act both parties considered to be marriage), is also strong evidence that her sexuality corresponds with what would today be described as lesbianism. However, the word did not come to be used to denote 'a woman sexually attracted to other women' until 1870, thirty years after Lister's death, only becoming commonplace in the early twentieth century. Should Lister be called a lesbian when it's not a term she would have used or recognized? The York Civic Society clearly felt not. In July 2018, the Society established a blue plaque dedicated to Lister at Holy Trinity Church in York, where she and Walker had taken the sacrament together. The plaque did not describe Lister as a lesbian. Rather, it referred to her 'marital commitment' to Walker and described her as 'gender nonconforming', perhaps in reference to the fact that she was notable among contemporaries for her masculine presentation and nicknamed 'Gentleman Jack' (the title of the BBC drama of Lister's life) and 'Fred'. Yet the Society's omission of the specific term 'lesbian' caused outcry and an online petition attracting 2,500 signatures. 'Anne Lister was, most definitely, gender nonconforming all her life. She was also, however, a lesbian,' the petition read. 'Don't let them erase this iconic woman from our history.' Apologizing, the York Civic Society affirmed that it hadn't intended to upset any element of the LGBT community, and replaced the plaque in January 2019 with a new inscription explicitly describing Lister as a lesbian.[9]

This fierce dispute over the precise description of a dead Victorian woman is more about contemporary LGBT politics than it is about history. The word 'lesbian' is still too often used as a misogynist pejorative in school playgrounds, in drunken jeers outside pubs, or as a tool for straight male gratification in online porn categories. Even within the LGBTQ community, lesbian culture often seems ignored and deprioritized, particularly when compared to that of gay men. The ongoing and rapid closure of LGBT venues in major UK cities has often affected lesbian scenes hardest: in London, only one lesbian venue exists in a city of almost 9 million people. In such a climate, it is understandable that the wording of Lister's blue plaque became an expression of modern angst over the recent disappearance and erasure of lesbian subcultures in Britain. When you feel your culture and identity endangered and ephemeral, the anchor of history and the celebration of antecedents can be empowering, and worth fighting fiercely for.

Given Lister's clear identity as a woman and unequivocal desire for other women, perhaps the anachronism of calling her a 'lesbian' had a net positive, since it has provided lesbians today with a historical icon. On other occasions, though, similar attempts to establish historic figures as trans people have been hotly contested. Contrast the example of Anne Lister with Dr James Barry, born Margaret Ann Bulkley in Cork, Ireland, in 1789, just two years before Lister. Raised female in childhood, Barry led his entire adult life in both public and private as a man, becoming a military surgeon who worked across the British Empire until his death in 1865. Despite his instructions that 'in the event of his death, strict precautions should be adopted to prevent any examination of his person,'[10] and, despite being initially recorded on his death certificate as male, Barry's natal sex was revealed to the press by one of the women who had prepared his body for burial, after she had unsuccessfully attempted to blackmail his physician into paying for her silence. The public revelation of his biological sex shocked all who had known Barry in life, including his military and medical colleagues. During the Crimean War he had got into an argument with the famous nurse Florence Nightingale, publicly berating her. After his death, Nightingale wrote of the incident:

> 'He' kept me standing in the midst of quite a crowd of soldiers, Commissariat, servants, camp followers, etc., etc., every one of whom behaved like a gentleman during the scolding I received while 'he' behaved like a brute . . . After 'he' was dead, I was told that [Barry] was a woman . . . I should say that [Barry] was the most hardened creature I ever met.[11]

Despite Barry's keenness to be remembered after death as a man, academic and popular historians have frequently claimed him as a woman, using female pronouns. Much like the lesbian reaction to the Lister blue plaque, this has caused outcry among trans communities. In February 2019, the latest iteration of this row was catalysed by novelist E. J. Levy, who had written a historical novel about Barry and described him publicly as a 'heroine' with female pronouns. Levy defended her choice to present Barry as a woman, tweeting that one thing is clear: she refused facile gender categories . . . To insist Barry is trans distorts complex history . . . There's no evidence Barry considered herself trans; she dressed as [a] man as needed to be [a] soldier, doctor . . . Shifting readings of her body are what my novel wrestles with; it's been taken into account; I use she / her as her biographers do.

As I mentioned in Chapter 5, such dismissals of historical trans men as women trying to seek professional advancement are common. The trans performance poet Jay Hulme called Levy's position 'abhorrent',[12] while the trans community historian Morgan Page tweeted:

The misgendering of one of the most blatant examples of an historical trans man is painful – both because it is a wilful attempt to erase us from our own history, and because he was clear that he wanted so badly to be recognized as a man after his death.[13]

As with the lesbians who had signed the Lister petition, Page essentially argued that Levy's and others' continued use of feminine pronouns and descriptions of Barry as a woman were not simply about historical accuracy but contemporary politics:

There is little that is more horrific for most trans people than the idea of being misgendered after death . . . it is an abject fate we have frequently been subjected to. Watching it happen to other members of our community, past or present, can feel traumatic.[14]

The biographer Jeremy Dronfield muddied the picture further: 'If Margaret had been born in 1989 instead of 1789, free to be a surgeon and soldier, would she have chosen to become a man?', he wondered in the *Guardian*. 'On balance, I don't think so, but Margaret might have identified as non-binary.'[15]

Dronfield's conception of non-binary identity as a halfway house or compromise between a woman in disguise and a trans man is both inaccurate and reductive, and causes even greater confusion about how we might understand LGBT history. In fact, some of the anxiety about describing Anne Lister as 'gender nonconforming' in the original plaque was the mistaken belief that she was being claimed as trans or non-binary and her womanhood was being qualified or erased, simply because she also went by typically male nicknames and wore masculine clothing. A concern that all butch or gender nonconforming women throughout history might retrospectively be declared to be not women at all, simply because they weren't stereotypically feminine, is reasonable from a feminist perspective – though it might also be used to erase people like Barry, who actually lived as a man. The contrast in how criticisms of Lister's plaque and the James Barry novel were received show us that much of how LGBT history is remembered is down to chance. It is dependent on the politics of those telling it, and of who holds more power in the context in which it is retold: the plaque was changed, the novel was not. The stories they will tell future generations will be shaped by these decisions. The combined abbreviation 'LGBT' acknowledges that the individual labels the four letters represent are still very new – no more than a century old – and that many of our forebears' lives evade our attempts to neatly label them in one of four boxes.

In my own experience of being a trans woman who is attracted to men, it isn't unusual for people to assume or insist I am 'really' an ultra-feminine gay man who is either confused, deluded or who has transitioned to 'entrap' more masculine partners than I could have if I had presented as male. At school my classmates and friends' insistence that I must be a feminine gay boy meant that I did actually come out as gay in my teens. It was years before I finally worked out that I did not feel comfortable living as male at all, and my desire to be female, not my attraction to men, was the central crisis of my life. I don't hold my classmates responsible for this mistake. After all, as we've seen, this confusion of gay and trans identities was also standard in medical practice throughout the twentieth century. In the 1960s, the husband of trans model April Ashley sought an annulment of their marriage on the basis that his wife was legally and medically a man. In giving medical evidence to the court, the psychiatrist John Randell described Ashley as a 'homosexual transsexual male', which suggested to the court that a trans woman was better considered a subtype of gay man rather a subtype of woman. As late as the 1980s, the sexologist Ray Blanchard maintained that being trans was an expression of sexual orientation. Like Randell, he argued that trans women who were solely attracted to men were a type of feminine homosexual who found it easier to live in imitation of women. Similarly, several of my gay male friends have stories about coming out to their parents as gay, and their tearful mothers asking if they ultimately intended to become a woman. That all gay men must have a desire to be women is the same confusion, reversed. Their mothers did not understand that sexual desire for men is not intrinsically connected to being a woman. In a society that has tended to simply label all LGBT people as 'queers', much of our oppression looks the same, too.

The picture is also complicated by the fact that, in the early days of the modern LGBT rights movement, the word 'gay' was used to describe everyone – including trans people. The birth of the modern movement in the twentieth century is generally dated to the riots at the Stonewall Inn in New York City in the early hours of 28 June 1969. It was an event which even those outside the LGBT family are likely to have heard of, and from which the UK charity takes its name. The Stonewall Inn was a mafia-owned gay club, whose clientele were predominantly gay men of a wide range of ethnicities, from their late teens to early thirties. Patrons also included, in smaller numbers, butch lesbians and street transvestites (a group which included gay men in female attire or 'queens', as well as transsexuals who had undergone or wanted to undergo sex changes). At just after 1 a.m., there was a police raid, which turned violent after police shoved and arrested a number of patrons. In some accounts of how the riots were sparked, a transvestite hit an officer over the head with her bag after being pushed. In others, a butch dyke (sometimes specified to be the black lesbian entertainer Stormé Delaverie) was seen fighting back after being hit by an officer for complaining her cuffs were too tight.

Given the varying accounts of a messy and complex situation (in which most of the rioters were angry and a little drunk), the riot now functions more as an origin myth or oral tradition, of which various branches of the LGBTQ+ community have championed different retellings, often with a somewhat cavalier attitude to the verifiable historical sources.[16] As the trans historian Susan Stryker puts it, the story of Stonewall is one where 'different identity groups go at each other, often quite vehemently, making historical claims that are ultimately objectively unverifiable, to wage contemporary struggles'.[17] These claims include rows over the prominence and identities of certain leading activists who were involved in the movement which the riots birthed. Two of the leading figures of the Stonewall story, Sylvia Rivera and Marsha P. Johnson, are sometimes called trans women. Neither ever used this description. They were gender nonconforming and expressed feminine identities (Rivera later called herself 'transgender'), but both tended to identify themselves as 'queens' or 'transvestites' rather than asserting that they were women. It is unlikely that Rivera was even present when the riots began. Both Rivera and Johnson (who undoubtedly did play a key role in them) also called themselves gay (because, as I mentioned earlier, everyone did at that time) and in the years after the riots spoke of their liberation struggle as 'gay power'. This doesn't mean that trans women of colour (in the modern sense – that is, trans people who identify consistently as female) did not take part in the Stonewall riot: a contemporary of Johnson and Rivera, Miss Major Griffin-Gracy, undoubtedly did. Alive at the time of writing, Miss Major identifies as a trans woman. However, most of her contemporaries are dead: to speculate on whether these people would identify themselves as trans women, non-binary people, drag queens, gender nonconforming or gay men if they were alive now misses the point. The Stonewall Uprising and the global movement of gay pride and gay liberation it instigated featured lesbians, gay men, bisexuals, trans and gender non-conforming people rioting against the same forces of state oppression and social stigma. At the very beginning of their modern movement, LGBT people stood shoulder to shoulder. Such solidarity has proved to be the most effective tool for advancing their shared interests.

The American story of Stonewall is better known to most British people than the early days of LGBTQ+ organizing in our own country. The British Gay Liberation Front had its first meeting on 13 October 1970, in a basement of the London School of Economics. Bob Mellors and Aubrey Walter, two of its founding members, had seen the effect of the Gay Liberation Front (GLF) in the United States and sought to create a parallel movement based on revolutionary politics.

The GLF sought not only to achieve equality or reforms within straight society but also to challenge that society itself: the nuclear family, gender roles and patriarchy. It was a socialist movement that rejected capitalism. 'We will show you how we can use our righteous anger to uproot the present oppressive system,' the GLF's 1971 manifesto declared, 'with its decaying and constricting ideology, and how we, together with other oppressed groups, can start to form a new order, and a liberated lifestyle, from the alternatives which we offer.' Contemporary accounts confirm that trans people were involved with the GLF from its early days – though not without some confusion over why and how they might be included. As one lesbian member of the GLF reflected:

> The problem about transsexuals was twofold. One, that trans-sexuality wasn't particularly well known at the time and a lot of people didn't believe it existed, and that maybe these people were gay men who weren't particularly well adjusted because of the way that straight society looked at them.[18]

Stuart Feather, another GLF member, also describes an early reluctance to accept trans members' perspectives on themselves:

> at first we thought transsexuals were gays with rigid black and white heterosexually polarized minds that could not perceive of any alternative to the heterosexual model, until surgery had corrected what the mind had partitioned off.[19]

It was only as certain gay and lesbian members came to know trans individuals that they realized this was not the case – not least because some trans women in the GLF were attracted not to men but to other women and identified themselves as lesbians. Rachel Pollack, a trans lesbian married to Edith, a cisgender woman, founded the first specific group within the British GLF for trans people in 1971: the Transvestite, Transsexual and Drag Queen Group. This was a space where those GLF members who were on the transgender spectrum could meet to examine their situation and political priorities together. They soon published their own political manifesto, *Declare Your Sex*, which clearly identified trans liberation as a part of wider gay liberation:

> Many gay people are confused by the separation between 'gay transvestites' and 'straight transvestites'. But this is an artificial split, imposed on us by those people who seek to isolate us and deny our identities. A transsexual or transvestite is gay because she or he is transsexual or transvestite. Some of us are into men and some of us are into women. Some of us are homosexual, some of us are heterosexual, some of us are lesbians. But we are all transsexual or transvestites and it's these identities that must be recognized and encouraged. To be gay means to break the rules of your official sex, to cross over the guidelines set up by the family, the schools, and the church. Some of us cross over by sleeping with the wrong person. Some of us dress the wrong way. Some of us do both. We are all gay.[20]

To modern ears, this is a peculiar claim. 'Trans', we are told, is strictly about gender identity and 'gay' is about sexuality. Or, as one truism observes: 'gender is who you go to bed *as*, sexuality is who you go to bed *with*.' The wording of the *Declare Your Sex* manifesto, however, captures an important point that remains true today: most trans people also identify their sexuality as queer or otherwise non-heterosexual. In a 2015 survey of 27,715 transgender and non-binary people, the American National Center for Transgender Equality found that 21 per cent said the term queer best described their sexual orientation, 18 per cent said pansexual, 16 per cent said gay, lesbian, or same-gender-loving, 14 per cent said bisexual and 10 per cent said asexual.[21] This means that most trans people are not straight. Arguably, the main inaccuracy of the term 'LGBT' is that it implies that trans people are a separate category to LGB, when in fact the T substantially overlaps.

Many trans people report that transitioning itself brings about a change in their sexual orientation, or how they perceive and describe it. In 2017, *Vice* ran a feature, 'The Trans Women Who Become Lesbians after Years as Gay Men', focusing on trans women who, while they were living as men exclusively dated men, and after transitioning to female exclusively dated women. As they changed, the gender of the people they were attracted to changed, and they went from living as gay men to living as gay women. Speaking to *Vice*, Dr Walter Bockting, a professor of medical psychology at Columbia University, suggested that the reason for this might be connected to how the act of changing gender role changes how you consider other people's gender: 'once a person challenges prevailing social norms about gender and sexuality, this person feels more free to explore sexual orientation in addition to having explored gender identity.'[22] In the same article, Alison, one of the trans women interviewed, offers an explanation for her change in attraction: '"I was in a different gender position," she said. Because she didn't identify as male anymore . . . she could "conceive of women as possible romantic or sexual interests" without having to stomach her "disgust at male heterosexuality" or having to view herself as complicit in it.'[23] In other words, Alison thinks that only as a woman could she feel comfortable desiring women. Desiring women before transition would have made her feel too much like a man: something that made her very distressed due to gender dysphoria. The twenty-first century has seen wider acknowledgment of the fact that human sexuality is much more complex than the rigid and unchanging categories of heterosexual, homosexual or bisexual can express; the experiences of trans people are just one part of this increased sexual diversity. In the case of non-binary people – whose gender identities and expressions may sit outside of the categories of man and woman, or move between the two – the nineteenth-century categories of human sexuality make little sense – which is why the term 'queer' has risen in popularity.

A wider range of medical and surgical options for trans people seeking to reassign their primary and secondary sex characteristics has also posed challenging questions for our understanding of human sexuality. What exactly is it we're attracted to? Genitals? An overall impression of masculine and feminine signifiers? Breasts? Voice? Hair? Or a varying combination of these? Instinctively, many people are inclined to think that sexual orientation is attraction to certain genitals – and, for many, genitals that are congruent with what we expect of men and women are a crucial component of their attraction to other people. However, the increased populations of, for example, trans women with a feminized appearance, body and breasts who have a penis, and trans men with chest hair, muscles, lowered voices, beards and a vagina, mean that it is possible to have a mixture of sex characteristics and signifiers on the same body. In my own personal acquaintance, I know men who identify themselves as solely attracted to women who will date women with penises; lesbians with vulvas in relationships with women with penises; gay men in relationships with men with vulvas and (naturally) women with penises in relationships with men with vulvas. Consequently, trans people's challenge to the gender binary is as physical and sexual as it is intellectual or political. In many ways, trans people present a challenge to traditional ways of understanding sexual attraction itself.

Unfortunately, this general challenge to our ways of understanding and categorizing our desires can make a small number of gay and lesbian people uncomfortable, as if they personally are being confronted or asked to reconsider their own sexuality. This is understandable, given that we live in a society where a preference for heterosexuality has usually tried to shame or force them out of their desires. However, the result of this discomfort is often discrimination against trans people in gay and lesbian venues and spaces. In October 2018, the British gay press reported that a trans man had been asked to leave Sailors Sauna, a gay sauna in Limehouse, east London, because he did not have a penis. Jason Smith (a pseudonym), a bisexual trans man, had reportedly been unsure about going to the sex-on-premises venue, so he checked their website beforehand for any trans-specific policies. There were none. Attending with a friend, he had been at the sauna for an hour before being told to leave by a member of staff, another customer having complained that a 'female' was on the premises. 'A staff member came over and requested I leave . . . as I was not allowed because of my genitals,' he later told *Gay Star News*.[24] Telling Smith it was a male space, the staff member (erroneously) suggested that local council regulations prevented Smith's presence. Smith then showed staff his passport, which showed his sex as male. The staff member allegedly said that if Smith had had 'tits and a dick' it would have been fine – but since he had a vagina it was not. The sauna staff and the cis gay male customer who complained about Jason's presence decided to use his genitals as the cue for how to categorize him: his other physical characteristics, his legal identification and, most importantly, his own stated identity as a bisexual man were disregarded. The other customer's discomfort with Jason's anatomy, even though he had no interaction with Jason whatsoever, was taken as more important than Jason's inclusion in the kind of place that historically existed to provide a queer space for sex without the dangers of homophobic violence. Of course, any man in the sauna had an absolute right to refuse sex with a trans man – but requesting pre-emptive removal of a trans man based on his body alone is an example of how overt transphobia can operate, even within the LGBT community.

If trans inclusion in gay spaces can be a fraught issue among queer men, then the anti-trans lesbian protest at 2018 Pride in

London showed how explosive it could be among queer and lesbian women. One reason cited for the rupture between a minority of lesbians and trans people, though, has nothing to do with trans women. It stems from a belief that butch lesbians, particularly young butch lesbians, are being recruited to become trans men by 'trans activists'. This idea, a recurring panic in some lesbian communities since the 1980s, is referred to as 'butch flight', that is, the dubious 'flight' of butch lesbians from womanhood itself to achieve a life of privilege as a straight man instead. The panic does have some roots in reality, since some trans men will initially identify as lesbians based on their attraction to women (just as I once identified as gay because of my attraction to men), and take refuge in queer female communities before ultimately deciding transition is right for them. A recent example would be the Hollywood actor Elliot Page, who initially came out as lesbian before subsequently transitioning. Having both cis LGB and trans friends, I know well that some families will accept a gay child but refuse to accept a trans one: the change in names, pronouns and physicality is simply too overwhelming for them to embrace. In cases like these, a trans man or a non-binary person may first try to embrace a butch female identity as part of a negotiation with their own fears of rejection, before ultimately realizing that they cannot co-exist with their unresolved dysphoria. But while there may exist a small number of women who experience deep confusion about their gender and are unsure for years about where they sit on the gender spectrum, there is no credible evidence that significant numbers of people initially identifying as lesbians are consciously abandoning a female identity to transition *en masse*, let alone that they are being pressured to do so.

A second explanation used for the rift between some lesbians and trans people is that cisgender lesbians may feel compelled or coerced to accept trans women as sexual partners. I have no doubt that many cisgender lesbians would not feel sexual desire for a trans woman, especially one with a penis, or that a lesbian may express interest in a woman until learning that the woman is trans and changing her mind. Ultimately everyone has a right to set sexual boundaries for any reason and to not feel pressured sexually on an individual basis. Yet, as with the trans man thrown out of a gay sauna, there is a crucial distinction to be made between this scenario and the mere presence of trans women on, for example, lesbian dating sites or in lesbian bars and their being cast as predatory by definition. Trans lesbians have as much of a right as any other lesbian to pursue sexual and romantic connections in an appropriate and consensual way, without being misrepresented as predatory men. Some lesbians are attracted to trans women and are open to dating them, and such couples risk total erasure of their sexuality by their peers and the media. These disputes often begin with the right of a trans woman to call herself a lesbian at all. 'Changing the concept of "woman" to include self-declared trans women also threatens a secure understanding of the concept "lesbian",' wrote the philosopher Kathleen Stock in the *Economist* in June 2018 (one month before the disruption of Pride in London by a group of lesbians who seemed to agree). 'Lesbians,' Stock argued, 'are traditionally understood as females* with a sexual orientation towards other females.' I'd argue, though, that the idea that there has been a longstanding 'secure' understanding of the term 'lesbian' is totally inaccurate.

Arguments about the legitimacy of trans lesbians are at least

---

* Stock's definition of 'female' here is rooted in the belief that biological sex at birth is the sole determiner of whether a person can be 'male' or 'female' for any purpose, and that this is immutable. I take a different view and would contend that, by virtue of her social, legal, political and sometimes medical reassignment or experience as a woman, a trans woman should also be considered 'female'.

as old as their first documented participation in lesbian organizing and scenes in the early 1970s. In 1971, the trans folk singer
Beth Elliott was elected vice president of the San Francisco
chapter of the Daughters of Bilitis, a US lesbian organization.
She was also embraced by the Orange County Dyke Patrol at
the Gay Women's Conference in Los Angeles, and was a member of the organizing committee for the West Coast Lesbian
Conference of 1973. During this time, arguments raged over her
legitimacy as a lesbian: when Elliott came to perform on stage at
that same conference, she was met with hostility by a lesbian
separatist group, the Gutter Dykes, who leafleted the crowd
with flyers calling Elliott a man who had no place performing at
a lesbian event. When the separatists approached the stage
aggressively, Elliott's performance was halted for the entire conference to vote on whether or not she should be allowed to
continue. An hour later, the votes of the 1,300 women present
were counted: a two-thirds majority had voted in favour of Beth
Elliott. (Sometimes, in focusing on the history of resistance to
trans women's inclusion in lesbian scenes, it's easy to overlook
the long history of overwhelming support for trans lesbians
from other women.)

As we've seen, some still disagree that trans women can be
lesbians. Yet the presence of trans lesbians like Rachel Pollack in
the earliest days of gay liberation in the UK, and the *Declare Your
Sex* manifesto's statement that trans people of all sexualities
ought to be part of gay liberation, suggest that there is no uniform 'tradition' that can be invoked to understand who gets to
use the terms 'gay', 'lesbian' and even 'straight'. This question
has always been contested. Concerns and debates over trans
people's relationship to their cis gay, lesbian and bisexual
counterparts and their membership of gay communities have
existed as long as the LGBT movement has existed.

This historical context to contemporary LGBT politics is

important, primarily because of the hostile and widespread media trope that trans people pose a threat to gay people. This idea is usually advanced by straight columnists for a largely straight audience. When in 2017 the pop singer Sam Smith came out as non-binary and invited the media to refer to them with gender neutral pronouns, the *Times* columnist Janice Turner (a straight woman) was scathing, flatly refusing to accept the legitimacy of Sam Smith's gender – or indeed the concept of non-binary trans people. In an article headlined 'Cult of Gender Identity is Harming Children', Turner referred to Smith not as a trans or non-binary person, but as a 'gay man'. Using male pronouns to refer to Smith, she wrote, 'That I refuse to call Sam Smith "they" is not from disrespect (I never misgender trans people) but because the concept "non-binary" is sexist, homophobic and, above all, damaging to the mental health of fragile young people.'[25] Turner's insistence that Smith, a person who has openly discussed the impact homophobia had on them growing up, is the real homophobe is egregious. It is even more outrageous in the context of Turner writing for a Murdoch-owned newspaper which, thirty years ago, was weaponizing the same rhetoric against gay people.

Back in 1991 *The Times* published a column about gay rights by Janet Daly. Headlined 'The Sad Fraud of Gay Equality', it used precisely the same analogy with cults that Turner reheated in 2019. 'Now gay life has become an aggressive freemasonry, for which recruits are required to stand up and be counted,' Daly wittered; 'the price [homosexuality] exacts in the form of childlessness, instability and now mortal danger from Aids is not something that most sixteen-year-olds have the capacity to evaluate.'[26] Back then, tabloids were even more explicit in their insinuation that gay people were 'recruiting' the young. In the 1992 general election campaign, the Murdoch-owned *Sun* ran a story warning of the risk from the extension of gay and lesbian rights that Labour planned to roll out were it to win. The piece was about a fifteen-year-old pupil, 'Niki', who attended a school run by Labour-controlled Haringey Council. Niki's mother thought she was in maths class, the story warned, but in fact she was 'being given a lesson in lesbianism by a gay teacher'.[27]

The homophobic press coverage of the 1980s and 1990s and transphobic headlines of recent years share this common image of predatory adults recruiting the young. Notable headlines include 'Children Sacrificed to Appease Trans Lobby' (*The Times*) and 'In Ten Years, We'll Ask How We Allowed the Trans Lobby to Hijack Childhood' (the *Telegraph*). In my own lifetime, however, it has become common for (heterosexual) commentators to see the development of gay rights in Britain as an evolutionary process towards an enlightened state, as we saw in Chapter 5. Such a position requires a liberal dose of hindsight and a collective – and convenient – amnesia about the viciousness and prevalence of homophobia at the time. It also usually focuses on the battles gay people fought for heteronormative rights which were tolerably divorced from sex, such as the right to get married or to enter the army, and ignores their struggles for the right of youth to receive proper education about LGBT people and the right to equality under the law regarding the age of consent. In both these battles, the conflation of a 'gay agenda' with sexual deviancy was widespread. In a startling interview for ITN News in 1998, the Conservative peer Baroness Young referred to the equal age of consent as 'a paedophiles' charter'; four years previously, the Tory MP Tony Marlow said gay campaigners were seeking to 'legalize the buggery of adolescent males', and that he wanted to 'protect young boys'.

This homophobic trope has been resurrected in recent years to repress the advancement of trans rights, because it is an effective sleight of hand. Moral panics rely on an inherent paradox: that the rights of a small minority of the population wielding little institutional power are in fact a risk to the majority. This is achieved by inciting in the population a mixture of moral disgust and anxiety about contagion. The problem group may be small now, but they will grow. They will grow by encouraging confused young people to join. For sexual minorities, this narrative of recruitment lends itself to the language of seduction and abuse, which helps direct the moral disgust society feels at paedophilia on to an innocent group. It is a shameful but highly effective propaganda tool.

Despite the obvious parallels and analogous struggles that trans people have had with the wider queer movement's struggle for sexual liberation, the claim that trans people are not only actively different but substantially harmful to the LGB movement has been readily embraced and promoted by extreme political conservatives. This includes even politicians who would themselves traditionally oppose lesbian, gay and bisexual rights. In October 2017, at a Washington DC networking event of the ultra-conservative Family Research Council (which, as an arm of the US Christian right, instinctively opposes all LGBTQ+ rights), campaigners openly discussed the need to create friction within the LGBT community. 'For all of its recent success, the LGBT alliance is actually fragile, and the trans activists need the gay rights movement to help legitimize them,' said Meg Kilgannon, a parent and director of the campaign group Concerned Parents and Educators of Fairfax County. 'Trans and gender identity are a tough sell, so focus on gender identity to divide and conquer,' she stated, adding that, 'if you separate the T from the alphabet soup, we'll have more success.'[28] Part of this success relies on substituting religious arguments against 'transgenderism' with secular, seemingly progressive, arguments rooted in feminism and protecting LGB people against the 'threat' of 'trans ideology'. The Family Research Council summit at which Kilgannon spoke was influential enough for then-President Donald Trump to speak at it the same year, in order to garner support from his Christian right voter base. Kilgannon's comments should be viewed for what they were: part of a wide, committed and well-funded strategy for dismantling LGBTQ+ rights and pushing a sexually conservative and anti-feminist agenda – beginning with trans people.

This strategy is all too evident in the founding of US-based organizations that aim to connect anti-trans feminists with Christian conservatives for the united purpose of resisting trans liberation. Hands Across the Aisle was co-founded by Miriam Ben-Shalom, a longstanding lesbian campaigner who, following a famous legal battle, was the first gay service person to be reinstated to military service in 1987 after being discharged from the US army for homosexuality in 1976. In 2015, she was named one of the LGBT website *Equality Forum*'s thirty-one 'Icons of the 2015 LGBT History Month'. Her co-founder, Kaeley Triller Haver, is by contrast a Christian conservative who has written opinion articles with titles such as 'Women Won't be Liberated Until We're Free from Abortion'. Triller Haver has admitted she believes homosexuality to be a sin, even if she restrains the impulse to tell that to her newfound allies: 'If I have a gay person in front of me with whom I have a friendship, and they ask me point-blank: "Kaeley, do you think homosexuality is a sin?" Then I'm going to talk to them about what I think and I have to tell them the truth,' she conceded in the *Christian Post* in 2018.

That Ben-Shalom and Triller Haver should be political bedfellows is a bizarre and alarming testimony to their vociferous and fanatical investment in transphobia. A year on from her fêting as an LGBT icon, Ben-Shalom was removed as Grand Marshal for Milwaukee's 2016 Pride Parade after adding her signature to an anti-trans petition online. 'I am tired of watching the so-called trans community try to extinguish us and extinct us,' Ben-Shalom wrote in the 'Reason for Signing' box on the Change.org website:

> I am enraged that young strong women, often called Butches, are being told they should 'transition and be men' as opposed to being strong, non-gender conforming/stereotypical women. I am tired of dealing with men in dresses who say they are women but who employ male power trips and threaten violence if Lesbians do not do it 'their way' . . . I do not want to shower next to a swinging dick which says the dick is a Lady wand.[29]

Having been rejected by her local LGBT community for bigotry, Ben-Shalom found a new home in the anti-abortion and anti-gay lobby, which accepted her with open arms. 'As the Hands Across the Aisle Coalition, we are committed to working together, rising above our differences, and leveraging our collective resources to oppose gender identity ideology,'[30] the group's website proclaims. Other similar groups include WoLF (The Women's Liberation Front), an anti-trans radical feminist group that has partnered with several anti-LGBTQ+ organizations on legal cases opposing trans rights in the US. In the fiscal year 2017 – the most recent year for which the feminist group's financial records are available – WoLF applied for and accepted a $15,000 grant from the ultra-conservative Alliance Defending Freedom.[31]

US anti-trans coalitions are all too happy to meddle in foreign politics. In the 2018 Irish referendum campaign on abortion, US Christian conservative groups supported anti-abortion campaigns in Ireland by buying up advertising space on social media platforms like Facebook, in the hope that Ireland could prove a test ground for future pro-life campaigns in the US. Such groups would probably support formalized attempts to create a split in the British LGBT movement – especially given the British liberal press's promotion of the idea that trans activism might be homophobic. The breeding ground for this message can be seen in the sudden appearance of groups like the LGB Alliance, a campaign group founded in London in October 2019 to campaign for homosexuals without the T, and in the committed campaign waged against Stonewall, the largest and best-funded LGBT organization in the UK, in right-wing publications like *The Times*, the *Telegraph*, the *Daily Mail* and the *Spectator*.

Indeed, these transatlantic links exist. In January 2019, WoLF assisted a group of British anti-trans campaigners visiting Washington DC, putting them in touch with various legislators and officials. One of these British visitors was Julia Long, one of the group of lesbians who stopped the Pride in London march the previous July. As part of her US tour alongside, and by the invitation of, WoLF, Long attended a panel event opposing pro-trans legislation hosted by the Heritage Foundation, a conservative and homophobic think tank. It bears repeating: this is an astonishing example of a link between ardent homophobes and transphobic campaigners who are themselves lesbians. Even if a tiny proportion of LGB people are willing to team up with right-wing homophobes to oppose trans civil rights, it only takes a handful of committed LGB people wilfully perpetuating these negative narratives for them to become normalized. Such narratives are then taken up by political conservatives and far-right voices, whose ultimate goal is the dismantling of all LGBTQ+ rights because of their profound disgust for us all.

The simple moral case for resisting transphobia as a form of cruelty should be enough for anyone who has been similarly victimized by society (as cisgender lesbians, gay men and bisexual people have all been in one way or another) to stand with us in solidarity. Yet it should also be a matter of self-interest. The world in which trans people's rights are restricted relies on narratives of dehumanization and myths of sexual predation. Restricting trans people's rights relies on policing other people's gendered appearance in toilets and changing rooms by arbitrating on who looks male or female *enough*, and by punishing deviation from rigid norms with intimidation and violence. It involves kids following the examples of adults and harassing their peers in the playground for being different. It relies on parents either beating into submission the child asserting their identity, or psychologically breaking them with conversion therapy. These traumatic experiences affect all 'queers', whether trans or cis. Advocating for them in any form for any letter will inevitably normalize their use against everyone judged queer. Politically, it is a gift to fascists at a time of growing far-right sentiment in Europe and North America alike.

The answer to these hateful challenges must be, as it was for the socialists of the Gay Liberation Front, solidarity between all oppressed groups, including lesbians, gay men, bi people and trans people and all other queer people, such as those with pansexual and asexual identities.

That summer of 2018, following Pride in London, all the other major UK Prides had cisgender lesbians and trans people walk at the front of parades together in a movement called 'LwiththeT'. It was a beautiful display of solidarity: one which recalled the support that the trans folk singer Beth Elliott was offered by lesbians in the vote at the West Coast Lesbian Conference all those decades ago. 'GwiththeT' and 'BwiththeT' slogans followed. These movements must continue to grow beyond social media rallying and affirmations. Together, an LGBTQ+ coalition with class consciousness and anti-racism at its core must recover its radicalism and reaffirm its opposition to capitalism and patriarchy. Infighting and division are in the interests of our right-wing oppressors. Gay people and trans people have had to battle similar arguments about being 'unnatural': homophobia still often rests on the prejudice that the worthiest form of sexuality is that which is capable of reproduction. Transphobia, too, emanates from a prejudice that a person's stated identity is more trust-worthy if it reflects their 'natural' role in human reproduction. Similarly, cisgender women's reproductive freedom is the first thing to be curbed by conservative regimes. Misogyny, homo-phobia and transphobia share much of the same DNA. To the patriarchy, we all do gender wrong.

7

The Ugly Sister: Trans People in Feminism

In May 2018, I compèred a one-day festival called 'Women Making History', organized by the UK human rights organization Amnesty International. Held at Amnesty's London HQ in Shoreditch, it celebrated and brought together women across the world who defend human rights. It featured women almost entirely (with the exception of one non-binary panellist in the afternoon). Speakers ranged from celebrities like the actress Olivia Colman to grassroots activists such as Seyi Akiwowo, the youngest black woman to be elected as a local councillor in the UK, who was also founder and director of Glitch, a non-profit campaign to end online abuse. The festival marked a century since women (or some of them) were given the vote.

At that point, I had been working for about a year as a volunteer with the Amnesty Collective, a new group of younger campaigners with a social media audience, who were tasked with amplifying Amnesty's campaigns. (I had come to Amnesty's attention through my work as a campaigner on trans issues, as well as creative work I had produced on the politics of mental health, including articles and YouTube videos.) When I was asked to host the 'Women Making History' event (to introduce all the panels, speakers and essentially keep the event to time), it was because I had prior experience as a performer on London's queer and cabaret scene and as a host of activist events. The role, I was told, would involve loosely following a script with some ad libbing; I was neither a panellist nor a speaker. Yet my involvement, as the sole trans woman named in the advance publicity for the event, was to plunge the festival into controversy.

A week before the festival, a petition appeared on Change.org titled 'Petition for the Removal of Shon Faye as Host of Amnesty International UK's Women Making History Festival'; soon, it was circulating on Twitter, Facebook and on the feminism boards of the British parenting website Mumsnet. Most of the people sharing the petition did so on the basis that I was a 'misogynist male' appropriating a space that should have been given to an 'actual' woman – or, worse, that I was too sexually 'inappropriate' to be a role model for young women and girls. This dog whistle was included because someone trawling my tweets for evidence to use in a smear campaign found jokes about sex. Within days, the petition acquired over 2,000 signatures – and, though it was probable that many repeatedly signed it to drive up the numbers, the momentum it gained was hard to ignore. Change.org later removed the petition permanently from the internet, after an internal investigation found it was being used for the purpose of harassment and hate speech, and at a glance it was immediately apparent why. Almost all the signatures referred to me as a 'man' with male pronouns. 'Sad to see Amnesty give space to an abusive pervert,' one read; another ran, 'Shon Faye is not a woman, he is a man performing a hideous pornified and hypersexualized parody of females. Including him in this event is gaslighting women and girls.' On Twitter, one feminist blogger shared a photo of me wearing a PVC skirt taken after I had been on stage at a cabaret night two years previously:

Did anyone imagine, 20, even 10 years ago, that this would be being presented as the pinnacle of feminism? A biologically male person, performing as a blow up doll, reclining in bondage gear, their eyes glazed, their mouth receptive. This is women's liberation? Or end of days?

The festival organizers received a barrage of phone calls and emails from the same small group of people, saying that they were cancelling longstanding donations to the charity because of my involvement, or simply demanding my removal. The charity's social media feeds swarmed with tweets, and comments were split between those incensed at my involvement and the people who – in far greater numbers, it turned out – vocally supported my inclusion. Then, inevitably, Amnesty fielded inquiries from *Daily Mail* reporters for a comment on the controversy. We braced ourselves for the smear story exposing me to the wrath of the public – but after two sleepless nights passed, nothing had materialized. Amnesty stood firmly by me, responding that they were proud to be associated with me. After a risk assessment, security for the event itself was hastily ramped up, and the other participants, from famous actresses to Instagram influencers, were told what had happened; Charlie Craggs, another trans woman originally booked as a panellist, pulled out of the festival after seeing the transphobia directed at me. It felt like I had become a bigger story than the festival itself; an irony, given that the self-described feminists who campaigned to remove me did so because they believed I was 'dominating' a space for women.

Worn down mentally and emotionally by a week-long hate campaign that had tried to imply that I was an abuser, I nonetheless wanted to continue as planned. I did, though, make a brief address at the festival's opening, stating how most of the vile abuse I had received focused on the belief that I was an impostor and had no right to be present at a festival celebrating women – simply because I am trans. I drew attention to Naomi Hersi, a black trans woman who, two months previously, was murdered by an intimate male partner in a London hotel room. Hersi's death went unreported for several days. When the British media finally got round to mentioning it, they frequently used the wrong name, misgendered her or otherwise belittled her identity as a woman. I stated that as long as trans women in the UK and around the world experience human rights violations and male violence as women, then it is right and just that we are able to access the support and solidarity of the feminist and women's community.

The day was a success – there were no disruptions – but I was left shattered by the whole episode. Notwithstanding the support from women at the festival, its organizers and many feminists from around the world who had contacted me with messages of support, insisting that I was welcome as a feminist voice and sister, it was driven home to me as never before that, for some cisgender women (and men), feminism was a justification for smears, abuse and cruelty, purely because I had been born with XY chromosomes.

As we've seen, hostility towards trans women participating in feminist spaces has a long and bleak history going back almost fifty years. What happened to me has resonances with the uproar surrounding Beth Elliott's appearance at the West Coast Lesbian Conference of 1973. Elliott, feeling rattled, left early. In her absence, the festival's keynote speaker, radical feminist Robin Morgan, denounced her, calling her 'an opportunist, an infiltrator, and a destroyer – with the mentality of a rapist'. This was exactly the tone adopted by my own online abusers. 'I will not call a male "she",' Morgan had said of Elliott:

> thirty-two years of suffering in this androcentric society, and of surviving, have earned me the title 'woman'; one walk down the street by a male transvestite, five minutes of his being hassled (which he may enjoy), and then he dares, he dares to think he understands our pain? No, in our mothers' names and in our own, we must not call him sister. We know what's at work when whites wear blackface; the same thing is at work when men wear drag.[1]

Instances of such harassment pervade British feminist organizing, too. Trisha McCabe, a radical feminist, recalled how, at the

10th Annual Women's Liberation Conference held in Birmingham in 1978, a group of feminists tried to print a leaflet attacking a trans woman at the event:

> I was looking after lost children at that point, having spent all my time Gestetnering endless reams of paper. The only one I wouldn't print was one from the Revolutionary Feminists, slagging off a transsexual who was at the Conference; I made them print their own.[2]

In British radical feminist circles of the 1970s, McCabe remembers, anxieties about trans women's presence were common: 'There were always incidents, like someone thinking they'd spotted a transsexual in the toilets,'[3]

Yet, historically and currently, feminists who oppose trans women's inclusion are almost always in the minority: the majority of cis feminists either have no issue with the presence of trans women in the movement, or actively encourage their involvement. But whatever their viewpoint, there's no getting away from the fact that much of the discussion about trans people and feminism has focused on the language of 'inclusion' (or exclusion) of trans women in feminist circles, events, consciousness or organizing. The debate over someone like Beth Elliott or me being offered a platform at specific events may well speak to profound feminist anxieties: 'What is a woman?', 'How and why are women oppressed?', 'What is the purpose of feminism?' Yet, while these deeper questions bubble away beneath the surface, the ultimate crux of the issue is always the same: 'do we let the trans woman in?' In the first two decades of this century, anxieties about who feminist space was for, and where feminists' energy should be directed, moved online, with conceptual arguments about who belonged in feminism raging on in feminist blogs, forums and social networking sites.

Online, the debate about trans women's inclusion only grew more polarized and tribal. The term 'trans-exclusionary radical feminist', once a descriptor for specific lesbian separatists and revolutionary feminists of the 1970s who rejected trans women's claim to be women, became popularized online as an acronym, 'TERF'. Almost always applied pejoratively by trans-inclusive feminists, the term was resoundingly rejected as a misogynist slur by those it was applied to. One thing is certainly true: the term 'TERF', once defining a specific kind of radical feminist, has expanded well beyond its original meaning. 'TERF' no longer solely denotes women with left-wing radical feminist politics (including the revolutionary political lesbians who left their male children behind to live in all-female separatist communes). Now, it is applied to any transphobic troll or bigot of almost any political persuasion who justifies their concerns about accepting trans women as women as being grounded in 'protecting [real] women'. In my view, its indiscriminate application doesn't make TERF a hugely useful term. Its use – or protests against its use – often denotes a tribal identity that is more about signalling which 'side' you're on in a Twitter war than about coherent feminist politics.

Today, the furious debate over whether or not to include trans people in feminist discourses is a peculiarly British phenomenon. Contemporary feminisms in other anglophone countries – including the United States, where anti-trans feminism originated – generally agree on the inclusion of trans people and have disavowed the exclusionary position. The same is not true in Britain. Here, suspicion over the presence of trans people (particularly trans women) has persisted, and hostility towards legal rights and protections for trans people has much more traction and influence both in the media and online. If Amnesty's 'Women Making History' festival had taken place in New York or Dublin or Toronto, the appearance of a trans woman as compère would hardly have raised an eyebrow. The abuse I faced had as much to do with me being a woman with a public profile in Britain, as it had to do with being trans.

This stark disconnection between British feminism, where transphobia is considered an orthodox feminist position, and feminism in North America, where it is now largely considered unacceptable in its overt forms, is viewed with bemusement by international feminists. As the Canadian feminist writer Nicole Cliffe joked on Twitter in 2017:

NORMAL-SEEMING UK PUBLIC FEMINIST: The pay gap!
ME: Right on!
NORMAL-SEEMING UK PUBLIC FEMINIST: Roving gangs of trans
    people are forcing lesbian children to date men!
ME: What just happened?!

By 2018 this transatlantic disparity was playing out in public spats between the British and American offices of the *Guardian*. In autumn that year, the paper ran an editorial that attempted to find the middle ground between those who supported reform of the UK Gender Recognition Act and those who alleged it was a threat to cis women's rights. The editorial drew its talking points from organizations hostile to trans rights. 'Women's concerns about sharing dormitories or changing rooms with "male-bodied" people must be taken seriously,' it stated.[4] While apparently this was acceptable phrasing in London, its casual scaremongering shocked the paper's American staff. To the ears of many American feminists, such language echoes the rhetoric that Republican ultra-conservatives employ when seeking to pass 'bathroom bills' criminalizing trans people for using public toilets aligned with their gender identity. Such was the shock at the editorial's transphobia that the *Guardian*'s US staff launched a public counter-strike against their own paper's official stance – in the *Guardian* itself: 'the *Guardian* published an editorial that we believe pro-

moted transphobic viewpoints, including some of the same assertions about gender that US politicians are citing in their push to
eliminate trans rights,' the piece proclaimed, adding that 'nearly
all reporters and editors from our New York, Washington DC and
California offices wrote to UK editors with our concerns.' It concluded that there exist 'fundamental divides between American
and British feminism and progressive politics – and [this] high-
lighted for us an alarming intolerance of trans viewpoints in
mainstream UK discourse.'[5]

Why are some strains of current British feminism so uniquely
transphobic? The answer partly rests in the concerted effort made
to normalize anti-trans feminism in Britain's left-leaning and liberal press in the past decade, making it a palatable and acceptable
talking point. This, Juliet Jacques suggests, is due to

> the longevity of a generation of journalists who established
> themselves when the argument was orthodox. Many still hold
> influential roles as columnists or editors and have used their pos-
> itions to keep the argument in the mainstream, while favouring a
> younger generation of writers who share their antipathy to trans
> people.[6]

It is certainly true that a cottage industry of feminist opinion
writers, whose main professional focus was writing pieces sceptical of so-called 'trans ideology', emerged in reaction to the new
wave of mainstream trans visibility in the mid-2010s. '[I]f Laverne
Cox on the cover of *Time* is the transgender tipping point, then it's
time to accept that trans politics and feminism have never been
headed to the same place,' the *New Statesman* columnist Sarah
Ditum wrote on her personal blog in response to the 2014 publication of Cox's celebrated cover.[7] This inherent incompatibility
between trans people's rights and feminism, Ditum wrote, was

obvious because of how Cox looked: 'a tight-tight dress, with breasts thrust forward and shoulders pulled back, facing down the camera but pouting seductively'. The problem seemed to lie in Cox's feminine presentation, which for Ditum was apparently regressive and inherently anti-feminist. Yet this willingness to judge trans politics as a whole by directly critiquing one television actress's body, posture, outfit and hair is exactly the kind of inference that would be plainly misogynist if made about a cis woman. Despite purporting to be a feminist analysis, Ditum's post seemed unconcerned by, or perhaps unaware of, the personal, political and professional pressures Cox may be under to appear satisfactorily feminine: a woman who is both trans and black in a media landscape where standards are set by the white, cis and male.

Similar analyses flourish in the UK media. Disputing the validity of the term 'cis', the *New Statesman* columnist Victoria Smith wrote in 2014: 'to break the stranglehold gender stereotypes have over human experience – distorting and restricting our experience of ourselves – should not involve telling whole swathes of humankind that they "match" their gender.'[8] The following year, the same magazine's deputy editor wrote that a failed campaign to 'no-platform' the celebrated feminist Germaine Greer from a talk she was due to give at Cardiff University was driven 'at least in part, by sexism'.[9] In fact, the campaign was driven by Greer's long history of transphobia in her own columns and articles in the British press, including her grotesque 1989 account of meeting a trans woman:

On the day that *The Female Eunuch* was issued in America, a person in flapping draperies rushed up to me and grabbed my hand. 'Thank you so much for all you've done for us girls!' I smirked and nodded and stepped backwards, trying to extricate my hand from the enormous, knuckly, hairy, be-ringed paw that clutched it . . . Against the bony ribs that could be counted through its flimsy scarf dress swung a polished steel women's liberation emblem.

I should have said, 'You're a man. *The Female Eunuch* has done less than nothing for you. Piss off.' . . . The transvestite held me in a rapist's grip.[10]

Cis feminists in the media rushed to defend bigots like Greer as sacred cows who should face minimal accountability for their years of unrestricted hate speech. Trans people's challenges to the legacy of lauded feminists who had abused them became caught up in the endless fetishization of 'debate' in British liberal media. Though one or two trans writers were often commissioned for 'balance', in the end most grew tired of constantly having to push back against other writers' scepticism of trans rights. When trans commentators challenged the validity of this confected debate, calling it out for what it was – a vehicle for increased hostilities towards and misunderstandings of trans people – they were accused of trying to silence women in a valid feminist discussion. This accusation was especially potent when directed at trans women, given that 'silencing women' is what sexist men have always done: the imputation being that trans women were just sexist men claiming womanhood. Anti-trans feminists' repeated claims that they were being silenced were in fact highly effective in getting their viewpoints aired on television, radio and in the press. As the (cisgender) feminist Sara Ahmed puts it:

Whenever people keep being given a platform to say they have no platform, or whenever people speak endlessly about being silenced, you not only have a performative contradiction; you are witnessing a mechanism of power.[11]

Such accusations of undue hostility and silencing were not only directed at trans women. Many of the above-quoted ex-amples come from the *New Statesman*, the UK's main centre-left liberal magazine. This mirrors something identified by the feminist Reni Eddo-Lodge in her analysis of white feminists' hostility to women of colour in her landmark 2017 book, *Why I'm No Longer Talking to White People about Race*: 'the most spirited takedowns of black women talking about race, racism and intersectionality,' she notes, 'were always published via the *New Statesman* . . . Because of the sheer frequency of these takedowns, I began to wonder if there was an editorial line.'[12]

That Eddo-Lodge and I point to similar sources for the normalization of white feminist hostility to both black women and trans women in the British feminist media is no coincidence. As the trans-inclusive British feminist Sophie Lewis wrote in an op-ed for the *New York Times*, titled 'How British Feminism Became Anti-Trans', the conditions for British feminism's transphobia arise out of a consensus in British academia and the press that is overwhelmingly middle class and white, both in its composition and outlook: 'middle- and upper-class white feminists have not received the pummelling from black and indigenous feminists that their American counterparts have, and thus their perspectives retain a credibility and a level of influence in Britain.'[13]

Lewis argues that the unique character of British feminism is infused with a strong disregard for Britain's history of colonialism and empire, and the impact of this history on women in colonized countries. This observation was at the heart of a 2018 letter, signed by thousands of Irish feminists, rebuking a delegation of British anti-trans feminists who planned to host a debate on trans rights in Dublin:

> We, the signatories of this letter, organize hand in hand with our trans sisters. Together, cis and trans, we are Irish feminism. Trans women are our sisters; their struggles are ours, our struggles theirs. They were our sisters before any state-issued certification said so and will always be no matter what any legislation says, either now or in the future.[14]

Crucially, the letter slammed British feminism's hostile focus on the supposed threat of trans women, and its contrasting lack of interest in the fight for abortion rights in Northern Ireland. The letter's authors were clear that British feminists' attempts to export their transphobia to their Irish neighbours was nothing more than chauvinism:

> Do you have any kind of concept of what feminism in a country shaped by struggle against Empire looks like? Did you take even a second to consider that, in assuming you have the right to come here in any kind of position of feminist authority, you're behaving with the arrogance of just that imperialism? . . . We have had enough of colonialism in Ireland without needing more of it from you . . . You're not welcome here.

The whiteness and unexamined colonialism of mainstream UK feminism correlate directly with its tendencies towards transphobia. First, they reinforce the central belief of most anti-trans feminism: that women are a global 'sex class' of everyone who shares female biology (including trans men and non-binary people born with vaginas and uteri), who are all raised as girls in a similar way (usually termed 'female socialization') and thus have a particular experience in common that no cis man and no trans woman could ever access, having been born into the other, dominant, 'sex class'. The concept of women as an undifferentiated global female sex class, more or less exploited in the same way for the same reasons, can only work by downplaying or minimizing any internal distinctions or hierarchies or exploitation *within* that class. Yet black and indigenous (or otherwise anti-colonial) feminisms render such a specious consensus on universal 'female experience' largely untenable.

The idea that after centuries of dehumanizing black women through slavery, and classing anyone not white as 'other', white women can claim a universal shared female experience with women of colour seems absurd. Female socialization may well describe a collection of experiences that some types of women share in common – but at a global level it is clear that the cultural expectations of what it is to be a woman, and how these expectations are imposed, vary significantly. The same expectations are applied to different women in different ways under a capitalist class system in which some women are racialized as inferior and exploited more readily for their labour. In reality, the ongoing predominance of white, middle-class and cisgender women in feminism means that any global definition of womanhood is often simply an extrapolation of these women's particular racial and class experience, as if it were universal.

Second, ignoring colonialism allows British (or other Western) feminists to disregard how the imposition of the strict gender binary of man and woman, with the accompanying hierarchy of male over female, was itself a mechanism of colonialism. Many pre-colonial societies and indigenous peoples did not view gender as binary. Some, as we have seen, had more than two genders, while the social roles around family and childrearing varied widely. To take one among a multitude of examples: in the seventeenth century, Paul Le Jeune, a Jesuit missionary to the Montagnais (Innu) people residing in Nitassinan (eastern Quebec and Labrador in Canada), described how the women held 'great power' and had 'in nearly every instance . . . the choice of plans, of undertakings, of journeys, of winterings'.[15] Often, Montagnais women would hunt, while men looked after children. Conversion to Christianity, encouraged by men by like Le Jeune, required the establishment of a new hierarchy and more rigid gender roles. Within ten years of colonial missionary activity and trading relations beginning, the Montagnais had started to insist on male authority and to inflict violence on wives and children.[16] Such accounts of colonial domination show how rapidly a society's understanding of gender can be changed as society itself changes. They demonstrate clearly that what it means to be a woman or a man (or neither) is not a fixed and stable entity, but a complex constellation of biological, political, economic and cultural factors, which may shift over time.

In contrast to this complexity, British anti-trans feminism – now known by its disciples, with unintentional irony, as 'gender critical' feminism (despite its lack of critical interest in how gender arises and varies according to time and place) – has tended to market itself as a common-sense approach that breezily waves nuance away. One 2018 campaign by a British anti-trans blogger involved posting the Google dictionary definition of the word 'woman' up on advertising billboards in British cities:

Woman

noun

an adult human female

The same definition, when later turned into a range of merchandise including T-shirts and tote bags, signalled that the adopter does not consider trans women to be 'female'. Leaving aside the fact that dictionary definitions are a product of a culture and not its arbiter, the definition of 'woman' as used here focuses solely on the biological and entirely disregards a point that feminists have largely agreed upon: the idea that being a woman is defined by *political* experience, how you are treated by others, especially those with power over you.

The extent to which socio-political experience defines what it means to be a woman has always been a contested aspect of feminist debate. The heterosexual feminist Betty Friedan notoriously referred to lesbians within the movement as the 'Lavender Menace', whose 'mannish' qualities – making them not-quite-women – were a risk to the success of feminism. While this was obvious homophobia, in 1978 even the lesbian radical feminist Monique Wittig argued that the socially constructed understanding of 'woman' is so bound up with compulsory heterosexuality that it necessarily excludes lesbians:

> it would be incorrect to say that lesbians associate, make love, live with women, for 'woman' has meaning only in heterosexual systems of thought and heterosexual economic systems. Lesbians are not women.[17]

Later, the black feminist bell hooks argued that a specific combination of racism and sexism directed at black women had estranged them from the social identity of being women:

> Contemporary black women could not join together to fight for women's rights because we did not see 'womanhood' as an important aspect of our identity.[18]

The gender critical feminist insistence on a straightforward biological definition of women and men, then, relies on an ignorance of cisgender women's own feminist intellectual history. The idea that a woman is simply an adult human female disregards the fact that the term 'female' refers to biological sex, which itself can denote a collection of traits (genitals, gonads, hormones, secondary sex characteristics and chromosomes), some of which can be modified. It also fails to consider that the term 'female' can have important social meanings for human beings beyond our reproductive role as mammals. It can, for instance, refer to legal sex (which, in many societies, can be changed), while in everyday vernacular, 'female' is used as an adjectival form to mean 'women' or 'things which relate to women'. If most of us heard a show or music concert had 'an all-female line up' we would imagine a group of women, not immediately and consciously consider that everyone involved produces eggs for reproduction (after all, there are cisgender women who do not produce eggs and cannot bear children). The word 'female' comes from the Latin 'femella', which means 'woman', not 'producer of eggs' or 'possessing XX chromosomes': such definitions came later. The 'common sense' argument of the 'adult human female' billboards is specious: there are many ways of legitimately interpreting the brief dictionary definition that would, in fact, include a trans woman as an adult human female.

Whichever way you look at it, the debate among cisgender feminists about whether or not trans women are to be included in both the definition of woman and the feminist movement still primarily envisions feminism as a project owned by cis women. In this vision, trans people are positioned either negatively, as impostors, or positively, as welcome guests. The case for inclusivity can often rest on whether it is 'kind' or 'good' or 'right' to welcome trans women as sisters, rather than any serious consideration of why their inclusion might be politically *necessary* for liberation from patriarchy. Rarely in mainstream debates over trans people and feminism do we consider the fatal flaw in any feminist movement that purports to be dismantling the patriarchy while disregarding the implications of trans people's existence. Their existence complicates cis feminism, and such complexity can only be erased by seeing the struggle as primarily about cis women fighting oppression by cis men. The reality, I would argue, is this: not only do trans people need feminism, but feminism also needs trans people.

Transfeminism is a term used to describe a collection of perspectives on feminism that centre the experiences of trans people. This perspective recognizes trans people as a group who, like cis women, suffer greatly at the hands of patriarchy, which punishes us for transgressing the roles laid out for us from birth. It is not a rival movement to other forms of feminism, nor is it a sub-division. It is a specific *approach* to feminist thought and organizing that begins with trans experience, rather than seeking to slot trans people into a cis feminist theory that is often articulated without us in mind. Naturally, cisgender women's feminism starts with the general principle that patriarchy is a system that benefits men to the detriment of women, and empowers men specifically by disempowering women. In some form or other, most cis feminist thought argues for a crucial distinction to be made between sex – one's biology – and gender, a social structure that dictates appropriate male and female behaviour.

Trans feminists also believe that, while the difference between bodies and the cultural narratives we use to interpret those bodies does exist, such difference is not always easily recognized or mapped. Our sexed bodies never exist outside social meanings: consequently, how we understand gender shapes how we understand sex.[19] The gender critical feminist idea – that there exists an objective biological reality which is real and observable to everyone in the same way and, distinct from that, a constructed set of subjective gender stereotypes that can be easily abolished – is an oversimplification. The way we perceive and understand sex differences and emphasize their significance is so deeply gendered that it can be impossible to completely divorce the two.

If this all seems a little crunchy, let me give you an everyday example. I believe most people, including feminists, would intuitively decide to momentarily leave a child, if absolutely necessary, in the care of a stranger they perceive as a woman rather than a stranger they perceive as a man. I would argue that this gut feeling – 'the woman is a safer bet' – arises from a deep-seated cultural idea that women are more likely to be kind, nurturing and capable with children and less likely than men to be risky, harmful or predatory. Yet it is a judgement that, on the spur of the moment, would be made solely based on observable physical traits, and would incorporate some pretty regressive gender stereotypes about women being 'natural' caregivers purely because of their physical appearance. The way we are all taught, from a young age, to make the link between visible biological sex traits and behaviour can be extremely powerful in shaping our intuitions about other people. This process of interpretation and the way it affects how we relate to and behave towards others is part of the system we call gender.

Feminism, though, ought always to interrogate biological essentialism (the idea that a person's nature or personality is innate; arising from, or connected to, their biological traits). The idea that anyone born with a penis is inherently more aggressive or violent because they have a penis is an anti-feminist idea: it actually suggests that male violence is linked to biological 'essence' and is therefore inevitable, immutable, perhaps not even truly men's fault. Yet anti-trans feminism is forced to rely on biological essentialism in its insistence that there is too great a similarity between trans women and cis men for the former to be regarded legally and politically as women. Transphobic feminism often uses imagery connected to penises (imagined or real) belonging to trans women as a powerful rhetorical tool, to suggest that trans women are exhibiting aggression or entitlement or are a threat. This was plainly evident in *Genderquake*, the live Channel 4 discussion between trans people and gender critical feminists that aired in May 2018: in it, the trans women on the panel, Caitlyn Jenner and model Munroe Bergdorf, were heckled by anti-trans feminists repeatedly shouting the word 'penis' across the studio (the behaviour led to 200 complaints to Ofcom from the viewing public).

One recent grassroots tactic by British anti-trans feminist groups involved placing transphobic stickers in public toilets around the UK. One of the more common slogans on these stickers, 'Women's sex-based rights are not for penises' (not the snappiest of phrases), carried with it the (false) allegation that trans women had no legal right to use women's facilities. Yet the stickers didn't actually mention trans women at all. Instead 'penises' was used as a demeaning metonym for trans women, in the same way 'suits' can be a derogatory term for callous business executives. The penis, so the sticker implied, tells you all you need to know about the human being. Conversations about biological sex or anatomy, then, almost always inadvertently become about gender and behaviour too, even in the kind of feminism that calls itself 'gender critical'.

Trans feminists seek to interrogate society's ingrained assumptions about the social and cultural meanings we ascribe to biology. They also generally incorporate an analysis of intersex people, who do not fit this reductive model, and who have suffered historical and ongoing mistreatment at the hands of a medical establishment obsessed with imposing binary biological sex on to bodies that don't 'fit'. The experiences of trans and intersex people show us that not all humans fit perfectly into two clear-cut categories of biological sex; indeed, the belief there are two separate sex categories is itself an erasure of sex variations that occur either naturally or through medical modification.

The global dominance of men over women can never be dismantled while simultaneously maintaining, preserving and reinforcing the binary model of sex and gender. As the philosopher Robin Dembroff neatly explains, patriarchy is based on three key ideas: that 'male' and 'female' are a natural, immutable and exhaustive binary; that all males should be masculine, and all females should be feminine; that masculinity is incompatible with and superior to femininity. The first belief asserts, says Dembroff, that 'every person, by virtue of their reproductive features (usually genitalia), decisively is male or female, and this can never be changed'; the second, 'that males and females should comply with pervasive and strict rules about the sexual attractions, clothing, emotions, work, family roles and behaviours expected of them'; and the third, 'that anything feminine is anti-masculine, and vice versa, and that masculine traits are more valuable than feminine traits'.[20]

Misogyny doesn't only occur when those assigned female at birth challenge the restrictions of femininity or sexist male superiority. That may be the most common scenario, given the fact that cis women are the *largest* group subject to misogyny, but it is not the only form that misogyny can take. Rather, misogyny consists of imposing, sometimes violently, all three of the beliefs Dembroff outlines on *anyone* who challenges them. Trans women, and other trans-feminine people assigned male at birth, potentially challenge all three beliefs. By socially transitioning and, in some cases, reassigning our sex characteristics medically, we challenge the stricture of an immutable sex binary. In some cases, feminine trans women will be punished as incongruous 'feminine males' (as I was at school), and our decision to rescind at least some aspects of masculinity in order to more safely and comfortably navigate the world challenges the superiority of masculinity and maleness. To many patriarchal men, trans women are a horror, having supposedly 'chosen' to surrender the higher status of being men under patriarchy for being women. This is one of the key reasons why, as I've shown in this book, trans women worldwide are subject to brutal forms of physical and sexual violence.

In hostile feminist analysis, trans women's apparent keenness to abdicate their maleness and 'become' women is typically explained away as either a pathology of maladaptive gay men who have internalized homophobia and want to become straight women instead, or, more commonly, simply as disturbing sexual fetishism. Both sexist men and transphobic feminists on some level find the desire to be a woman perverted; moreover, they consider the act of male-to-female transition itself to be a form of dishonesty and deception – which is perhaps why, when dealing with anonymous transphobic abuse online, I've often found it difficult to tell sexist men and transphobic feminists apart. Janice Raymond, who is considered the pioneer of anti-trans radical feminism, infamously wrote in her 1978 text *The Transsexual Empire: The Making of the She-Male* that in transitioning all trans women are committing an act of rape: 'All transsexuals rape women's bodies by reducing the real female form to an artefact, appropriating this body for themselves.'[21] The idea that the transsexual female body is inherently violent also lingers in Germaine Greer's 1999 book *The Whole Woman*. In a frankly unhinged chapter on transsexuals, Greer argues that all trans women are in fact committing matricide: 'Whatever else it is, gender reassignment is an exorcism of the mother. When a man decides to spend his life impersonating his mother (like Norman Bates in *Psycho*) it is as if he murders her and gets away with it.'[22] As she does elsewhere, Greer goes on to compare trans women to rapists.

This image of the trans woman as a living, breathing act of rape is a potent and persistent trope in the transphobic discourses of both right-wing men and anti-trans feminists: both groups are capable of providing cover for the other to perpetuate it. If transition itself is a rape, so this argument goes, then the trans woman is already guilty by the mere fact of her existence and can expect to be punished.

Such rhetoric is of course a way of distracting the general public from the reality. The reality is that transition is an act most trans women and girls see as lifesaving, and one for which they can be punished severely: with violence, with community and familial rejection, with poverty, with mental illness, with sexual abuse, with domestic violence and, yes, with murder. That we can be both highly at risk of rape by men and blamed for rape by feminists is made possible because the media constructs trans women simultaneously as deviant men and as dangerous women.

The transfeminist Julia Serano has described this as 'transmisogyny': a unique and severe form of misogyny specifically directed at trans women (and, I would add, transfeminine non-binary people). While trans women, trans men and non-binary people alike experience transphobia, transmisogyny is reserved for those whose gender identity sits closer to womanhood on the spectrum:

> When a trans person is ridiculed or dismissed not merely for failing to live up to gender norms, but for their expressions of femaleness or femininity, they become the victims of a specific form of discrimination: transmisogyny. When the majority of jokes made at the expense of trans people center on 'men wearing dresses' or 'men who want their penises cut off,' that is not transphobia – it is transmisogyny.[23]

In my own experience, it is entirely possible for a person to know a woman is trans, insist they do not believe she is really a woman, and yet still treat her misogynistically. This may seem a paradox – but, as Serano argues, it is because our popular culture and media has spent decades depicting trans women as extreme embodiments of very misogynistic tropes.[24] First, we are represented as agents of vapid and regressive femininity – vain, obsessed with how we look, stupid, weak, childish and entitled. We are simultaneously hypersexualized: either as grotesque sexual deviants, particularly if we are unconventionally feminine (or lesbians); or, as yielding, sexually passive and deceptive if we are more feminine in appearance and/or if we date men. Consider again Sarah Ditum's derogatory description of Laverne Cox's 'breasts thrust forward' while 'pouting seductively' on the cover of *Time*; or the descriptions of me by those seeking my removal from the Amnesty women's festival as 'pornified' and a 'blow up doll . . . eyes glazed . . . mouth receptive'. These highly sexualized descriptions of trans women by cisgender people, including feminists, are used to detract from our work and our agency. It is a form of misogyny to which we are subjected even by those who would insist that they don't believe we're women. This is particularly the case for trans women of colour, who have to contend simultaneously with the specific ways in which, for example, all black women or all East Asian women are sexually stereotyped alongside the ways trans women are pruriently objectified in media and culture.

The misogynist trope that women are by nature temptresses or deceivers has influenced our culture since the Book of Genesis; for trans women, it combines all too neatly with the idea that trans people's bodies are inherently deceptive. Growing up, the first time I ever saw another trans woman depicted in the media in Britain was in 2004, on a reality television show called *There's Something about Miriam.* The premise of the show was simple and cruel: six men were competing for the affections of a beautiful twenty-one-year-old Mexican model, Miriam Rivera. The television audience knew one crucial fact that the men did not. Miriam was trans and, it was emphasized repeatedly, still had a penis. Throughout the series, the contestants attempted to woo Miriam; multiple scenes were shown of them kissing and caressing her. In the show's excruciating finale, Miriam picked one man, who won a luxury trip with her and £10,000 prize money, then announced to him and his fellow competitors that she was trans. The male contestants later began a lawsuit against the producers, alleging conspiracy to commit sexual assault, defamation, breach of contract, and personal injury in the form of psychological and emotional damage.

The entire premise of the show was unpleasant and exploitative of all the onscreen participants. Yet most of the critics blamed Miriam. At best, media commentary at the time seemed confused as to whether Miriam should be pitied or reviled. There was even greater confusion, both among reviewers and the show's producers, about whether she should rightly be considered as a kind of woman or a kind of man. Speaking about the lawsuit, a spokesperson for the programme said: 'As Miriam is a transsexual, I would never refer to her as male or female. She is a gorgeous creature':[25] othering language that still genders Miriam primarily as feminine, but as somehow a kind of third gender or hybrid. But Miriam was portrayed as a deceptive and other-worldly seductress of men: an ancient misogynist trope, which I have never heard applied to a man. Again, even where trans women are not seen as authentically female, neither do they tend to be simply thought of, regarded or discussed as if they are men.

Femininity in external appearance or styling can certainly be distinct from womanhood: many men enjoy expressing femininity and feel a deep connection to it; many women reject traditional femininity, some preferring traditionally masculine aesthetics. Nonetheless, femininity is still largely seen and perceived as a proxy for femaleness and is denigrated as such. In some cases, a trans woman will embody enough physical traits of culturally approved femininity, including female secondary sex characteristics, to 'pass' to others as a cisgender woman. Some may pass only in certain contexts; others might consistently be perceived as a cis woman. Many trans women still aim to live and work in 'stealth' (not disclosing their history to others at all). Naturally, in these instances, a trans woman can be subject to sexism identical to that endured by cisgender women around her.

Different trans women have hugely different experiences of navigating the world and of gender-based prejudice and violence; much like cis women, their particular experience will be shaped by class, racism, age and so on. Yet it is safe to say that trans women as a group are either subject to misogyny in one form or another, or are at perpetual risk of being so. Understanding that patriarchy polices and punishes trans women with the same weapons it forged to punish women generally is crucial to understanding why feminism needs trans women's perspective to succeed.

Dismantling patriarchy requires a full analysis of all the ways it manifests itself. Ignoring the concerns of any woman or person subject to misogyny will mean that, instead of abolishing patriarchy, all the feminist movement will achieve is the creation of a sub-class of woman against whom gendered violence and misogyny remain acceptable. At present, feminist discourses that focus only on the 'problem' of a trans woman's presence in women's spaces or services, and disregard the very material issue of why she may need the space or service, are aiding and abetting systemic transmisogyny and, therefore, patriarchy itself. As someone who has lived in a variety of gender presentations, my personal experience is that the kinds of violent men who sexually harass and demean women, homophobically abuse gay and bi people, and engage in transphobic violence, are usually the same. It is therefore regrettable that some feminists happily align themselves with Conservative politicians, who have repeatedly supported austerity policies that disproportionately harm working-class women and disabled women, all because trans women fall outside of their personal definition of womanhood, and that this is the hill on which they have chosen to die.

In January 1972, the transsexual women of the UK Gay Liberation Front wrote in the *Lesbian Come Together* newsletter

> think how much more inspiring and beautiful the women's revolution will be when it joyously includes all women. Think of a Holloway demo with transvestite, transsexual and drag-queen women, gay women and heterosexual women, black, yellow [*sic*], brown and white women, mothers, daughters, poor women, rich women, working women, housewives and career women.[26]

Some of the language here is jarring to a modern ear, but the essential point – made about feminism being stronger with solidarity between all women – is an enduring one.

The controversy surrounding trans women's relationship to feminism and their access to women's spaces, particularly in Britain, is so central to transphobic discourse generally that it devours all other discussion regarding trans people and feminism. While trans women are perpetually forced to prove their legitimacy as women and their oppression under patriarchy in the face of incessant critique, trans men can find themselves erased and ignored by cis feminism entirely. Even among trans people, the extent to which trans men ought to be a part of feminism can be a matter of some debate. Anti-trans feminism's insistence that 'women' are purely a sex class of everyone born into the world with a vulva and recorded as female means that transphobic feminists frequently claim to welcome trans men as part of their movement. A common reply to the claim that gender critical feminism is 'trans-exclusionary' is 'No, my feminism includes trans people – it includes trans men because they are female!' Of course, this supposed inclusion is nothing of the sort, since it only works through overt misgendering and outright dismissal of trans men's experience of their own bodies and of society. As the poet Jay Hulme puts it:

> The approach transphobes take towards trans men is far more insidious [than transmisogyny directed at trans women] and is much more difficult to explain and identify. Because transphobes see trans men as women, and because much of the political and online transphobia at the moment is perpetrated by women under the guise of 'feminism', there is a sense that trans men are misguided allies, that we are mistaken, and simply need to be welcomed back into the fold, and into womanhood itself. This

welcoming seems like a kindness. It is not, and needs to be called out for what it is – a form of conversion therapy . . . As a trans man, I am, and always will be, belittled, disrespected, spoken down to, and patronised, by transphobes.[27]

When I spoke to Henry, the eighteen-year-old trans man who featured in the second chapter of this book, he pointed out how the belief that trans boys are in fact 'young girls' leads to a greater moral panic about access to medical transition in transmasculine people, because 'girls' are seen as more delicate and more easily influenced, so more in need of adult intervention and protection. Jay Hulme agrees: '[Transphobes] obsess over our surgeries, our ages, and our presentations. The prospect of a trans man exercising his right to bodily autonomy horrifies them.' Echoing Henry, Hulme says that a key tactic of transphobic feminist discourse is infantilizing trans men and body horror:

> They speak of trans men as 'girls' even when we're well into our twenties, and even beyond . . . They speak of 'testosterone poisoning' (having normal male levels of testosterone in our bodies and maybe growing facial hair), of 'mutilation', of 'hacking off healthy body tissue' – they care more about the sexist ideal of the perfect untouched female form, than about the people whose bodies they actually are.[28]

With such a confusing combination of being welcomed to feminism by the very same voices who describe them as brainwashed and broken, some trans men fight shy of seeking any feminist solidarity or support. For a trans man to state publicly that he is still subject to gender-based oppression or sexism on the basis that others still perceive him as a woman must be very hard, in a culture so frequently determined to tell him he's not actually a man. For trans women, the debate over our relationship to feminism usually involves debating the extent to which we are oppressed as women. For trans men the debate is the inverse: the extent to which trans men can enjoy the privileges and advantages afforded to men under patriarchy.

Trans men who medically transition with testosterone will grow facial hair and visibly masculinize; their voices will break. For some, this undoubtedly means that in some or all contexts they are simply read as male by society. In an article for *Time*, Charlotte Alter interviewed more than twenty trans men about work, relationships and family: 'Over and over again, men who were raised and socialized as female described all the ways they were treated differently as soon as the world perceived them as male.' Alter's interviews revealed that many trans men started to realize, for the first time, the workplace sexism to which they had been subject prior to transition. As they began to be read as men, and afforded male privilege, 'they found their missteps minimized and their successes amplified. Often, they say, their words carried more weight: they seemed to gain authority and professional respect overnight.' The better treatment the trans men reported was balanced by greater awareness of sexism and misogyny among other men: 'They also saw confirmation of the sexist attitudes they had long suspected. They recalled hearing female colleagues belittled by male bosses, or female job applicants called names.' The men reported other downsides. One interviewee, trans man James Gardner, told Alter: 'I have to be very careful to not be staring at kids . . . I can look at a mom and her baby, but I can't look for too long. I miss being seen as not a threat.'[29] (Gardner's observation echoes my earlier point about leaving a child with a stranger: how people may instinctively assess risk based solely on observable sex differences.)

The fact that some trans men do acquire male privilege, and can be perceived by women as a threat, is typically ignored in anti-trans feminist discourse. The reason for this is simple. If – as most gender critical feminists do – you subscribe to a feminism which preaches that sex is immutable and that trans women should be compelled to use male toilets, changing rooms and refuges, regardless of whether or not they medically transition, then, similarly, a trans man must be compelled and encouraged to use female spaces. The logical endpoint of their ideology is that a person with a deep voice, full beard, masculine clothing, a typically male name and in some cases a penis will be permitted to enter a female space because he is a trans man or, in fact, just because he says he is (you cannot test for chromosomes in a public toilet). Anti-trans feminist rhetoric about female spaces tends to rely on the false premise that it is always possible to detect a trans woman on sight and challenge her access to the space. This simply is not true in many instances, and could easily lead to a situation where masculine cis women and intersex women are challenged erroneously as 'male' based on their appearance. In reality, most trans men I know would not want to make cis or trans women uncomfortable in spaces set aside for people currently subject to the kinds of misogyny women experience, even if those same trans men did once experience it themselves.

That there is tension between the respective interests of trans men and trans women is a trope beloved of some cis feminists, who believe that trans women 'dominate' the entire trans movement and shut out the interests of trans men. This idea is usually rooted in the fact that well-known or celebrity trans women far outnumber trans men. '[Trans women] are both more visible in the LGBT movement – trans men only seem to make the news when they have babies – and pose harder questions,'[30] the journalist Helen Lewis wrote (again in the *New Statesman*) in 2019. That trans men are less visible in the 'mainstream media' (the kinds of media created and controlled by cis and straight people) is true: trans women have received much more coverage, both good and bad. But it is wrong to equate the mainstream media with the LGBTQ+ movement or, more specifically, the trans movement. The idea that greater visibility automatically leads to greater political power is a misapprehension, particularly when some of the most celebrated trans women in media are actresses, models and writers – industries in which all women are sexualized and obsessed over. To use trans women's commodification and objectification in the media (because femininity has always been more easily commodified than masculinity) to suggest that trans women speak over, control or 'dominate' trans men is transmisogyny. That's to say, it falsely implies that trans women, deep down, are really still men and afforded the privileges of being male, while erasing the ways in which famous trans women are still exploited, sexualized and fetishized in the media, just as cis women are.

Many of the major trans organizations around the world are led by white trans men. The list is a long one. In Britain, one of the leading legal scholars in trans rights and a founder of the trans lobby group Press for Change, Stephen Whittle, is a trans man; so too is Jay Stewart, the only chief executive of a trans-run charity. The manager of the Scottish Trans Alliance until November 2020, James Morton, is a trans man; as is Dr Richard Curtis, the only openly trans doctor to have worked as a gender clinician for trans patients in private practice. The same goes for Masen Davis, acting executive director of the pan-European NGO Transgender Europe, and Broden Giambrone, director of the International Trans Fund and formerly CEO of Ireland's trans organization TENI. In the US and Canada, the situation is the same. The reality is that at all levels of well-funded and staffed trans activism and political lobbying, trans men can and do take leading roles. As, of course, they should. But the view that all trans men are spoken over and silent, simply because a handful of palatably feminine trans women make the covers of glossy magazines, is both patronizing and wrong, and devalues the contribution many trans men make to the progress of trans liberation.

Nonetheless, it's also true that trans men suffer from the sense

of being invisible in our culture. (This, as ever, will be complicated by race and class. Just as white cis women can wield and
have historically wielded their whiteness as power over cis men
of colour, the same can be true if the parties are trans.) It must be
acknowledged that there has not been a nuanced conversation
about what trans men need from feminism, and that in this regard
they continue to be failed. Helen Lewis is right about trans men
and pregnancy being headline news: the problem is, in Britain the
headlines are always sensationalized, and always tailored to and
by cis people. In this, once again, Britain is well behind the curve.
The lack of consideration for trans men and non-binary people in
the way society cares for the pregnant, or those able to become
pregnant, contrasts markedly with the situation in Ireland: the
successful campaign to repeal the Eighth Amendment to the Irish
Constitution, which gave the unborn equal right to life with the
mother, was strikingly inclusive of trans people. Likewise, the
Abortion Rights Campaign (ARC) for free safe and legal abortion
in Ireland was trans inclusive from its inception: the presence of
trans speakers at its events reflected the reality that, while abortion is predominantly a women's issue, trans men and some
non-binary people in Ireland were also affected by this aspect of
the Constitution.

After the Eighth Amendment was repealed by referendum in
May 2018, ARC continued to push publicly for meaningful legislation that would finally allow legal abortion in Ireland to be
explicitly inclusive of trans men and non-binary people. British
feminism must take its cue from this approach and recognize that
the desire for autonomy over one's own body regarding pregnancy, and the right to have one's gender identity acknowledged
in law, are two concerns that overlap in the lives of trans men and
non-binary people. Acknowledging that people other than cis
women are politically oppressed on the basis of their capacity to
reproduce does not erase these women; rather, it acknowledges

the very real existence of trans men trapped in a culture in which, in order to talk about their reproductive health, they are pressured into denying their gender identity as men. It is a cruel ultimatum imposed on people who have often suffered greatly because of their gender and their sex, and no feminist should be party to it.

Trans men should never be forced into a reactive position of denying their experiences of sexism, misogyny or transphobia in order to have their identity as men respected. Feminist solidarity for anyone who has been treated as a girl or woman at any point, regardless of their current gender expression, should be instinctive. While a trans man might acquire some forms of male privilege if he transitions in a particular way, in a transphobic society such privilege is always conditional on passing as a cisgender male to others and suppressing knowledge of his history. Even where this is the case, there is substantial evidence that trans men as a group still need the support and care of feminism. While, globally, the vast majority of trans people murdered are trans women, vicious violence is also unleashed on trans men. In South Africa, to cite just one example, trans men have – like butch lesbians – been subjected to so-called 'corrective' rape: a use of rape as punishment for gender deviance intended to force them 'back' into being (heterosexual) women. (It's telling that one of the most famous cultural depictions of a trans man in mainstream cinema remains that of Brandon Teena, played by Hilary Swank in *Boys Don't Cry* (1999), a trans man who was gang raped and later murdered aged twenty-one in 1993.)

Research shows that trans men in contemporary Britain report significant levels of physical, sexual and emotional abuse. The 2018 National LGBT Survey, referred to in Chapter 1, found that, while trans women experienced higher degrees of some forms of abuse and harassment by people outside their home, trans men were at significantly greater risk from perpetrators in their own home: 58 per cent of trans men had experienced some form of abuse at home, compared to 40 per cent of trans women and 47 per cent of non-binary people. More trans men reported physical or sexual violence towards them in their own home than trans women or non-binary people.[31] Further research and open discussion are needed on the emotional, sexual and domestic violence that trans men suffer. Trans women and cis feminists, meanwhile, should avoid the pitfalls of either erasing trans men's male identity or presuming that their male identity protects them automatically from misogyny.

It is notable that the domestic and sexual violence support sector (often, ironically, referred to as the 'women's sector') currently cannot provide trans men with the support they need. While men's crisis services for male survivors of abuse do exist, their specialist counsellors and support workers are typically trained to deal with cis men's experiences. Trans men may have been subjected to abuse by perpetrators who saw them as women, and will need support by sensitive professionals who are aware of that experience. All feminists should acknowledge trans men's struggle to have access to services that work for them, and should include such concerns in the fight against the broader Conservative funding cuts for specialist domestic violence services.

It is clear that trans men still experience gendered violence grounded in misogyny. To apply Robin Dembroff's test: they challenge the existence of a sex binary, they can be punished as 'masculine females' when they don't pass as male to others, and, whereas trans women are seen as perverted for abandoning maleness and masculinity, trans men are seen as deluded or confused women who have been misled into wanting to be male. In the views of some anti-trans feminists, they are even considered 'traitors' for trying to acquire male privilege for themselves instead of fighting oppression as feminists. Misogyny, as we've seen, is multifaceted and polices different people and different kinds of bodies in different ways: all must be resisted in order for feminism to truly challenge patriarchy.

Readers acquainted with feminist theory may be surprised that, in this exploration of trans feminism, I have mostly cited the thoughts of second-wave feminists (some of whom are now controversial in younger feminist circles because of their focus on criminalizing pornography and sex work) instead of Judith Butler, Jack Halberstam and others whose later writing in feminism and queer theory might be a more obvious place to start in a defence of trans people's existence. However, I believe it is important to debunk the myth that transfeminism is a new departure from the feminist theory of the past. As we have seen, ambivalence about the categories of man and woman, challenging biological essentialism, and championing a multifaceted analysis of the harm that misogyny does to every human being (including men) have always been central to feminist thought. As the second-wave feminist Catherine MacKinnon put it,

> I always thought I don't care how someone becomes a woman or a man; it does not matter to me. It is just part of their specificity, their uniqueness, like everyone else's. Anybody who identifies as a woman, wants to be a woman, is going around being a woman, as far as I'm concerned, is a woman.[32]

This is especially important when considering feminist attitudes to non-binary trans identities. People who say they are something other than a man or a woman, or both, or always in flux between the two, are living proof of one of feminism's central ideas: that gender is a reductive trap which limits freedom and curbs individuality, forcing people to deform themselves and their desires in the service of an exploitative and violent system. As the artist Travis Alabanza puts it:

When I say trans, I also mean escape. I mean choice. I mean autonomy. I mean wanting something greater than what you told me. Wanting more possibilities than the one you forced on me.[33]

Non-binary people's spirited refusal to yield so completely to this process ought to be a breath of fresh air, and feminism should concern itself with the harms such people face. It should, but, frequently, it doesn't. 'Too often, discussions of gender today, rather than expanding boundaries, only contract them,' the *Guardian* columnist Hadley Freeman wrote in 2017:

> When people say they're 'non-binary', it sounds to me more like they swallowed the lie of the pink and blue onesies [for babies]. Because the point is everyone, really, is non-binary – no one's a wholly pink butterfly or blue car onesie.[34]

Freeman seems to accept that binary gender is a construct that confines us all, and that we are all more complicated than this, something that non-binary trans people do evidence. But her simplistic metaphor about baby clothing diminishes the all-encompassing way in which the gender binary shapes law, politics, medicine, culture, violence and sexuality: basically, the whole gamut of human discourse. It is strange for Freeman's feminist analysis to stop at clothing and ignore the wider implications. When non-binary people ask for legal recognition or a rethinking of gendered language (for instance through neutral pronouns, or new words for new genders), they are asking for more freedom for us all. In one sense, the claim that everyone is non-binary isn't wrong: the binary is a powerful and pervasive myth, and everyone is somewhere on a spectrum. 'Non-binary' is only useful insofar as it is a term which can be used to make such ideas legible to policymakers, families, schools and societies. It is a term designed to make conversation easier; it is not the end point.

The existence of trans people ought to make everyone take a long hard look at their own dearly held ideas about gender, and wonder whether these ideas are quite as stable and certain as they once thought. This would be healthy. The distinction between men and women is often arbitrary. The distinction between 'binary' trans men and women and non-binary trans people is equally arbitrary and, in reality, the precise distinction between people we call cis and people we call trans isn't rigid either. The fact that definitions can be so unstable is clearly deeply troubling to many – which is why it is easier to belittle challenges to binaries than to take on their contradictions, complications and exceptions. 'We are all non-binary' is potentially a radical new analysis for how we might reorder society, but conventionally it is used by gender critical feminists to mock those people making political demands to dismantle the binary's imprint on our culture. Yet those critics provide no alternative for how we would otherwise emancipate society from binary gender stereotypes and roles. Once more, feminist hostility to non-binary people reasserts the notion of an inescapable biological sex that should be given more social and legal credence than a variant gender identity, a notion that merely replicates patriarchy's own logic. Back in 1974, the radical feminist Andrea Dworkin wrote on humanity's growing consciousness of the arbitrariness of both sex and gender categories:

> Hormone and chromosome research, attempts to develop new means of human reproduction (life created in, or considerably supported by, the scientist's laboratory), work with transsexuals, and studies of formation of gender identity in children provide basic information which challenges the notion that there are two discrete biological sexes. That information threatens to transform the traditional biology of sex difference into the radical biology of sex similarity. That is not to say there is one sex, but

that there are many. The evidence which is germane here is simple. The words 'male' and 'female', 'man' and 'woman', are used only because as yet there are no others.[35]

Dworkin knew forty years ago what many non-binary trans people and progressive cis feminists are still forced to defend in feminist circles now. More recently, the British feminist Lola Olufemi has described the concept of 'woman' as

> a strategic coalition, an umbrella under which we gather in order to make political demands. It might be mobilized in service of those who, given another option, would identify themselves in other ways. In a liberated future, it might not exist at all.[36]

The same is true, of course, of the concept of 'man'. Feminism must concern itself with radical possibilities for our future, a future in which gender-based violence and harm is abolished, freeing us all to lead more joyful lives. That cannot begin with barring the freedom to find other ways to look at, understand or *do* gender.

Trans people do not all have radical ideas about gender: most will have ideas that are no more and no less binary, reductive, stereotypical and anti-feminist than the cis people around them. The demand that trans people all have radical analyses of gender can itself be a form of transphobia, because we do not hold cis people to this standard. It also frames cis claims about gender as natural and default, and trans people as proponents of a new ideology which must be tested and probed. Trans people deserve social dignity and personal respect, regardless of whether or not they wish to immerse themselves in feminist politics. At a time of growing populist authoritarianism, which seems determined to entrench sexism, misogyny and transphobia across the globe, one may even wonder why a theoretical framework for understanding trans people should be the prime concern for any feminist. Theory is important: it shapes our society, whether or not we engage with it intellectually, which is why I've discussed it extensively here. But theory should only ever play second fiddle to the practical work of movement-building, resource-allocation, care and solidarity. Political coalitions rarely achieve full mutual understanding of every facet of one another's reality. Rather, they are practical collaborations based on shared goals: we need only look at the huge mobilization of people to secure victory for the Repeal campaign in Ireland to see what can be achieved by working in concert. For those cis feminists who still feel daunted by accepting trans people into their consciousness, the sheer urgency of the situation facing women and trans people alike in the 2020s ought to give them pause. As the writer Jo Livingstone puts it:

> Agendas do not have to melt together or shed their distinctness or lose their efficacy when they 'correspond or get along'. They do not have to align, at all . . . Why waste your breath hurting people? There is no time, and there is so much work to be done.[37]

Conclusion: A Transformed Future

There can be no trans liberation under capitalism. This is a fact. Yet it's not a popular view among liberal and centrist LGBTQ+ advocacy groups, who – as we've seen in the course of this book – talk about 'trans rights' in isolation as a range of personal freedoms and protections; and who cling to corporations and brands as potential 'allies' in the fight for social acceptance. So how can true justice be achieved?

It has become popular, in those liberal spaces that consider themselves trans-inclusive, to assert that people who engage in transphobic behaviour are 'on the wrong side of history'. The idea that there are right and wrong sides of history is, of course, a fallacy. The myth that the passage of time reveals moral truth and that history marches forward toward progress is ancient, seductive – and surprisingly persistent. It only works, however, by carefully editing the histories we choose to remember and giving after-the-fact praise to transformative social revolutions – praise that often plays down their more problematic elements, such as the use of force or violence. In modern Britain, the claim that to be supportive of trans equality is to be on the 'right' side of history is usually rooted in a comparison with the social and legal advances of gay people by the beginning of the new millennium, and the perception that overt homophobia is now *verboten* in many liberal spaces. Trans people, so it's hoped, are following the same trajectory, albeit with a twenty-year time lag. Those in the press and politics who are virulently transphobic now, we are told, will in a few years find themselves embarrassed.

Perhaps, for some liberals, the lurking fear that they might be on the wrong side of moral progress – peer pressure, in other words – is potent enough to make them disavow transphobia. I think, however, that it's naïve to pin all our hopes for trans people's wellbeing, safety, dignity and liberation on liberal squeamishness. The reality is that many who were homophobic twenty years ago remain so today, and a clear record of past homophobia is no bar to power or popularity. The current British prime minister, Boris Johnson, has a long history of opposition to gay rights, including gay men serving in the military, LGBTQ+ inclusive education in schools and equal marriage. He has never retracted the 'tank-topped bum boys' line – then again, he has never needed to. Given that the British prime minister gets away with it, it's hardly surprising that overt homophobia, while remaining stigmatized in liberal spaces, has witnessed a huge resurgence in far-right groups across Europe, from Golden Dawn in Greece to the French neo-fascist group Génération Identitaire. Even in British schools, surveys of teachers suggest that overt homophobia is still more common than many straight liberals might imagine.

The 2010s saw the Conservatives under David Cameron and Theresa May attempt to rebrand themselves as socially liberal, even as they made brutal cuts to housing, welfare and education, and enabled the creeping privatization of healthcare. In the 2020s, however, the political landscape is very different. British trans people can no longer be enticed by crumbs of acceptance, like those offered by the May government when it announced it would reform the Gender Recognition Act and the parallel GRA reform currently under review in Scotland. In truth, the Tory party was always the enemy of trans people. The brazen social conservatism of the Johnson era has simply made it more accept-able for them to be open about the fact that we are, fundamentally, antithetical to their values. It is unclear what lies ahead regarding Scottish independence and whether Irish reunification may become more likely. At this juncture, it has to be said that the only hope trans people have of achieving beneficial policy changes enacted in Parliament is through internal lobbying and, ultimately, the election of the Labour Party.

Being trans, of course, is not a consciously adopted political position, just as claiming a trans identity is not, usually, an expression of a consciously held ideology. A trans person is just a person. We see our daily lives through the same everyday lens as most human beings; after all, we are simply trying to live. However, as with all stigmatized social identities, the very ability to articulate being trans, or to work, seek healthcare, or participate in civic life while trans, *is* political. This is why the material conditions needed for trans people's prosperity have always come from the policies and practices of the left. In Britain, we have free healthcare because of the NHS, a socialist model created by the left; and we cannot legally be fired for being trans or transitioning, because of the labour movement. Right-wing parties and governments offer us little hope. For the past decade, too, the centre has also offered no real vision, frequently conspiring with the architects of austerity while refusing to work with the left.

This is not to say that Labour itself is innocent of transphobia, both within its membership and from some of its key figures, who have failed to show full and public solidarity with trans communities. Anti-trans discourse is very much alive on the left in Britain, in trade unions and in local party branches. In 2017, the election of a nineteen-year-old trans woman, Lily Madigan, as a Labour women's officer for Rochester and Strood provoked a particularly vicious transphobic backlash within the party. In early 2018, a GoFundMe page set up by a Labour Party activist, Jennifer James, called for trans women not to be included in all-women's shortlists: it quickly raised tens of thousands of pounds before James was eventually suspended from the party. Lewis Moonie, a Labour life peer, former defence minister and trained psychiatrist, left the Labour Party in May 2019 after being suspended for repeated derogatory comments about trans women, whom he referred to as 'nonces' and 'someone with a cock in a frock'.[1] Those opposed to GRA reform included a number of leading trade unionists, notably Len McCluskey, general secretary of Britain's second largest union, UNITE (a key Labour donor). Woman's Place UK, the most well-known grassroots anti-trans feminist group, was founded by Ruth Serwotka, wife of Mark Serwotka, general secretary of the Public and Commercial Services Union. In 2020, the *Morning Star*, a socialist newspaper that amplified many anti-trans voices during the GRA campaign, had to apologize for and retract a transphobic cartoon it published. The cartoon in question, by Stella Perrett, showed a salivating and predatory crocodile slithering into a small pond containing newts. In speech bubbles, the newts could be seen saying, 'But you can't come in here! This is our safe space!', to which the crocodile replies, 'Don't worry your pretty little heads! I'm transitioning as a newt!' This open depiction of trans people as animalistic predators was a new low for British left-wing transphobia.

The intellectual justification for transphobia on the left is usually framed as concern about a mythological 'trans ideology', which is individualist, bourgeois and unconcerned with class struggle. As we've seen, however, the majority of trans people are working class, and the oppression of trans people is specifically rooted in capitalism. In short, capitalism across the world still relies heavily on the idea of different categories of men's work and women's work, in which 'women's work' (such as housework, child-rearing and emotional labour) is either poorly paid or not paid at all. In order for this categorization to function, it needs to rest on a clear idea of how to divide men and women.

Capitalism also requires a certain level of unemployment to function. If there were enough work to go round, no worker would worry about losing their job, and all workers could demand higher wages and better conditions. The ever-present spectre of unemployment, on the other hand, enables employers to dictate conditions. Equally, in times of severe crisis this 'reserve army' of unemployed people can be called into employment as and when the economy requires it. This system of deliberate unemployment needs ways to mark who will work and who will be left unemployed. In our society this is principally achieved through race, class, gender and disability. Social exclusion and revulsion at the existence of trans people usefully provides another class of people more likely to be left in the ranks of the unemployed (even more so if they are trans and poor, black or disabled – which is why unemployment is highest among these trans people).[2]

There should be more debates on the left about the extent to which policy and legal protections within a capitalist system can ever truly rectify this fundamental need for some people to be marginalized. Arguably, 'trans inclusion' within capitalism will only ever be partial, favouring the white and the middle class among us. While such debates are beyond the scope of this book, it must be emphasized that criticisms of the trans movement being inherently 'capitalist' or irredeemably individualist are very wide of the mark. Of course, this does not mean that capitalism won't sometimes cloak itself in the language of social justice. The demands, slogans, aesthetics and culture of feminism, anti-racism and gay rights have all, at times, been similarly co-opted and sold back to consumers by corporations: one need only look at the explosion of feminist tote bags, Gay Pride T-shirts and cor-porate #BlackLivesMatter platitudes in the past five years to see that. This misappropriation of activists' language doesn't mean that the radical demands for transformative politics they are mak-ing are a sham. The same is true of trans justice and trans freedom.

While I believe that, in England if not the rest of the UK, the Labour Party is the only instrument by which trans people's rights are championed in electoral politics, our full emancipation will never come through parliamentary politics alone. It is entirely possible for trans people to make certain gains in legal rights or social acceptance – and for these gains to be subsequently reversed. The very first wave of modern scientific trans research and advocacy took place in inter-war Berlin, a city with a thriving queer social scene: all this was quickly suppressed by fascists in the early 1930s. In Hungary, a modern EU member state, the same suppression of already-won legal rights is starting to happen right now, in the early 2020s. British people cannot assume that we are immune from these forces. There is a real risk that the UK will lean so far to the right that trans people's emancipation is suppressed by the state once again.

Already, we are seeing profound changes to our social and political lives brought about by the coronavirus pandemic, the resulting recession and the resurgence of the Black Lives Matter movement. The climate crisis rages on, unaddressed. With the next decade set to be one of continuing upheaval, scientists have warned of the possibility of severe societal breakdown in our lifetimes caused by unrest resulting from extreme climate events. Climate-crisis-fuelled mass migration might well lead to increased surveillance, militarization and anti-immigrant racism in the global north. All this will disproportionately impact oppressed minorities, including trans people.

In this context, the idea of linear political struggles, which are confined to formal parliamentary politics, is a chimera. Protest, civil disobedience, local community work, care work, and bridge-building with other oppressed people are all politics: all will be necessary in our struggle.

At the outset of this book, I said I would refuse the pressure on trans people, particularly trans women, to engage in personal writing or memoir. Much of what I have discussed in this book, from homelessness to domestic violence, lies outside my experience. This is by virtue of my class and race but also because of my good luck: thanks to a family who embraced me when I came out, good friends and relationships, and a modestly successful career, I will never be marginalized in the way the majority of my trans siblings are. Yet – to speak personally – I can say that, ever since I was a child, I have had to learn to keep on going in a world which signalled to me at every turn that I was mad, bad, sick, deluded, disgusting, a pervert, a danger, unlovable. I still do. I still struggle, at times, to like myself, and there are days I have to remind myself, consciously, that I have done nothing wrong in being trans, being feminine, being a woman. This has left its scars. Often, in the course of writing and researching this book, I spoke to younger trans people and their families and found myself hoping that, at the deep psychic level, they would not have to abide with the recurrent narratives of disgust and shame that this world has always imposed on me. This is not intended to be self-pitying; hope, including mine, is precious and powerful. My hope wrote this book, and, while I have used the language and conceptual tools of structural politics and collective action, the thing that will liberate trans people is our shared hope for a better world. Hope is part of the human condition and trans people's hope is our proof that we are fully human. We are not an 'issue' to be debated and derided. We are symbols of hope for many non-trans people, too, who see in our lives the possibility of living more fully and freely. That is why some people hate us: they are frightened by the gleaming opulence of our freedom. Our existence enriches this world.

Acknowledgements

Writing my first book on one of the most fraught and heated topics in politics, both here in the UK and beyond, a topic that has and will continue to profoundly determine the course of my own life, was not without its challenges. I am immensely grateful, then, to have worked with an editor of the experience and calibre of Tom Penn, whose insight and suggestions helped to loosen some of the tension in my prose and who was able to guide me into knowing what the reader needed to be better able to engage with the central argument. The book also benefited greatly from Eva Hodgkin's reflections as assistant editor. I'd also like to thank Richard Duguid at Penguin, who copy-edited the manuscript himself thereby giving me the benefit of another person with formidable experience in publishing. I am also so lucky to have had the expertise of Pen, my publicist, and Micca, who has handled the marketing.

This book simply would not exist were it not for Emma Paterson, the best agent and confidante one could wish for. I had no intention of writing a book about trans politics at all until Emma got the train down to Bristol on a cold December afternoon and within an hour had somehow inspired me to articulate an idea that would ultimately become this text. Her ability to convince authors from minorities or backgrounds underrepresented in publishing that they also have voices that should be heard is something her industry should cherish. I also have to thank her for putting up with what must have been hundreds of text messages with questions, concerns and panics – often out of office hours – and never once complaining about it. The same is also true for her assistant Monica, who has pretty much imposed order on my professional life where there was none.

I owe so much to trans people. One of the greatest by-products of my own transition was gaining a community of friends who never fail to astonish me in their capacity to find wit, laughter and hope in the face of the hostility and unkindness that society can sometimes show to them. I am particularly grateful to the trans people and their families who agreed to be interviewed for this book and trusted me with their experiences. I am truly proud to be trans, and that is in large part because of my siblings. In particular, I would like to say thank you to those trans people who kept me sane while writing this book during a pandemic and unprecedented government and media aggression towards trans liberation, especially Robin Craig, Cara English and Rose Dommu, all of whom have the capacity to make me laugh aloud even when I'm sitting alone staring at my phone. I am lucky to know Kuchenga, who can make me hysterical with laughter but who has also been a huge personal support and listened to me in some of my darkest times. She is a brilliant writer whose work and thinking has hugely informed my own. The same can be said of Travis Alabanza, a trailblazer for British trans artists and creatives. I have learned so much about politics from the brilliance of my trans colleagues and friends, especially Crash Wigley and Morgan Page. Morgan kindly gave her time to read an early draft of Chapter 4 to help make sure I did justice to sex workers, and her insight was invaluable. Writing about British trans history was made infinitely easier by the knowledge and tips given to me by Roz Kaveney, who has been part of trans life in the UK for forty years and remains welcoming to young upstarts.

Thanks to Huw Lemmey for also reading an early fragment of this book and providing me with suggestions and thoughts for further research, as well as my former editor at *Dazed*, Thomas Gorton, who championed my writing career from the very beginning. The same is true of the crew at Novara Media, who provided me with a platform early in my career and allowed me to make video content in ludicrous outfits, and to Owen Jones, who has been consistent in using his own platform to provide trans people with a voice.

In the isolation and loneliness we have all experienced in the pandemic I could not have written this book without the support of all my friends. My own personal life had several tumultuous periods during the time I was writing, and I couldn't have coped without the wisdom and kindness of Ellie Mae O'Hagan. I am thankful for beautiful Otamere, my constant hype man even when I don't believe in myself. Few are so lucky as to have in their life someone as kind and loyal as my darling friend Gemma Pharo. I relied so much upon her daily voicenotes from the opposite side of the country during the lockdowns. Thank you to Rob, Patrick and Matt for the much-needed escapism and fun over the past few years. Shoutout to the alt-Twitter crew (you know who you are), who have been there for me so much online, and to Will Swannell, who supported this book in its early days by his care for its author. Though now far away in geography, I still feel close in spirit to my friends Josie and Jo – the first people to whom I ever blurted out my big trans secret – and who were the perfect friends to tell. I hope the three of us will be together soon.

Finally, I am so lucky to have the family I do. There are no words to describe how much I owe to my powerful and generous mother, Helen, to whom this book is dedicated, and to my brother, Ciarán, and my sister, Enya. Thank you for everything, but especially for putting up with me while writing this book, locked down together, in a pandemic.

Notes

Introduction

1 Bannerman, L., 'Trans Movement Has been Hijacked by Bullies and Trolls', *The Times*, 1 October 2018, https://www.thetimes.co.uk/article/trans-movement-has-been-hijacked-by-bullies-and-trolls-lwl3s73vj.

2 House of Commons Women and Equalities Committee, 'Transgender Equality', report, 14 January 2016, https://publications.parliament.uk/pa/cm201516/cmselect/cmwomeq/390/390.pdf , p. 6.

3 Namaste, V., *Sex Change, Social Change: Reflections on Identity, Institutions, and Imperialism*, Women's Press (2nd edn, 2011), p. 63.

1. Trans Life Now

1 Wood, C. and Jones, S., 'World War 2 Veteran Decides to Live as Transgender Woman at Age 90 and Begins Taking Female Hormones', *Daily Mirror*, 29 March 2017, https://www.mirror.co.uk/news/uk-news/world-war-2-veteran-comes-10119089.

2 Gilligan, A., 'Parents' Anger as Child Sex Change Charity Mermaids Puts Private Emails Online', *The Times*, 16 June 2019, https://www.thetimes.co.uk/article/parents-anger-as-child-sex-change-charity-puts-private-emails-online-3tntlwqln.

3 'The Paris Lees One', *Political Thinking*, BBC Radio Four, 9 February 2018, https://www.bbc.co.uk/programmes/p05xp3z2.

4 Ibid.

5 *School Report: The Experiences of Lesbian, Gay, Bi and Trans Pupils in Britain's Schools,* Stonewall (2017), https://www.stonewall.org.uk/school-report-2017.

6 Ibid.

7 Durwood, Lily, et al., 'Mental Health and Self-worth in Socially Transitioned Transgender Youth', *Journal of the American Academy of Child & Adolescent Psychiatry,* 56(2) (2017), pp. 116–23, https://www.jaacap.org/article/S0890-8567%2816%2931941-4/fulltext; Gurevich, R., 'Using Transgender Youths' Chosen Names May Lower Suicide Risk', Reuters, 10 April 2108, https://www.reuters.com/article/us-health-youth-transgender-idUSKBN1HH2WH.

8 Todd, M., *Straight Jacket: How to be Gay and Happy,* Bantham Press (2016), p. 73.

9 Hudson-Sharp, N., 'Transgender Awareness in Child and Family Social Work Education: Research Report', National Institute of Economic and Social Research, Department for Education, May 2019, https://assets.publishing.service.gov.uk/government/uploads/system/uploads/attachment_data/file/706344/Transgender_awareness_in_child_and_family_social_work_education.pdf.

10 'School Report'.

11 'School Report', p. 4.

12 Davies-Arai, S., *Supporting Gender Diverse and Trans-Identified Students in Schools,* Transgender Trend (2018), https://www.transgendertrend.com/wp-content/uploads/2019/08/Transgender-Trend-Resource-Pack-for-Schools3.pdf.

13 Ibid.

14 Ibid.

15 'School Report'.

16 Goode, Erich, and Ben-Yehuda, Nachman, *Moral Panics: The Social Construction of Deviance Oxford,* Blackwell (2nd edn, 2009). pp. 57–65.

17 Both were headlines in *The Times*: Turner, J., 'Children Sacrificed to Appease Trans Lobby', *The Times,* 11 November 2017, and Turner, J.

'Cult of Gender Identity is Harming Children', *The Times*, 21 September 2019.

18 Here I draw on the characteristics of a 'folk devil' first outlined by sociologist Stanley Cohen. See Cohen, S., *Folk Devils and Moral Panics*, Paladin (1973).

19 Rayer, G., 'Minister to Order Inquiry into 4000 Per Cent Rise in Children Wanting to Change Sex', *Telegraph*, 16 September 2019.

20 Manning, S., 'I've Seen Girls Who've Changed Gender Groom Younger Ones to Do the Same . . .', *Mail on Sunday*, 17 November 2018, https://www.dailymail.co.uk/news/article-6401583/Ive-seen-girls-whove-changed-gender-groom-younger-ones-same.html.

21 'School Report', p. 11.

22 'National LGBT Survey Research Report', Government Equalities Office, July 2018, p. 58, https://assets.publishing.service.gov.uk/government/uploads/system/uploads/attachment_data/file/721704/LGBT-survey-research-report.pdf.

23 *The LGBTQ+ Youth Homelessness Report*, akt (2021), https://www.akt.org.uk/report.

24 Mukherjee, K., ' "We're just as human as you": One Woman's Experience of being Transgender and Homeless', *Bristol Cable*, 17 July 2016, https://thebristolcable.org/2016/07/transgender-homeless/.

25 Smith, J., 'Homeless Woman's Possessions Burnt In Front of Her by Kingswood Arsonists', *Bristol Post*, 21 July 2017, https://www.bristolpost.co.uk/news/bristol-news/homeless-womans-possessions-burnt-front-225743.

26 Mukherjee, ' "We're just as human as you" '.

27 *LGBT in Britain – Trans Report*, Stonewall (2018), p. 6, https://www.stonewall.org.uk/lgbt-britain-trans-report.

28 Ingala-Smith, K., 'An End to Violence against Women' (speech), Woman's Place UK, https://womansplaceuk.org/end-to-violence-against-women/.

29 Ingala-Smith, K. 'The Importance of Women Only Spaces and Services for Women and Girls Who've been Subjected to Men's

Violence' (speech), 20 January 2020, https://kareningalasmith.com/2020/01/20/the-importance-of-women-only-spaces-and-services-for-women-and-girls-whove-been-subjected-to-mens-violence/.

30 Lothian McLean, M., ' "If they sound like a man, hang up": How Transphobia Became Rife in the Gender-based Violence Sector', *gal-dem*, 1 February 2021, https://gal-dem.com/transphobia-sexual-violence-sound-like-a-man-hang-up-vawg-investigation/.

31 *Supporting Trans Women in Domestic And Sexual Violence Services*, Stonewall (2018), p. 15, https://www.stonewall.org.uk/system/files/stonewall_and_nfpsynergy_report.pdf.

32 For more on this, see Finlayson, L., et al., ' "I'm not transphobic, but . . . ": A Feminist Case against the Feminist Case against Trans Inclusivity' (blog), Versobooks.com, 17 October 2018, https://www.versobooks.com/blogs/4090-i-m-not-transphobic-but-a-feminist-case-against-the-feminist-case-against-trans-inclusivity.

33 *Supporting Trans Women in Domestic And Sexual Violence Services*, p. 11.

34 'The Challenges of being Transgender and Over 60', BBC News, 11 October 2015, https://www.bbc.co.uk/news/magazine-34454576.

35 Fisher, F., and Fisher, O., 'Growing Older as Me: Cat Burton', My Genderation (Youtube channel), 6 March 2019, https://www.youtube.com/watch?v=ngWdYClıbUo.

36 'For Aging Trans People, Growing Old is Especially Isolating', *Vice*, 14 June 2016, https://www.vice.com/en_us/article/jpyym3/aging-transgender-people-growing-old-care-home-abuse.

37 Ibid.

38 'Dementia Care Advice for Transgender Patients Drawn Up', BBC News, 12 March 2018, https://www.bbc.co.uk/news/uk-wales-43365446.

2. Right and Wrong Bodies

1 Leigh, R., 'Transsexual Former Builder Left "half man, half woman" After being "refused NHS boob job"', *Mirror*, 29 December

2011, https://www.mirror.co.uk/news/uk-news/transsexual-former-builder-left-half-188250.

2 House of Commons Women and Equalities Committee, 'Transgender Equality', report, 14 January 2016, https://publications.parliament.uk/pa/cm201516/cmselect/cmwomeq/390/390.pdf , p. 35.

3 Long Chu, A., 'On Liking Women', *n+1*, 30 (winter 2018), https://nplusonemag.com/issue-30/essays/on-liking-women/.

4 See https://web.archive.org/web/20140301110310/http://www.salon.com/2014/01/07/laverne_cox_artfully_shuts_down_katie_courics_invasive_questions_about_transgender_people/.

5 Kowlaska, M., 'The Heroines of My Life: Interview with Helen Belcher' (blog), 1 September 2014, http://theheroines.blogspot.com/2014/09/interview-with-helen-belcher.html.

6 Pollack, R., et al., 'Don't Call Me Mister You Fucking Beast!', *Lesbian Come Together*, 11 (January 1972).

7 Bilek, J., 'Who are the Rich, White Men Institutionalizing Transgender Ideology?', *Federalist*, 20 February 2018, https://thefederalist.com/2018/02/20/rich-white-men-institutionalizing-transgender-ideology/.

8 Balfe, A., 'Don't Leave Breeding to the Breeders', in *Dysphoria: A Map of Wounds*, zine published by the Trans Health Collective, London, 2017.

9 Savage, W., 'Fifty Years On, the Abortion Act Should be Celebrated – and Updated', *Guardian*, 27 October 2017, https://www.theguardian.com/commentisfree/2017/oct/27/50-years-abortion-act-law-women.

10 See Dhejne, C., et al., 'An Analysis of All Applications for Sex Reassignment Surgery in Sweden, 1960–2010: Prevalence, Incidence, and Regrets', *Archives of Sexual Behavior*, 43(8) (May 2014); and Bowman, C., and Goldberg, J., *Care of the Patient Undergoing Sex Reassignment Surgery (SRS)*, Medical Student Association (2006), https://www.amsa.org/wp-content/uploads/2015/04/CareOfThePatientUndergoingSRS.pdf.

11 Simpson, F., 'Theresa May: "being trans is not an illness"', *Evening Standard*, 19 October 2017, https://www.standard.co.uk/news/uk/theresa-may-being-trans-is-not-an-illness-a3662451.html.

12 Pearce, R., *Understanding Trans Health*, Policy Press (2018), p. 21.

13 Feiner, N., 'Endocrinology, "Transsexual Agency", and the boundaries of Medical Authority', http://humanities.exeter.ac.uk/media/universityofexeter/collegeofhumanities/history/exhistoria/volume7/Endocrinology,_Transsexual_Agency,_and_the_Boundaries_of_Medical_Authority.pdf.

14 Page, M., 'One from the Vaults' Podcast, 4: Valentine's Day Special! (2016).

15 Green, R., et al., 'Attitudes towards Sex Transformation Procedures', *Archives of General Psychiatry*, 15(2) (1966), pp. 178–82 (p. 180).

16 Randell, J., 'Indications for Sex Reassignment Surgery', *Archives of Sexual Behaviour* 1 (1971), 153–61 (p. 159).

17 King, D., and Ekins, R., 'Pioneers of Transgendering: John Randell, 1918–1982', paper given at the Seventh International Gender Dysphoria Conference, http://www.gender.org.uk/conf/2002/king22.htm.

18 Barrett, J., 'Written evidence submitted by British Association of Gender Identity Specialists to the Transgender Equality Inquiry' cited in House of Commons Women and Equalities Committee, 'Transgender Equality', report, 14 January 2016, https://publications.parliament.uk/pa/cm201516/cmselect/cmwomeq/390/390.pdf.

19 Davis, N., '"Are you a man or a woman?": Trans People on GP Care', *Guardian*, 26 February 2019, https://www.theguardian.com/society/2019/feb/26/trans-man-woman-gp-care-healthcare.

20 *LGBT in Britain – Trans Report*, Stonewall (2017).

21 NHS England GP Patient Survey 2019 results. Percentage taken from Q. 31, 'Overall, how would you describe your experience of your GP practice?'; 83 per cent of respondents responded 'good' or 'fairly good' and 6 per cent responded 'poor' or 'very poor'.

22 Parkins, K., 'Meet the Gender Reassignment Surgeons: "Demand is going through the roof"', *Guardian*, 10 July 2016, https://www.the guardian.com/society/2016/jul/10/meet-the-gender-reassignment-surgeons-demand-is-going-through-the-roof.

23 Ibid.

24 Kaveney, R., 'Transphobia is the Latest Weapon in a Raging Culture War', *Red Pepper*, 5 December 2017, https://www.redpepper.org.uk/transphobia-is-the-latest-weapon-in-the-culture-war/.

25 Roberts, A., 'Dispelling the Myths around Trans People "Detransitioning"', *Vice*, 17 November 2015, https://www.vice.com/en_uk/article/kwxkwz/dispelling-the-myths-around-detransitioning.

26 Ibid.

27 Imbimbo, C., et al., 'A Report from a Single Institute's 14-year Experience in Treatment of Male-to-Female Transsexuals', *Journal of Sexual Medicine*, 6 (2009), 2736–45.

28 Pearce, *Understanding Trans Health*, p. 60.

29 Ibid., p. 64.

30 Pearce, R. (@NotRightRuth), 'In other news, Leeds and York Gender Identity Clinic literally ask for referring GPs to perform a genital exam', Twitter, 18 August 2017, https://twitter.com/NotRightRuth/status/898531765270302721.

31 Barrett, J., *Transsexual and Other Disorders of Gender Identity: A Practical Guide to Management*, Radcliffe (2007), p. 73.

32 'Black Patients Half as Likely to Receive Pain Medication as White Patients, Study Finds', *Guardian*, 11 August 2016, https://www.theguardian.com/science/2016/aug/10/black-patients-bias-prescriptions-pain-management-medicine-opioids

33 Ansara, Y. G., 'Beyond Cisgenderism: Counselling People with Non-assigned Gender Identities', in Moon, L. (ed.), *Counselling Ideologies: Queer Challenges to Heteronormativity*, Ashgate (2010), pp. 167–200.

34 Roche, J., 'Pleasureless Principle: Who Gets to Decide What Your Anatomy is Capable Of?', *Bitch Media*, 81 (winter 2019), https://www.bitchmedia.org/article/pleasureless-principle-anatomy.

35 Turner, J., 'Meet Alex Bertie, the Transgender Poster Boy', *The Times*, 11 November 2017, https://www.thetimes.co.uk/article/meet-alex-bertie-the-transgender-poster-boy-z88hgh8b8.

36 Giordano, S., *Children with Gender Identity Disorder: A Clinical, Ethical and Legal Analysis,* Routledge (2013), p. 104.

37 Giordano, S., 'Is Puberty Delaying Treatment "Experimental Treatment"?', *International Journal of Transgender Health*, 21(2) (2020), 113–21, https://www.tandfonline.com/doi/full/10.1080/26895269.2020.1747768.

38 Baral, S. D., et al., 'Worldwide Burden of HIV in Transgender Women: A Systematic Review and Meta-analysis', *Lancet Infectious Diseases*, 13(3) (2012), 214–22.

39 See https://tgeu.org/trans-rights-europe-central-asia-index-maps-2020/.

40 Balfe, 'Don't Leave Breeding to the Breeders'.

3. Class Struggle

1 Calnan, M., 'Transgender Primark Employee Told She Had a "Man's Voice" Was Harassed, Tribunal Rules', *People Management*, 12 February 2018, https://www.peoplemanagement.co.uk/news/articles/transgender-primark-worker-harassed.

2 *LGBT in Britain – Hate Crime and Discrimination*, Stonewall (2017), https://www.stonewall.org.uk/lgbt-britain-hate-crime-and-discrimination.

3 EU Agency for Fundamental Rights, 'Being Trans in the EU: Comparative Analysis of the EU LGBT Survey Data – Summary' (2015).

4 Survey by Crossland Employment Solicitors, quoted in Andersson, J., 'One in Three Employers Say They are "less likely" to Hire a Transgender Worker', *Pink News*, 18 June 2018.

5 Rundall, E. C., ' "Transsexual" People in UK Workplaces: An Analysis of Transsexual Men's and Transsexual Women's Experiences', PhD thesis, Oxford Brookes University, 2010.

6 O'Driscoll, S., 'Half of Transgender People are Unemployed', *The Times*, 21 July 2016, https://www.thetimes.co.uk/article/half-of-transgender-people-are-unemployed-mkqfmb3d2.

7 *LGBT in Britain – Hate Crime and Discrimination*.

8 Clery, E., et al. (eds.), 'Moral Issues: Sex, Gender Identity and Euthenasia', *British Social Attitudes*, 34 (2017), https://www.bsa.natcen.ac.uk/media/39147/bsa34_moral_issues_final.pdf.

9 Godfrey, C., 'This is What Workplace Discrimination is Like for Transgender People', *Buzzfeed News*, 21 May 2016, https://www.buzzfeednews.com/article/chrisgodfrey/this-is-what-workplace-discrimination-is-like-for-transgende.

10 Ibid.

11 Pipe, E., 'Hate Crime Destroys Lives and Won't be Tolerated in Bristol', *B24/7*, 1 December 2017, https://www.bristol247.com/news-and-features/news/hate-crime-destroys-lives-wont-tolerated-bristol/.

12 Burchill, J., 'Transsexuals Should Cut It Out', *Observer*, 13 January 2013.

13 Moore, S., 'I Don't Care if You Were Born a Woman or Became One', *Guardian*, 9 January 2013, https://www.theguardian.com/commentisfree/2013/jan/09/dont-care-if-born-woman.

14 Krauthammer, C., 'For Democrats, the Road Back', *Washington Post*, 24 November 2016.

15 Lilla, M., 'The End of Identity Liberalism', *New York Times*, 18 November 2016, https://www.nytimes.com/2016/11/20/opinion/sunday/the-end-of-identity-liberalism.html.

16 *Saturday Night Live*, Season 42, Episode 7, NBC (aired 19 November 2019).

17 Lott, T., 'Jordan Peterson and the Transgender Wars', *Spectator*, 20 September 2017.

18 O'Neill, B., 'The Orwellian Nightmare of Transgender Politics', *Spiked*, 25 July 2017, https://www.spiked-online.com/2017/07/25/the-orwellian-nightmare-of-transgender-politics/.

19 Bunce, P., 'Transformed: The Credit Suisse Director Known as Pippa and Philip', *Financial News*, 2 December 2018, https://www.fnlondon.com/articles/mistranslated-i-split-my-time-as-pippa-and-philip-20171002.

20 *LGBT in Britain – Hate Crime and Discrimination*, p. 10.

21 Shenje, K., 'Why Trans People Need More Safe Spaces to Get Our Hair Done', *Dazed*, 8 October 2018, https://www.dazeddigital.com/beauty/head/article/41725/1/safe-trans-friendly-hairdressers.

22 Raha, N., 'The Limits of Trans Liberalism' (blog), Versobooks.com, 21 September 2015, https://www.versobooks.com/blogs/2245-the-limits-of-trans-liberalism-by-nat-raha.

23 See https://prideandprejudice.economist.com/why-attend/.

24 Filar, R., 'Trans ™: How the Trans Movement Got Sold Out', *Open Democracy*, 25 November 2015, https://www.opendemocracy.net/en/transformation/how-trans-movement-sold-out/.

25 McCheyne, S., '"You are more oppressive than our oppressors": Transphobia and Transmisogyny in the British Left', *New Socialist*, 15 March 2018, https://newsocialist.org.uk/you-are-more-oppressive-than-our-oppressors-transphobia-and-transmisogyny-in-the-british-left/.

26 Editorial, 'Who Decides Your Gender?', *The Economist*, 27 October 2018, https://www.economist.com/leaders/2018/10/27/who-decides-your-gender.

4. Sex Sells

1 Curtis, R. (dir.), *Love Actually* (2003), Universal Pictures.

2 Kidron, B. (dir.), *Bridget Jones: The Edge of Reason* (2004), Universal Pictures.

3 Coulter, A. (dir.), *Sex and the City*, Season 3, Episode 18, 'Cock-A-Doodle-Do', HBO (aired 15 October 2000).

4 Brooks-Gordon, B., 'Calculating the Number of Sex Workers and Contribution to Non-Observed Economy in the UK', 2015, https://www.researchgate.net/publication/323796831_Calculating_the_number_of_sex_workers_and_their_contribution_to_the_non-observed_economy_in_the_UK.

5 Weisman, C., 'Why Trans Porn is Hugely Popular among Hetero Men', AlterNet, 2 June 2016, alternet.org.

6 Beresford, M., 'Trans Porn is Super Popular in Russia and with Over-65s', *Pink News*, 12 January 2018.

7 'Trans Rentboys: Love Don't Pay the Rent', SWARM Collective, https://www.swarmcollective.org/zine/.

8 Fantz, A., et al., 'Turkish Police Fire Pepper Spray at Gay Pride Parade', CNN, 29 June 2015, https://edition.cnn.com/2015/06/28/world/turkey-pride-parade-lgbt-violence/index.html.

9 'Hande Kader: Outcry in Turkey over Transgender Woman's Murder', BBC News, 21 August 2016, https://www.bbc.co.uk/news/world-europe-37143879.

10 Fedorko, B., and Berredo, L., *The Vicious Circle of Violence: Trans and Gender-Diverse People, Migration, and Sex Work*, TvT Publication Series, Vol. 16 (October 2017).

11 Ibid.

12 Cunningham, S., et al., 'Sex Work and Occupational Homicide: Analysis of a U.K. Murder Database', *Homicide Studies*, 22(3) (2018), https://researchonline.lshtm.ac.uk/id/eprint/4647626/1/Sex%20Work_GOLD%20VoR.pdf.

13 Goldberg, J., 'John Rykener, Richard II, and the Governance of London', *Leeds Studies in English*, 45 (2014), 49–70.

14 Norton, R. (ed.), 'Newspaper Reports, 1728', in *Homosexuality in Eighteenth-Century England: A Sourcebook* (online resource), http://rictornorton.co.uk/eighteen/1728news.htm.

15 Transgender Europe, 'Overdiagnosed but Underserved: Trans Health Survey', available at https://tgeu.org/healthcare.

16 Smith, M., and Mac, J., *Revolting Prostitutes: The Fight for Sex Workers' Rights*, Verso (2018), p. 51.

17 Fedorko and Berredo, *The Vicious Circle of Violence*.

18 Smith and Mac, *Revolting Prostitutes*, p. 141.

19 Ibid.

20 Filar, R., 'Are Sex Workers the Original Feminists?' (blog), Versobooks.com, 30 March 2020, https://www.versobooks.com/blogs/4618-are-sex-workers-the-original-feminists.

21 Syndicat du Travail Sexuel, 'Notre collègue Vanessa [*sic*] Campos a été assassinée', STRASSsyndicat.org, at https://www.liberation.fr/debats/2018/08/17/notre-collegue-vanessa-campos-a-ete-assassinee_1815411/.

22 'Police Officer Had Sex with Prostitute after She was Arrested in Brothel Raid', *Daily Mirror*, 13 July 2015, https://www.mirror.co.uk/news/uk-news/police-officer-sex-prostitute-after-6061472.

23 For more on benefits of the New Zealand model, see Smith and Mac, *Revolting Prostitutes*, pp. 195–202.

24 Stahl, A., ' "We're Monumentally Fucked": Trans Sex Workers on Life under FOSTA/SESTA', *Vice*, 2 August 2018, https://www.vice.com/en/article/ev8ayz/trans-sex-workers-on-life-under-fosta-sesta.

25 Ibid.

5. *The State*

1 https://libcom.org/library/dr-angela-davis-role-trans-non-binary-communities-fight-feminist-abolition-she-advocates.

2 See https://www.businessinsider.com/pentagon-transgender-medical-comparison-2017-7?r=US&IR=T.

3 Puar, J., 'Rethinking Homonationalism', *International Journal of Middle East Studies*, 45 (2013), p. 33.

4 *LGBT in Britain – Trans Report*, Stonewall (2017), p. 6.

5 'Transgender Hate Crimes Recorded by Police Go Up 81%', BBC News, 27 June 2019, https://www.bbc.co.uk/news/uk-48756370.

6 *LGBT in Britain – Trans Report*, p. 9.

7 Bindel, J., 'Why the Transbullies are a Threat to Us All', *UnHerd*, 10 October 2018, https://unherd.com/2018/10/why-the-transbullies-are-a-threat-to-us-all/.

8 Jacques, J., 'Cross-dressing in Victorian London', *Time Out*, 16 February 2012, http://www.timeout.com/london/lgbt/cross-dressing-in-victorian-london.

9 *LGBT in Britain – Trans Report*, p. 8.

10 Bryant, B., and Stephenon, W., 'How LGBTQ+ Hate crime is Committed by Young People', BBC News, 21 December 2018, https://www.bbc.co.uk/news/uk-46543874.

11 Fae, J., 'Trans Woman: Police pinned me down and pulled off my bra', *Gay Star News*, 20 June 2017, https://www.gaystarnews.com/article/trans-woman-police-pinned-pulled-off-bra/.

12 Reid-Smith, T., 'Police Handcuff Trans Protestors at Glasgow Pride', *Gay Star News*, 20 August 2017, https://www.gaystarnews.com/article/police-handcuff-trans-protestors-glasgow-pride/.

13 Townsend, M., 'Black People "40 times more likely" to be Stopped and Searched in UK', *Observer*, 4 May 2019, https://www.theguardian.com/law/2019/may/04/stop-and-search-new-row-racial-bias.

14 Owusu, M., 'Black Trans People are Disrespected in Life and Barely Acknowledged in Death – Our Lives Matter Too', *Independent*, 2 June 2020, https://www.independent.co.uk/voices/george-floyd-black-lives-matter-racism-tony-mcdade-transgender-a9544131.html.

15 'James Baldwin: The Last Interviews', *Village Voice*, 24 February 2017, https://www.villagevoice.com/2017/02/24/james-baldwin-the-last-interviews/.

16 Roach, A., 'Female Prison Officers Raped by Inmates Who Self-Identify as Trans', *Sun*, 12 April 2020, https://www.thesun.co.uk/news/11381963/female-prison-officers-raped-trans-rory-stewart/.

17 Abraham, A., 'What It's Like to be Trans in the UK Prison System', *Dazed*, 6 November 2019, https://www.dazeddigital.com/life-culture/article/46703/1/what-its-like-to-be-transgender-in-the-uk-prison-system.

18 Ibid.

19 Shaw, D., 'Eleven Transgender Inmates Sexually Assaulted in Male Prisons Last Year', BBC News, 21 May 2020, https://www.bbc.co.uk/news/uk-52748117.

20 Community Innovations Enterprise, *Inside Gender Identity: A Report into the Health and Social Care Needs of Transgender Offenders*, CIE (2017), p. 49.

21 'HMP Eastwood Park: Concern over Segregated Transgender Women Prisoners', BBC News, 18 March 2020, https://www.bbc.co.uk/news/uk-england-bristol-51928421.

22 Light, M., et al., *Gender Differences in Substance Misuse and Mental Health amongst Prisoners*, Ministry of Justice (2013).

23 Hopkins, K., et al., *Associations between Ethnic Background and being Sentenced to Prison in the Crown Court in England and Wales in 2015*, Ministry of Justice (2016).

24 Grierson, J., 'More than 2,500 Prison Staff Disciplined In Five Years, MoJ Figures Show', *Guardian*, 29 April 2019, https://www.theguardian.com/society/2019/apr/29/more-than-2500-prison-staff-disciplined-in-five-years-moj-figures-show.

25 Prison Reform Trust, *Prison: The facts* (Bromley Briefings, summer 2019), http://www.prisonreformtrust.org.uk/Portals/0/Documents/Bromley%20Briefings/Prison%20the%20facts%20Summer%202019.pdf.

26 Davis, A. Y., *Are Prisons Obsolete?*, Seven Stories Press (2003), p. 108.

27 Knopp, F. H., *Instead of Prisons: A Handbook for Abolitionists*, Prison Research Education Action Project (1976), Chapter 1, at https://www.prisonpolicy.org/scans/instead_of_prisons/chapter1.shtml.

28 *No Safe Refuge: Experiences of LGBT Asylum Seekers in Detention*, Stonewall (2016), p. 17.

6. *Kissing Cousins*

1 Southwell, H., 'Anti-Trans Group Allowed to Lead Pride in London March after Hijack', *Pink News*, 7 July 2018, https://www.pinknews.co.uk/2018/07/07/anti-trans-group-allowed-to-lead-pride-in-london-march-after-hijack/.

2 Ibid.

3 Bindel, J., 'It's Not Me. It's You', *Guardian*, 7 November 2008, https://www.theguardian.com/commentisfree/2008/nov/08/lesbianism.

4 Jacques, J., 'On the "Dispute" between Radical Feminism and Trans People', *New Statesman*, 6 August 2014, https://www.newstatesman.com/juliet-jacques/2014/08/dispute-between-radical-feminism-and-trans-people.

5 Ibid.

6 Jones, O., 'Stonewall is Right to Bring Our Trans Brothers and Sisters in from the Cold', *Guardian*, 18 February 2015, https://www.theguardian.com/commentisfree/2015/feb/18/stonewall-trans-issues-neglected-progressives.

7 Ibid.

8 Norton, R., 'Anne Lister, the First Modern Lesbian', at http://rictornorton.co.uk/lister.htm.

9 'Anne Lister: Reworded York Plaque for "First Lesbian"', BBC News, 28 February 2019, https://www.bbc.co.uk/news/uk-england-york-north-yorkshire-47404525.

10 du Preez, M., and Dronfield, J., *Dr James Barry: A Woman Ahead of Her Time*, Oneworld (2016), pp. 251, 252, citing Bradford, E., 'The Reputed Female Army Surgeon', *Medical Times and Gazette*, 2 (1865), 293.

11 Letter from Florence Nightingale to Parthenope, Lady Verney, Wellcome Institute for the History of Medicine, n.d., quoted at https://www.ed.ac.uk/medicine-vet-medicine/about/history/women/james-barry.

12 Flood, A., 'New Novel about Dr James Barry Sparks Row over Victorian's Gender Identity', *Guardian*, 18 February 2019, https://www.theguardian.com/books/2019/feb/18/new-novel-about-dr-james-barry-sparks-row-over-victorians-gender-identity.

13 Page, M., Twitter, 16 February 2019, https://twitter.com/morganmpage/status/1096739245132300289.

14 Ibid.

15 Flood, 'New novel about Dr James Barry'.

16 Page, M., 'It Doesn't Matter Who Threw the First Brick at Stonewall', *The Nation*, 30 June 2019, https://www.thenation.com/article/trans-black-stonewall-rivera-storme/.

17 Londoño, E., 'Who Threw the First Brick at Stonewall?', *New York Times*, 26 August 2015, https://takingnote.blogs.nytimes.com/2015/08/26/who-threw-the-first-brick-at-stonewall/.

18 Power, L., *No Bath but Plenty of Bubbles: An Oral History of the Gay Liberation Front, 1970–73*, Continuum (1995), p. 244.

19 Feather, S., *Blowing the Lid*, Zero Books (2014), p. 324.

20 Ibid., p. 326.

21 Jame, Sandy E., et al., *The Report of the 2015 U.S. Transgender Survey*, National Center for Transgender Equality (2016), https://transequality.org/sites/default/files/docs/usts/USTS-Full-Report-Dec17.pdf.

22 Tourjee, D., 'The Trans Women Who Become Lesbians after Years as Gay Men', *Vice*, 23 February 2017, https://www.vice.com/en_uk/article/8qezbp/the-trans-women-who-become-lesbians-after-years-as-gay-men-412.

23 Ibid.

24 Besanville, J., 'Trans Man Kicked Out of London Gay Sauna for Not Having a Penis', *Gay Star News*, 31 October 2018, https://www.gaystarnews.com/article/trans-man-sauna/.

25 Turner, J., 'Cult of Gender Identity is Harming Children', *The Times*, 21 September 2019, https://www.thetimes.co.uk/article/cult-of-gender-identity-is-harming-children-pjvbkjzxq.

26 Daley, J., 'The Sad Fraud of Gay Equality', *The Times*, 3 December 1991.

27 Tides of History (@labour_history), Twitter, 7 August 2019, https://twitter.com/labour_history/status/115899502761755852 8?s=20.

28 Barthélemy, H., 'Christian Right Tips to Fight Transgender Rights: Separate the T from the LGB', Southern Poverty Law Center, 23 October 2017, https://www.splcenter.org/hatewatch/2017/10/23/christian-right-tips-fight-transgender-rights-separate-t-lgb.

29 'Statement: L is out of GBT', Change.org, 2 April 2016, https://www.change.org/p/hrc-statement-l-is-out-of-gbt.

30 See https://handsacrosstheaislewomen.com/home/.

31 Burns, K., 'The Rise of Anti-trans Radical Feminists, Explained', *Vox*, 5 September 2019, https://www.vox.com/identities/2019/9/5/20840101/terfs-radical-feminists-gender-critical.

7. The Ugly Sister

1 Stryker, S., *Transgender History*, Seal Press (2008), pp. 102–4.

2 Birmingham LGBT Community Trust, 'Gay Birmingham Remembered' (2008), http://www.gaybirminghamremembered.co.uk/interview/41/.

3 Ibid.

4 Editorial, 'The *Guardian* View on the Gender Recognition Act: Where Rights Collide', *Guardian*, 17 October 2018, https://www.theguardian.com/commentisfree/2018/oct/17/the-guardian-view-on-the-gender-recognition-act-where-rights-collide.

5 Levin, S, et al., 'Why We Take Issue with *The Guardian*'s Stance on Trans Rights in the UK', *Guardian*, 2 November 2018, https://www.theguardian.com/commentisfree/2018/nov/02/guardian-editorial-response-transgender-rights-uk.

6 Jacques, J., 'Transphobia is Everywhere in Britain', *New York Times*, 9 March 2020, https://www.nytimes.com/2020/03/09/opinion/britain-transphobia-labour-party.html.

7 Ditum, S., 'A Hot Woman on a Magazine Cover' (blog), SarahDitum.com, 24 June 2014, https://sarahditum.com/2014/06/24/a-hot-woman-on-a-magazine-cover/.

8 Smith, V., 'I Don't Feel I "Match" My Gender, So What Does It Mean to be Called Cis?', *New Stateman*, 6 February 2014, https://www.newstatesman.com/lifestyle/2014/02/i-dont-feel-i-match-my-gender-so-what-does-it-mean-be-called-cis.

9 Lewis, H., 'What the Row over Banning Germaine Greer is Really About', *New Statesman*, 27 October 2015, https://www.newstatesman.com/politics/feminism/2015/10/what-row-over-banning-germaine-greer-really-about.

10 Greer, G., 'On Why Sex Change is a Lie', *Independent*, 22 July 1989.

11 Ahmed, S., 'You are Oppressing Us!', feministkilljoys, 15 February 2015, https://feministkilljoys.com/2015/02/15/you-are-oppressing-us/.

12 Eddo-Lodge, R., *Why I'm No Longer Talking to White People about Race*, Bloomsbury (2017), p. 162.

13 Lewis, S., 'How British Feminism Became Anti-Trans', *New York Times*, 7 February 2019, https://www.nytimes.com/2019/02/07/opinion/terf-trans-women-britain.html.

14 Redmond, S., et al., 'An Open Letter to the Organisers of the "We Need to Talk" Tour from a Group of Feminists in Ireland', *Feminist Ire*, 22 January 2018, https://feministire.com/2018/01/22/an-open-letter-to-the-organisers-of-the-we-need-to-talk-tour-from-a-group-of-feminists-in-ireland.

15 Leacock, E., *Myths of Male Dominance: Collected Articles on Women Cross-Culturally*, Monthly Review Press (1981), p. 135, as cited in 'Marxism and Transgender Liberation: Confronting Transphobia in the British Left', Red Fightback, https://redfightback.org/read/transphobia_in_the_left.

16 Ibid.

17 Wittig, M., *The Straight Mind and Other Essays*, Beacon Press (1992), p. 32.

18 hooks, b., *Ain't I a Woman*, South End Press (1981), p. 1.

19 See Butler, J., *Gender Trouble: Feminism and the Subversion of Identity*, Routledge (2nd edn, 1999).

20 Dembroff, R., 'Trans Women are Victims of Misogyny, Too – and All Feminists Must Recognise This', *Guardian*, 19 May 2019, https://www.theguardian.com/commentisfree/2019/may/19/valerie-jackson-trans-women-misogyny-feminism.

21 Raymond, J., *The Transsexual Empire: The Making of the She-Male*, Teachers College, Columbia University (2nd edn, 1994), p. 104.

22 Greer, G., *The Whole Woman*, Black Swan (reissue, 2007), p. 93.

23 Serano, J., *Whipping Girl: A Transsexual Woman on Sexism and the Scapegoating of Femininity*, Seal Press (2007), p. 11.

24 Ibid., pp. 11–12.

25 Dean, J., 'Contestants in Transsexual Show to Sue Sky', *Guardian*, 30 October 2003, https://www.theguardian.com/media/2003/oct/30/bskyb.broadcasting.

26 Pollack, et al., 'Don't Call Me Mister You Fucking Beast!', *Lesbian Come Together*, 11 (January 1972).

27 Hulme, J., 'Transphobes and Trans Men' (blog), jayhulme.com, 20 July 2019, https://jayhulme.com/blog/transmen.

28 Ibid.

29 Alter, C., 'Seeing Sexism from Both Sides: What Trans Men Experience', *Time*, 16 June 2016, https://time.com/4371196/seeing-sexism-from-both-sides-what-trans-men-experience/.

30 Lewis, H., 'How an Email with a Secret Location Led Me to the Most Vibrant Feminist Meeting of the Year', *New Statesman*, 22 May 2019, https://www.newstatesman.com/politics/feminism/2019/05/how-email-secret-location-led-me-most-vibrant-feminist-meeting-year.

31 *National LGBT Survey Research Report*, Government Equalities Office (2018), pp. 57–61, https://assets.publishing.service.gov.uk/

government/uploads/system/uploads/attachment_data/file/721704/ LGBT-survey-research-report.pdf.

32 Williams, C., 'Sex, Gender, and Sexuality: An Interview with Catharine A. MacKinnon', The Conversations Project, 27 November 2017, http://radfem.transadvocate.com/sex-gender-and-sexuality-an-interview-with-catharine-a-mackinnon/.

33 Cited in Olufemi, L., *Feminism, Interrupted: Disrupting Power*, Pluto Press (2020), p. 49.

34 Freeman, H., 'Let's Drop the Gender Stereotypes – We are All Non-Binary', *Guardian*, 16 September 2017, https://www.theguardian.com/society/2017/sep/16/drop-gender-stereotypes-we-are-all-non-binary.

35 Dworkin, A., *Woman Hating*, Dutton (1974), pp. 175–6.

36 Olufemi, *Feminism, Interrupted*, p. 65.

37 Livingstone, J., 'Transphobia Redefined', *New Republic*, 17 February 2017, https://newrepublic.com/article/140703/transphobia-redefined.

Conclusion

1 Power, S., 'Labour Peer Lord Lewis Moonie Quits Party after Transphobic Tweets', *Gay Star News*, 15 May 2019, https://www.gaystarnews.com/article/labour-peer-lord-lewis-moonie-resigns-after-transphobic-tweets/.

2 Escalante, A., 'Marxism and Trans Liberation', *Medium*, 12 July 2018, https://medium.com/@alysonescalante/marxism-and-trans-liberation-1066d09b7e8f.